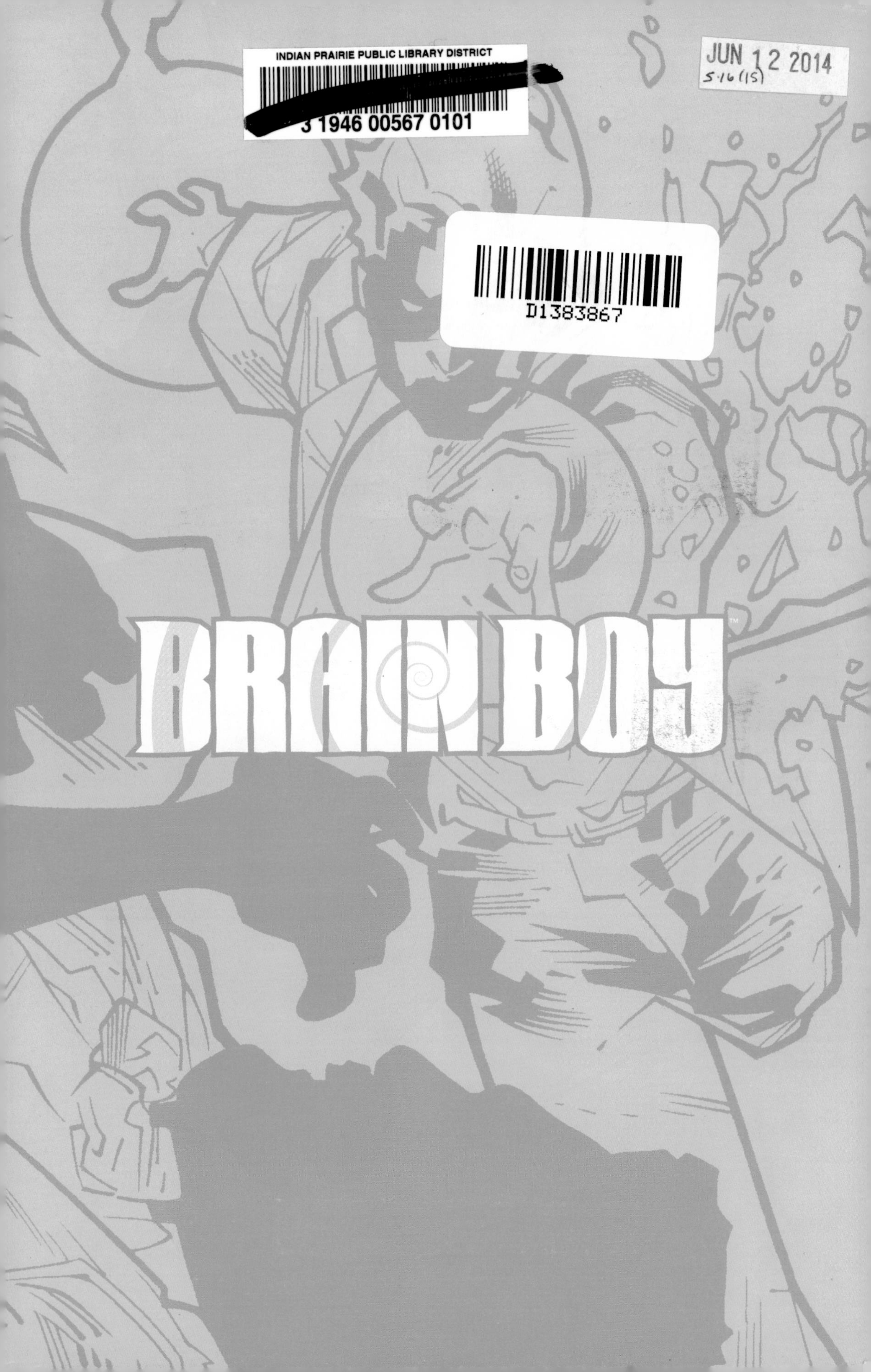
BRAIN BOY™

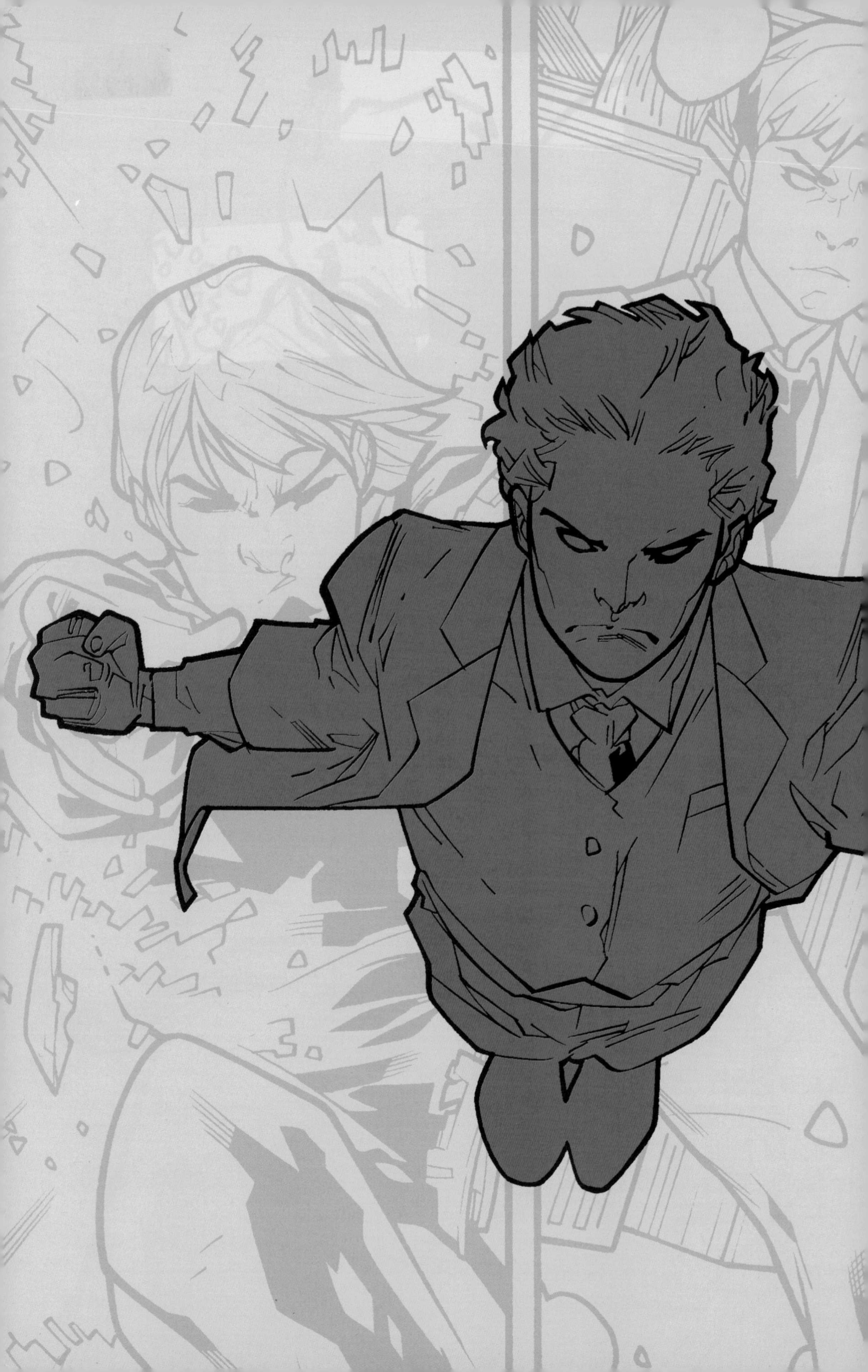

BRAIN BOY™

VOLUME 1 PSY VS. PSY

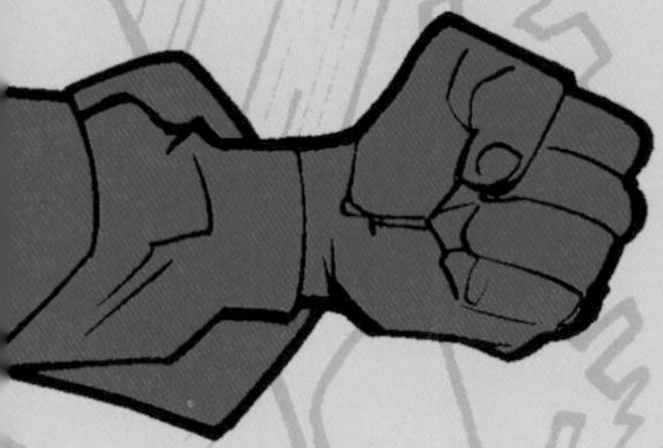

STORY BY
FRED VAN LENTE

ART BY
FREDDIE WILLIAMS II
(CHAPTER 0)
R. B. SILVA AND ROB LEAN
(CHAPTERS 1–3)

COLORS BY
EGO

LETTERS BY
NATE PIEKOS OF BLAMBOT®

COVER BY
ARIEL OLIVETTI

CHAPTER BREAK ART BY
ARIEL OLIVETTI
(CHAPTERS 0–3 , PINUP)
JUAN DOE
(PINUP)

DARK HORSE BOOKS

PUBLISHER........................**MIKE RICHARDSON**

EDITOR................................**JIM GIBBONS**

ASSISTANT EDITOR..........**SPENCER CUSHING**

DIGITAL PRODUCTION..........**ALLYSON HALLER**

COLLECTION DESIGNER...........**JIMMY PRESLER**

Special thanks to Mike Richardson, Randy Stradley,
Scott Allie, and Space Goat Productions.

Mike Richardson, President and Publisher | Neil Hankerson, Executive Vice President | Tom Weddle, Chief Financial Officer | Randy Stradley, Vice President of Publishing | Michael Martens, Vice President of Book Trade Sales | Anita Nelson, Vice President of Business Affairs | Scott Allie, Editor in Chief | Matt Parkinson, Vice President of Marketing | David Scroggy, Vice President of Product Development | Dale LaFountain, Vice President of Information Technology | Darlene Vogel, Senior Director of Print, Design, and Production | Ken Lizzi, General Counsel | Davey Estrada, Editorial Director | Chris Warner, Senior Books Editor | Diana Schutz, Executive Editor | Cary Grazzini, Director of Print and Development | Lia Ribacchi, Art Director | Cara Niece, Director of Scheduling | Tim Wiesch, Director of International Licensing | Mark Bernardi, Director of Digital Publishing

Published by Dark Horse Books
A division of Dark Horse Comics, Inc.
10956 SE Main Street
Milwaukie, OR 97222

First edition: April 2014
ISBN 978-1-61655-317-3

1 3 5 7 9 10 8 6 4 2
Printed in China

International Licensing: (503) 905-2377
Comic Shop Locator Service: (888) 266-4226

BRAIN BOY VOLUME 1: PSY VS. PSY

This volume collects the one-shot *Brain Boy #0* and *Brain Boy #1–#3*, from the ongoing comic series from Dark Horse Comics.

CHAPTER 0

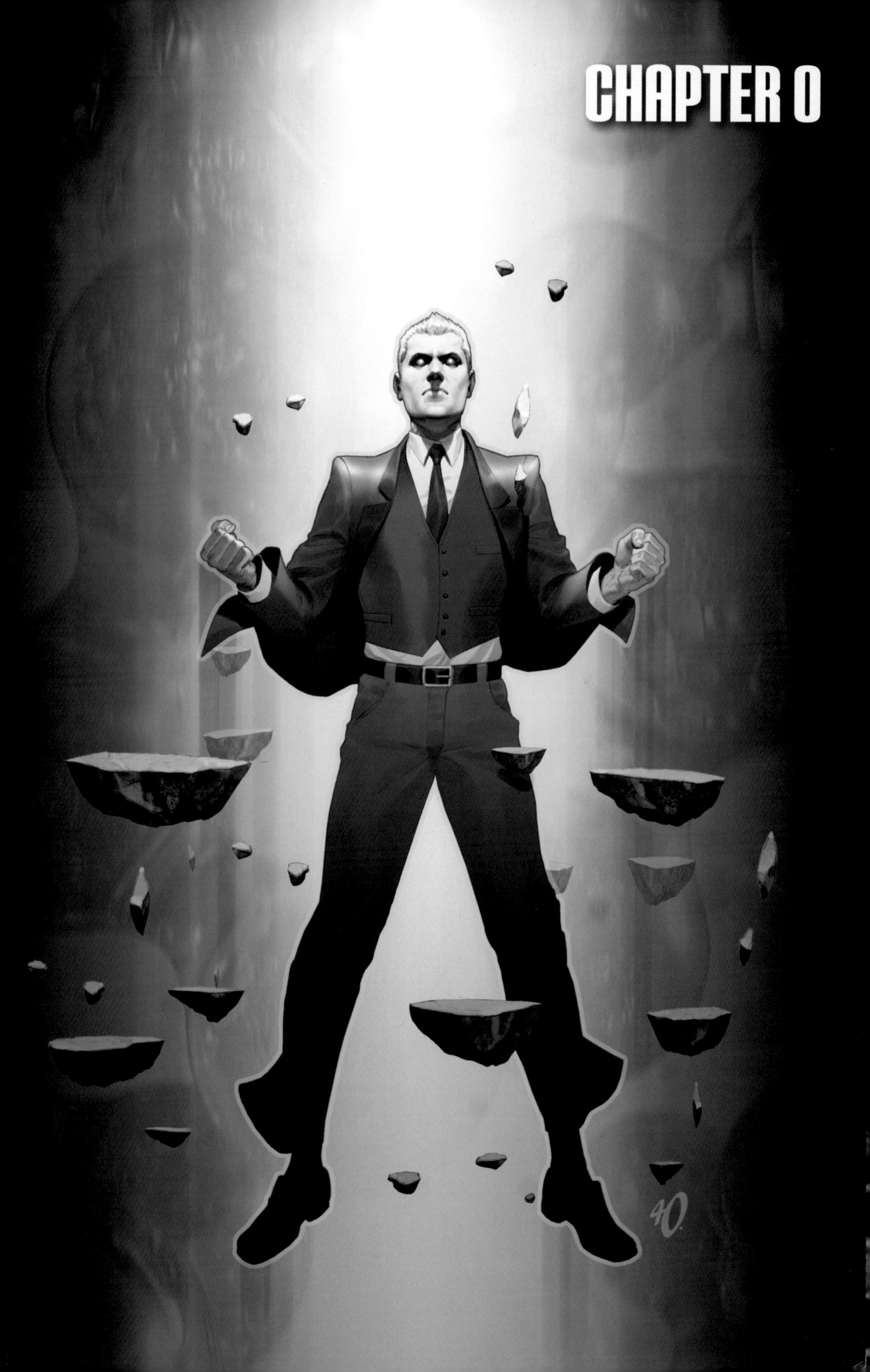

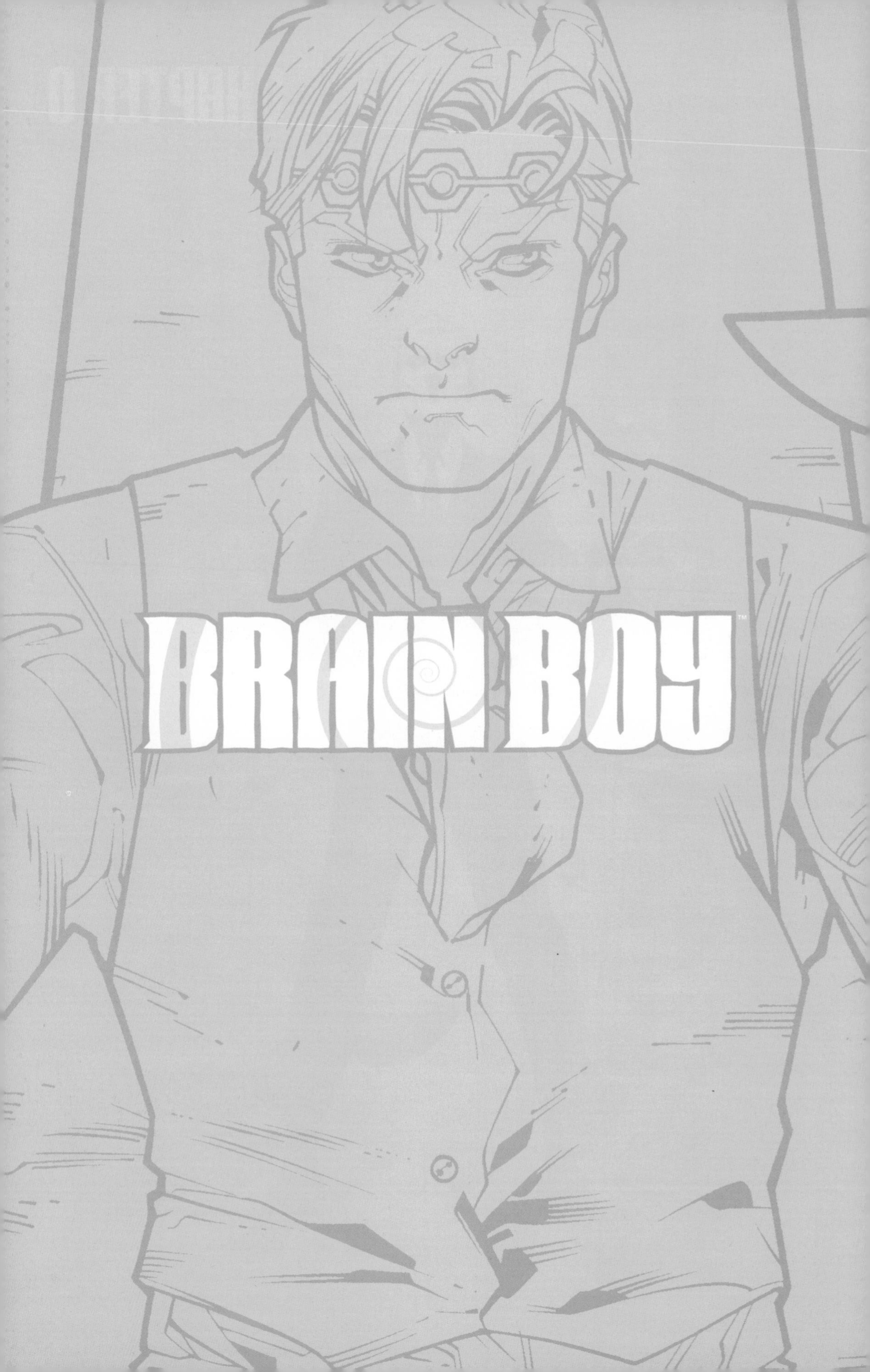
BRAIN BOY™

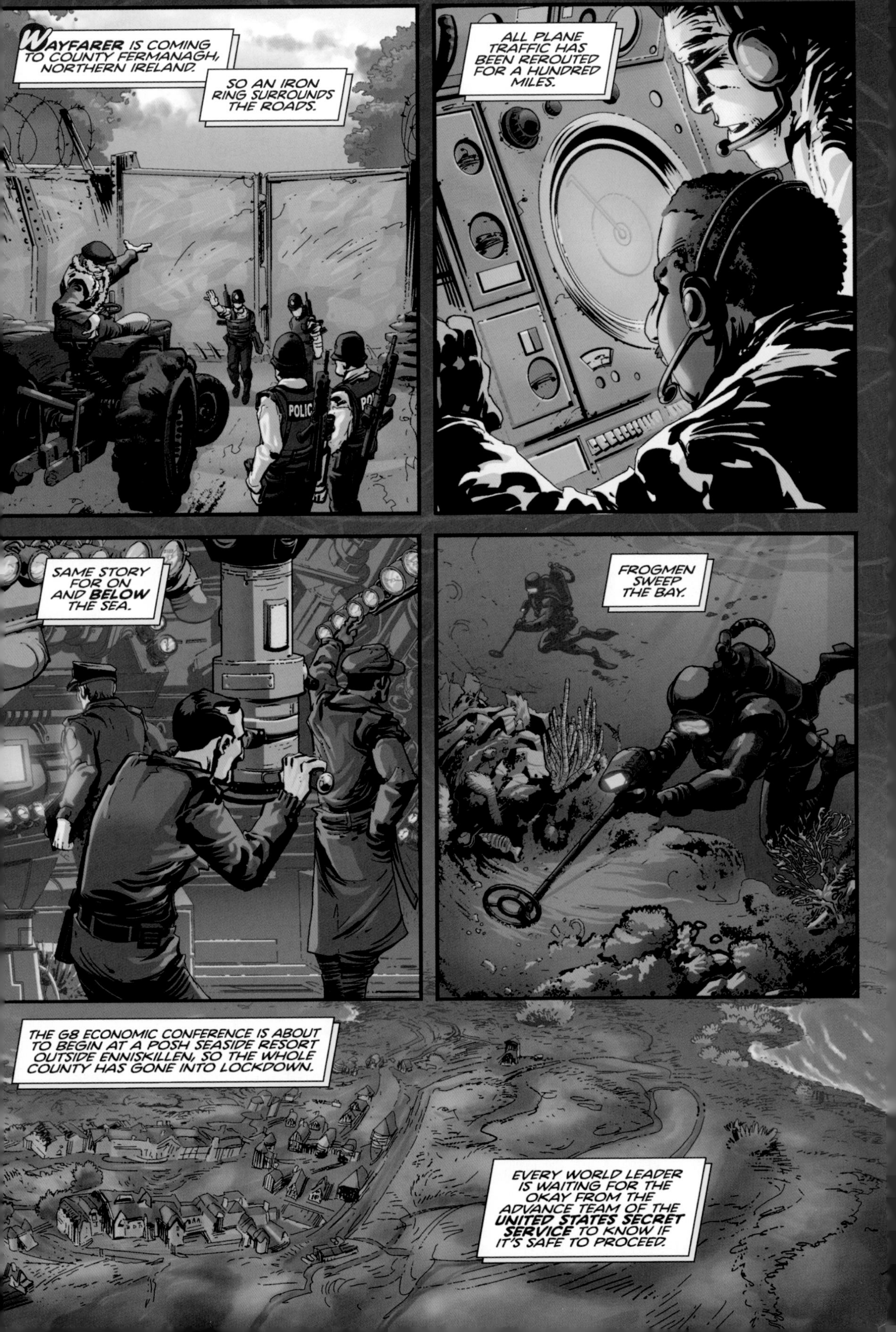
WAYFARER IS COMING TO COUNTY FERMANAGH, NORTHERN IRELAND.
SO AN IRON RING SURROUNDS THE ROADS.
POLICE
ALL PLANE TRAFFIC HAS BEEN REROUTED FOR A HUNDRED MILES.
SAME STORY FOR ON AND BELOW THE SEA.
FROGMEN SWEEP THE BAY.
THE G8 ECONOMIC CONFERENCE IS ABOUT TO BEGIN AT A POSH SEASIDE RESORT OUTSIDE ENNISKILLEN, SO THE WHOLE COUNTY HAS GONE INTO LOCKDOWN.
EVERY WORLD LEADER IS WAITING FOR THE OKAY FROM THE ADVANCE TEAM OF THE UNITED STATES SECRET SERVICE TO KNOW IF IT'S SAFE TO PROCEED.

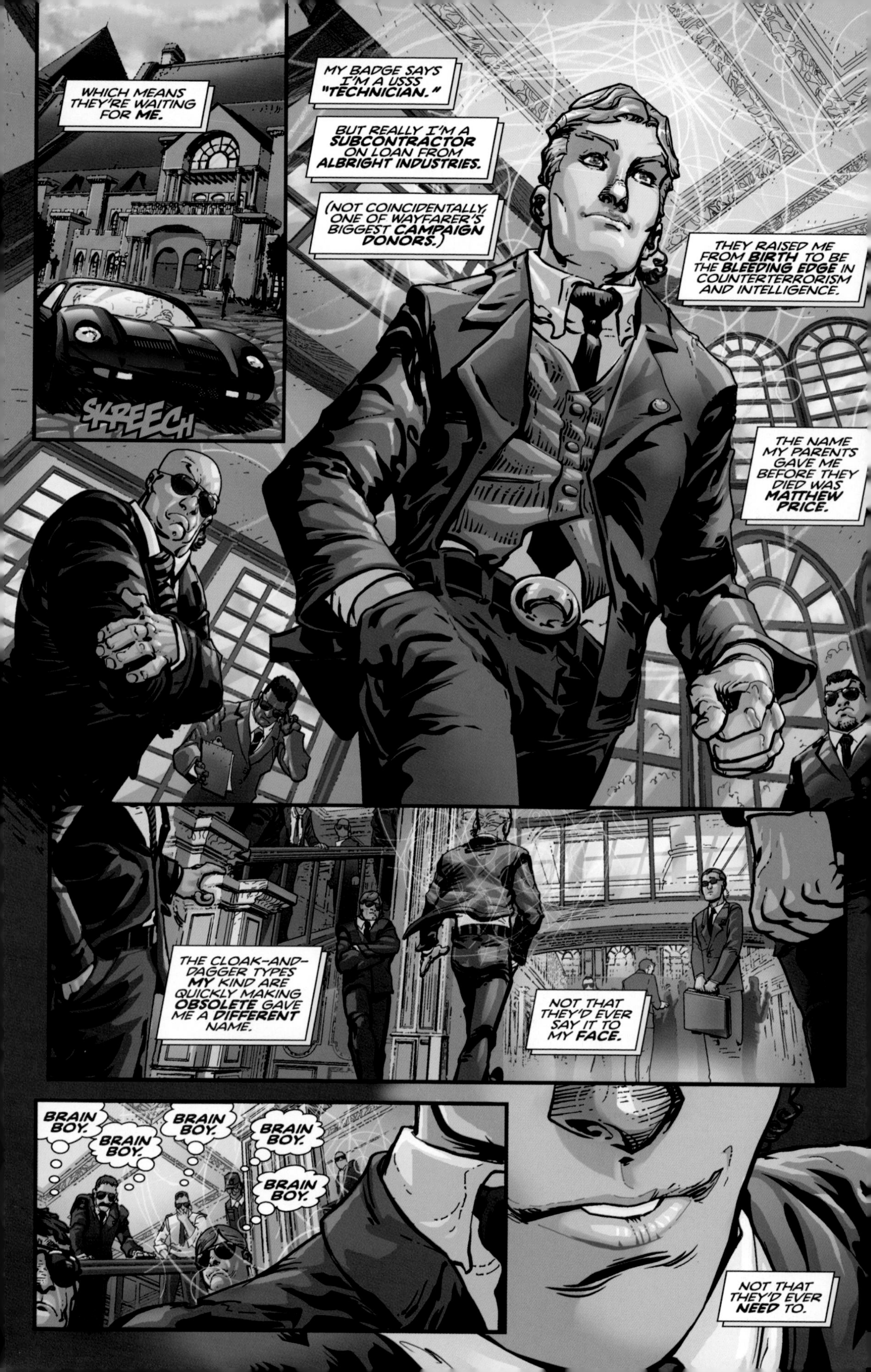

WHICH MEANS THEY'RE WAITING FOR ME.
SKREECH
MY BADGE SAYS I'M A USSS "TECHNICIAN."
BUT REALLY I'M A SUBCONTRACTOR ON LOAN FROM ALBRIGHT INDUSTRIES.
(NOT COINCIDENTALLY, ONE OF WAYFARER'S BIGGEST CAMPAIGN DONORS.)
THEY RAISED ME FROM BIRTH TO BE THE BLEEDING EDGE IN COUNTERTERRORISM AND INTELLIGENCE.
THE NAME MY PARENTS GAVE ME BEFORE THEY DIED WAS MATTHEW PRICE.
THE CLOAK-AND-DAGGER TYPES MY KIND ARE QUICKLY MAKING OBSOLETE GAVE ME A DIFFERENT NAME.
NOT THAT THEY'D EVER SAY IT TO MY FACE.
BRAIN BOY.
BRAIN BOY.
BRAIN BOY.
BRAIN BOY.
BRAIN BOY.
NOT THAT THEY'D EVER NEED TO.

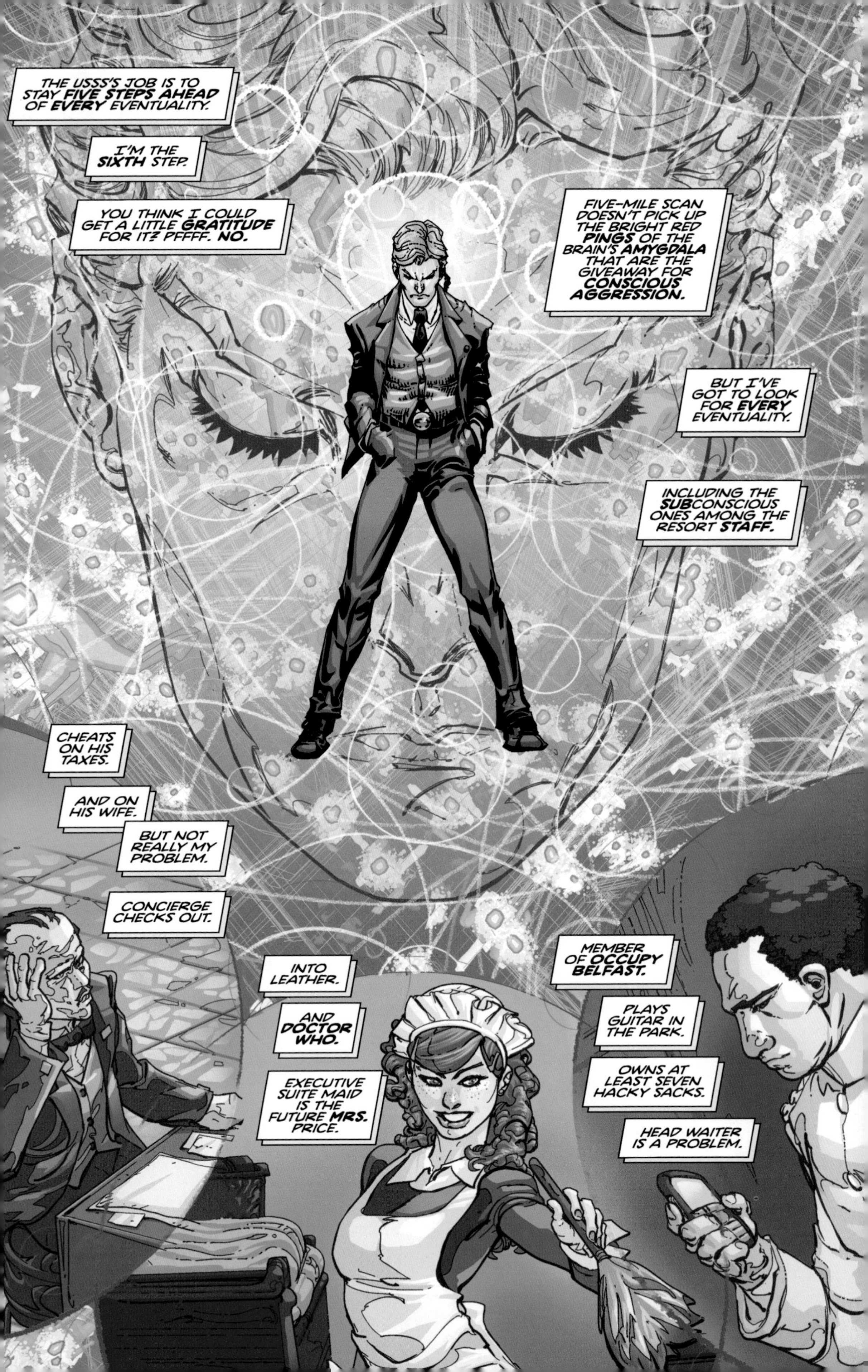

THE USSS'S JOB IS TO STAY **FIVE STEPS AHEAD** OF **EVERY** EVENTUALITY.
I'M THE **SIXTH** STEP.
YOU THINK I COULD GET A LITTLE **GRATITUDE** FOR IT? PFFFF. **NO.**
FIVE-MILE SCAN DOESN'T PICK UP THE BRIGHT RED **PINGS** OF THE BRAIN'S **AMYGDALA** THAT ARE THE GIVEAWAY FOR **CONSCIOUS AGGRESSION.**
BUT I'VE GOT TO LOOK FOR **EVERY** EVENTUALITY.
INCLUDING THE **SUB**CONSCIOUS ONES AMONG THE RESORT **STAFF.**
CHEATS ON HIS TAXES.
AND ON HIS WIFE.
BUT NOT REALLY MY PROBLEM.
CONCIERGE CHECKS OUT.
INTO LEATHER.
AND **DOCTOR WHO.**
EXECUTIVE SUITE MAID IS THE FUTURE **MRS.** PRICE.
MEMBER OF **OCCUPY BELFAST.**
PLAYS GUITAR IN THE PARK.
OWNS AT LEAST SEVEN HACKY SACKS.
HEAD WAITER IS A PROBLEM.

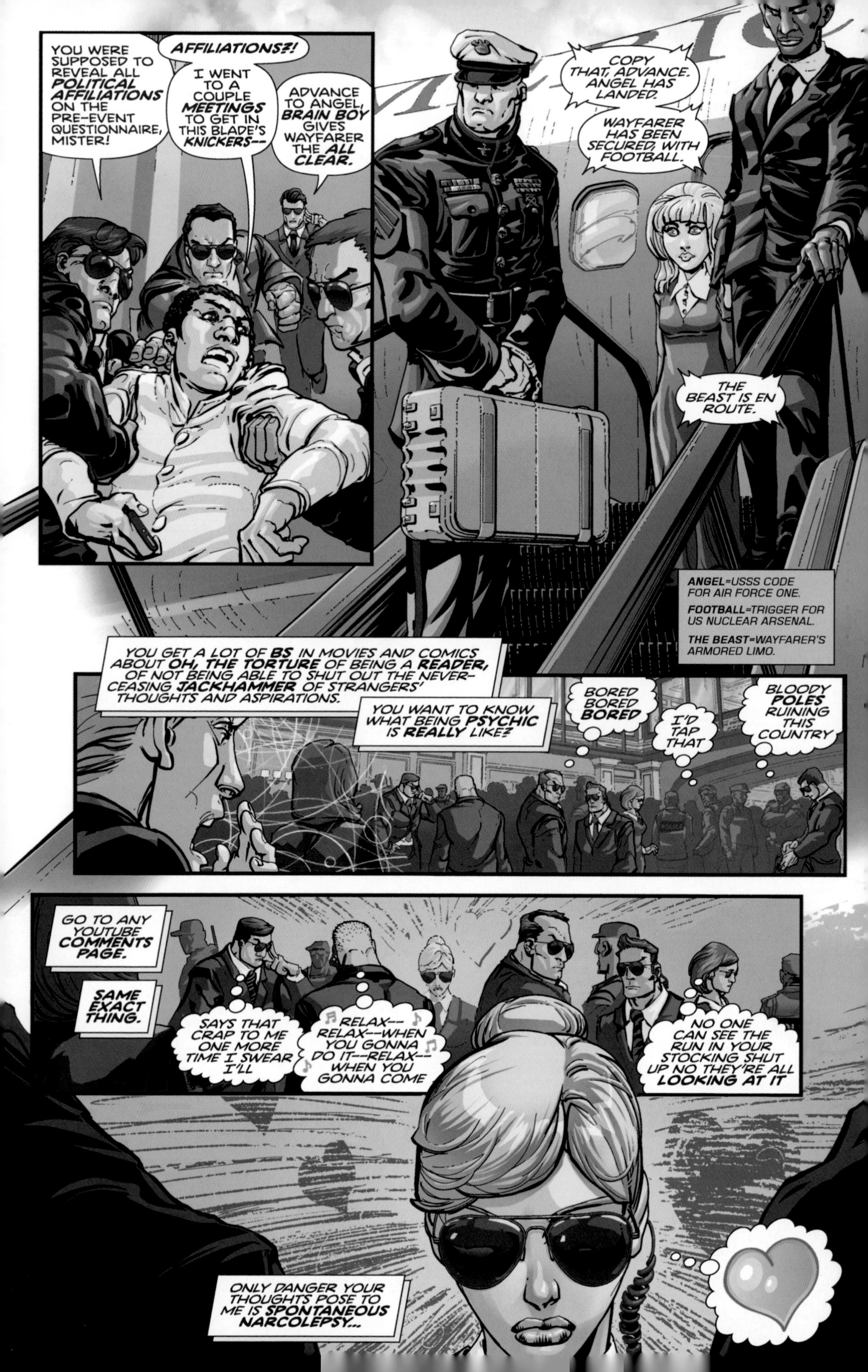
YOU WERE SUPPOSED TO REVEAL ALL POLITICAL AFFILIATIONS ON THE PRE-EVENT QUESTIONNAIRE, MISTER!
AFFILIATIONS?!
I WENT TO A COUPLE MEETINGS TO GET IN THIS BLADE'S KNICKERS--
ADVANCE TO ANGEL, BRAIN BOY GIVES WAYFARER THE ALL CLEAR.
COPY THAT, ADVANCE. ANGEL HAS LANDED.
WAYFARER HAS BEEN SECURED, WITH FOOTBALL.
THE BEAST IS EN ROUTE.
ANGEL=USSS CODE FOR AIR FORCE ONE.
FOOTBALL=TRIGGER FOR US NUCLEAR ARSENAL.
THE BEAST=WAYFARER'S ARMORED LIMO.
YOU GET A LOT OF BS IN MOVIES AND COMICS ABOUT OH, THE TORTURE OF BEING A READER, OF NOT BEING ABLE TO SHUT OUT THE NEVER-CEASING JACKHAMMER OF STRANGERS' THOUGHTS AND ASPIRATIONS.
YOU WANT TO KNOW WHAT BEING PSYCHIC IS REALLY LIKE?
BORED BORED BORED
I'D TAP THAT
BLOODY POLES RUINING THIS COUNTRY
GO TO ANY YOUTUBE COMMENTS PAGE.
SAME EXACT THING.
SAYS THAT CRAP TO ME ONE MORE TIME I SWEAR I'LL
RELAX-- RELAX--WHEN YOU GONNA DO IT--RELAX-- WHEN YOU GONNA COME
NO ONE CAN SEE THE RUN IN YOUR STOCKING SHUT UP NO THEY'RE ALL LOOKING AT IT
ONLY DANGER YOUR THOUGHTS POSE TO ME IS SPONTANEOUS NARCOLEPSY...

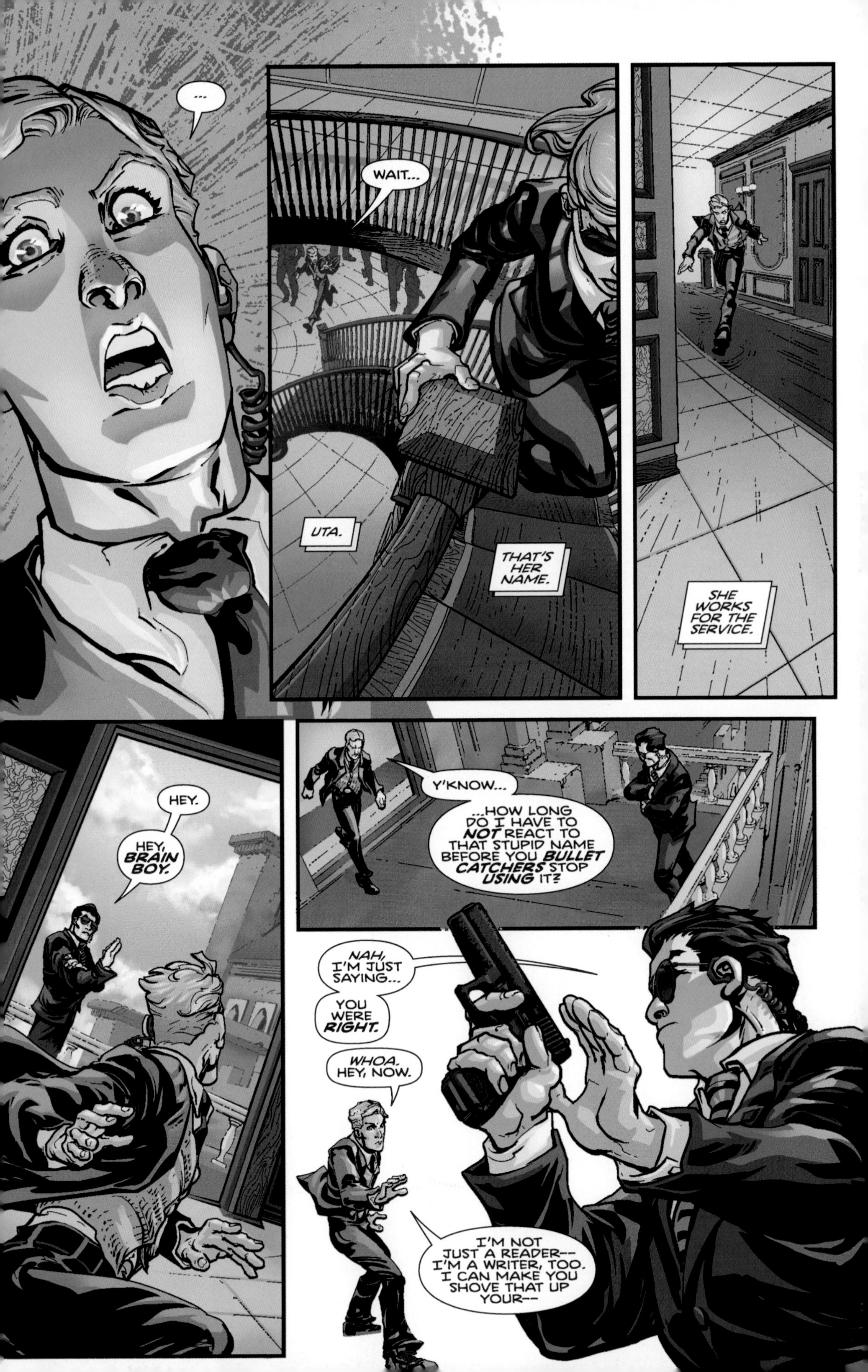
...
WAIT...
UTA.
THAT'S HER NAME.
SHE WORKS FOR THE SERVICE.
HEY.
HEY, BRAIN BOY.
Y'KNOW...
...HOW LONG DO I HAVE TO NOT REACT TO THAT STUPID NAME BEFORE YOU BULLET CATCHERS STOP USING IT?
NAH, I'M JUST SAYING...
YOU WERE RIGHT.
WHOA. HEY, NOW.
I'M NOT JUST A READER-- I'M A WRITER, TOO. I CAN MAKE YOU SHOVE THAT UP YOUR--

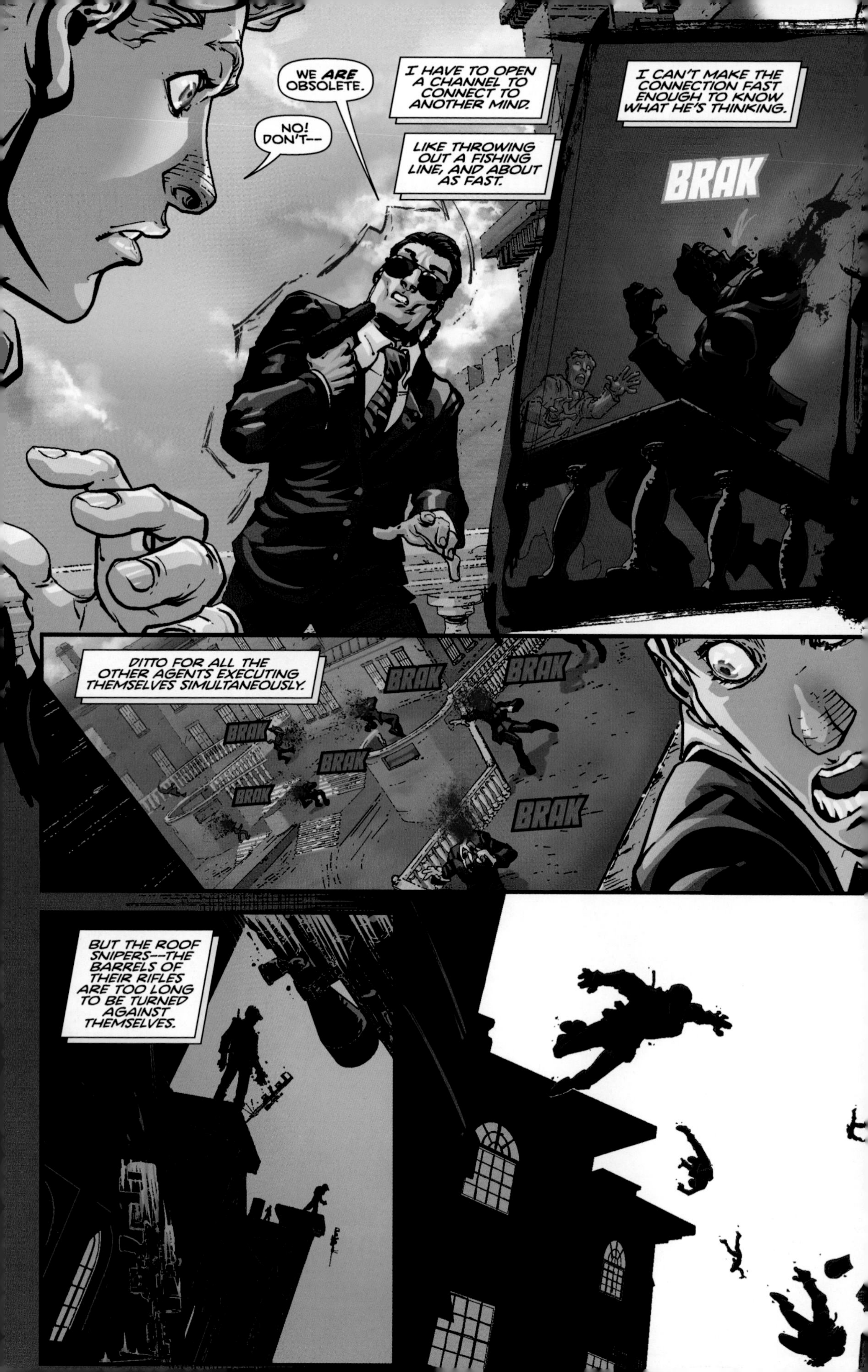
WE ARE OBSOLETE.
NO! DON'T--
I HAVE TO OPEN A CHANNEL TO CONNECT TO ANOTHER MIND.
LIKE THROWING OUT A FISHING LINE, AND ABOUT AS FAST.
I CAN'T MAKE THE CONNECTION FAST ENOUGH TO KNOW WHAT HE'S THINKING.
BRAK
DITTO FOR ALL THE OTHER AGENTS EXECUTING THEMSELVES SIMULTANEOUSLY.
BRAK
BRAK
BRAK
BRAK
BRAK
BRAK
BUT THE ROOF SNIPERS--THE BARRELS OF THEIR RIFLES ARE TOO LONG TO BE TURNED AGAINST THEMSELVES.

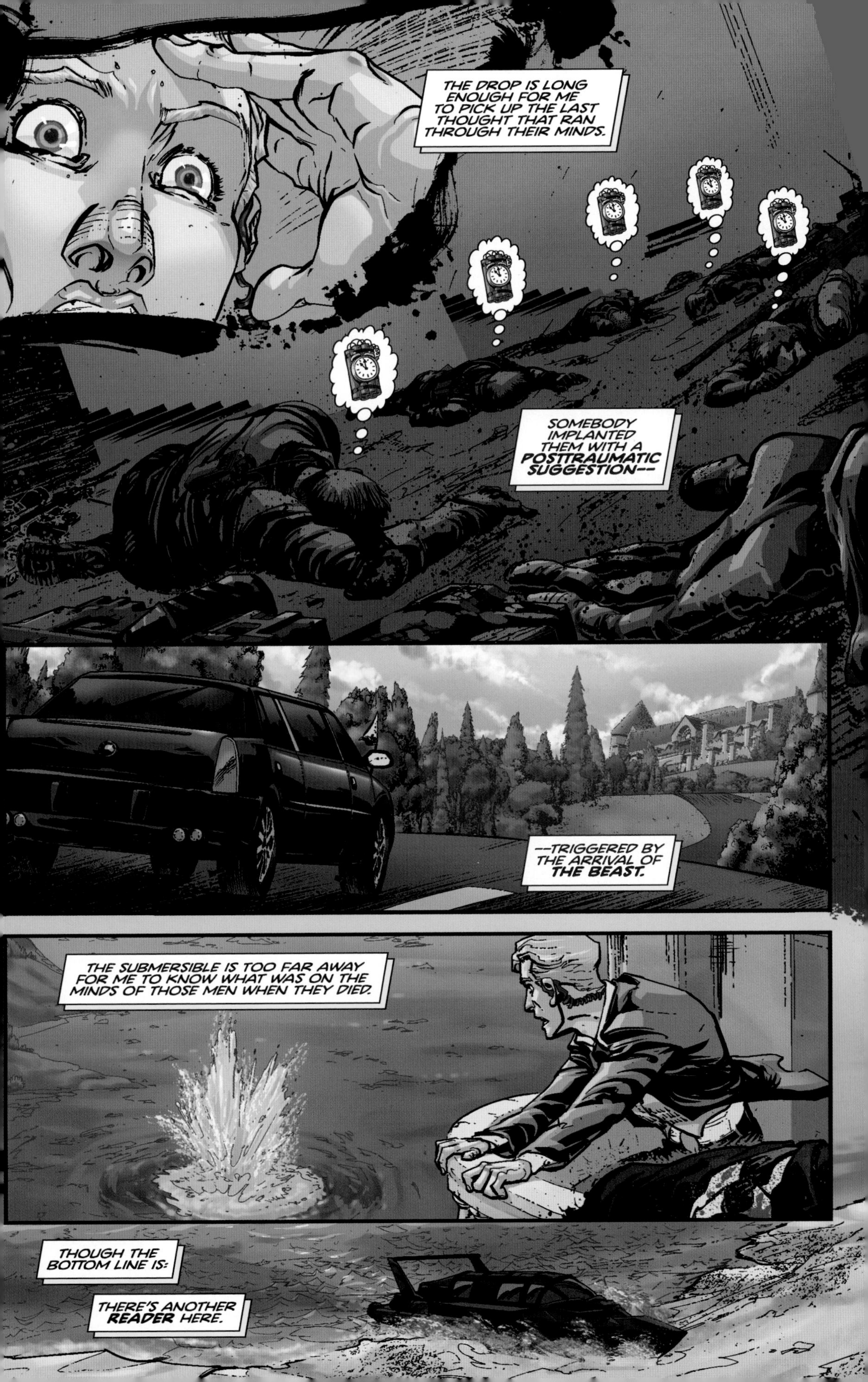
THE DROP IS LONG ENOUGH FOR ME TO PICK UP THE LAST THOUGHT THAT RAN THROUGH THEIR MINDS.
SOMEBODY IMPLANTED THEM WITH A POSTTRAUMATIC SUGGESTION--
--TRIGGERED BY THE ARRIVAL OF THE BEAST.
THE SUBMERSIBLE IS TOO FAR AWAY FOR ME TO KNOW WHAT WAS ON THE MINDS OF THOSE MEN WHEN THEY DIED.
THOUGH THE BOTTOM LINE IS:
THERE'S ANOTHER READER HERE.

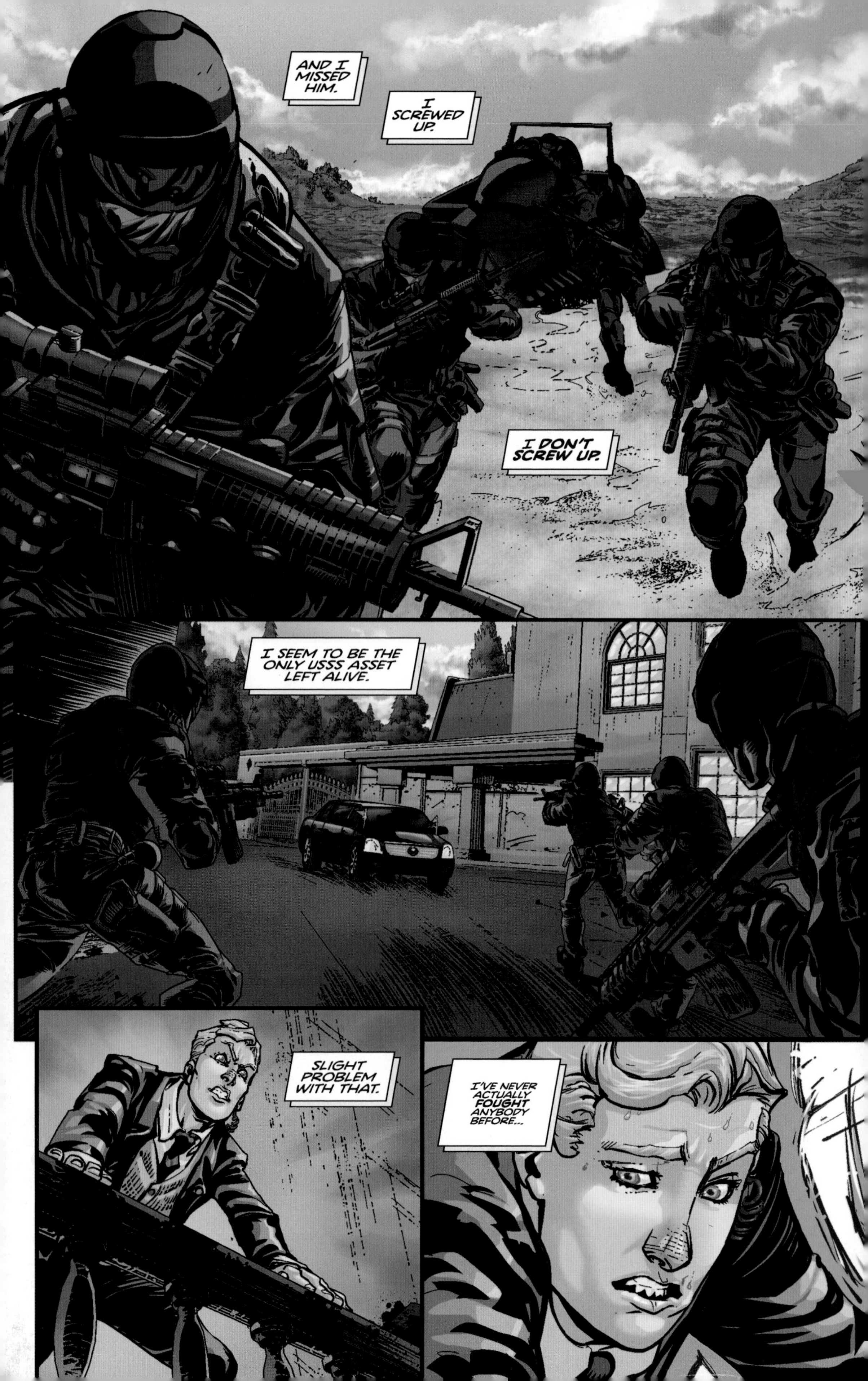
AND I MISSED HIM.
I SCREWED UP.
I DON'T SCREW UP.
I SEEM TO BE THE ONLY USSS ASSET LEFT ALIVE.
SLIGHT PROBLEM WITH THAT.
I'VE NEVER ACTUALLY FOUGHT ANYBODY BEFORE...

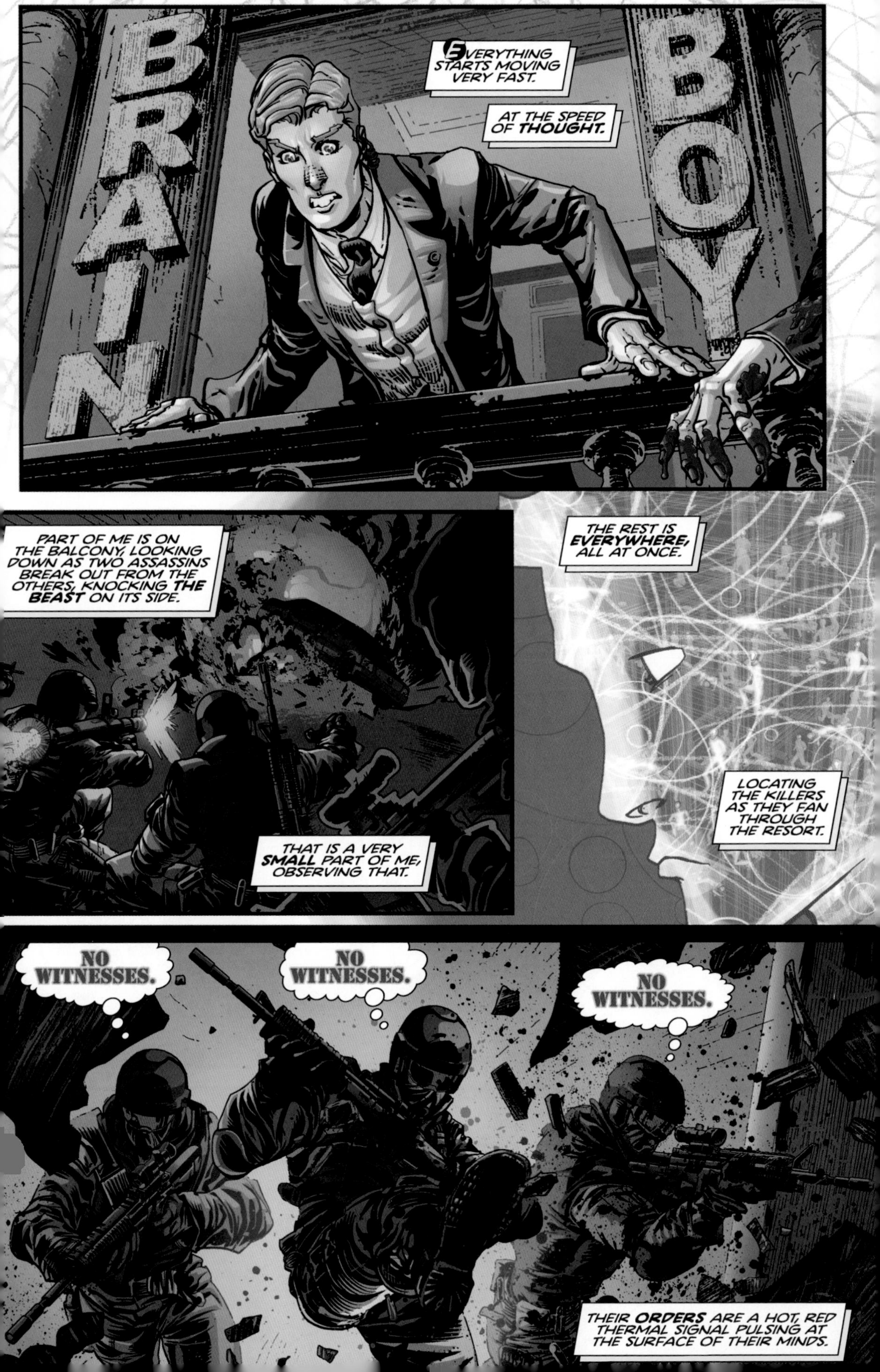
BRAIN
BOY
EVERYTHING STARTS MOVING VERY FAST.
AT THE SPEED OF THOUGHT.
PART OF ME IS ON THE BALCONY, LOOKING DOWN AS TWO ASSASSINS BREAK OUT FROM THE OTHERS, KNOCKING THE BEAST ON ITS SIDE.
THAT IS A VERY SMALL PART OF ME, OBSERVING THAT.
THE REST IS EVERYWHERE, ALL AT ONCE.
LOCATING THE KILLERS AS THEY FAN THROUGH THE RESORT.
NO WITNESSES.
NO WITNESSES.
NO WITNESSES.
THEIR ORDERS ARE A HOT, RED THERMAL SIGNAL PULSING AT THE SURFACE OF THEIR MINDS.

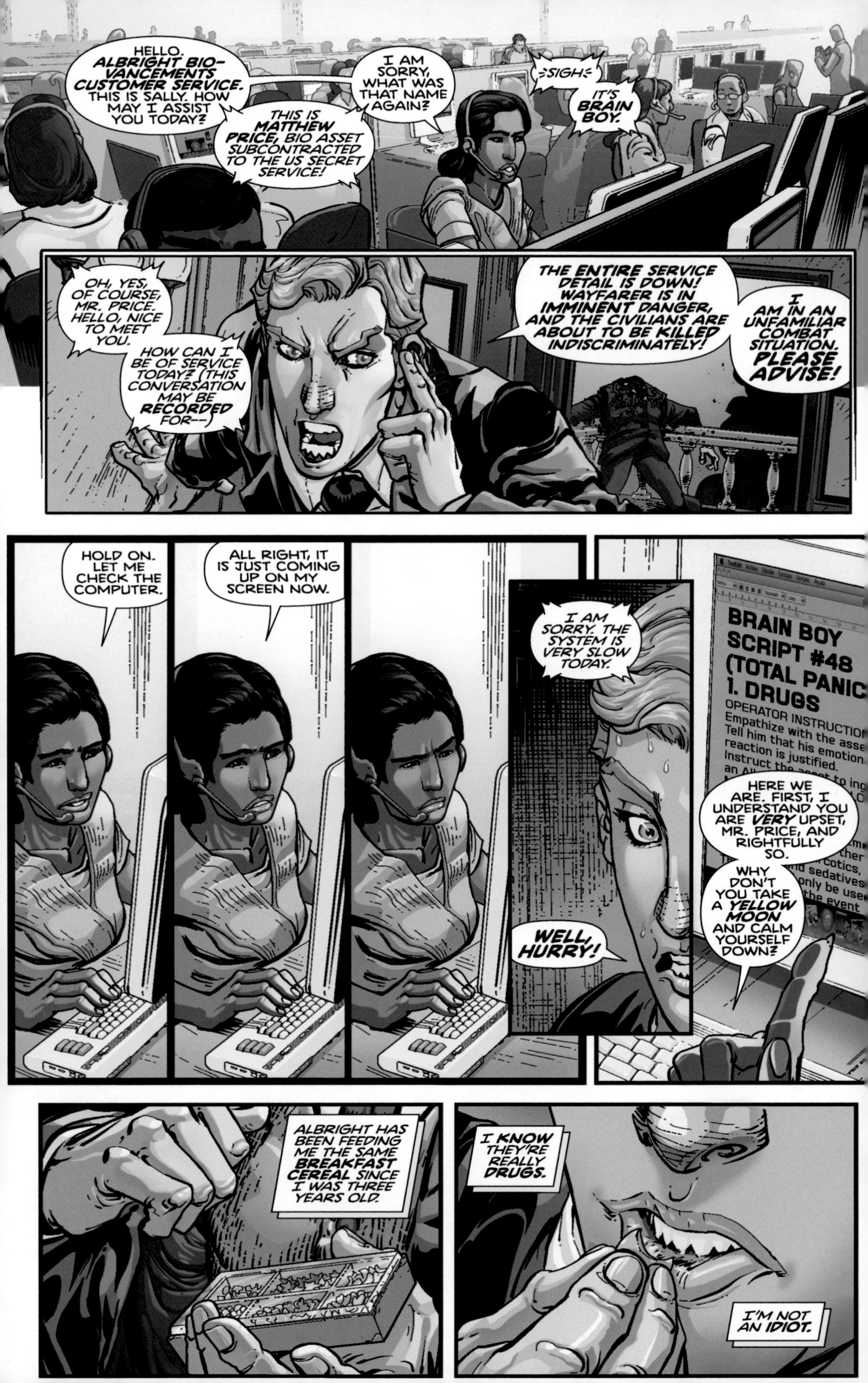
HELLO. ALBRIGHT BIO-VANCEMENTS CUSTOMER SERVICE. THIS IS SALLY. HOW MAY I ASSIST YOU TODAY?
THIS IS MATTHEW PRICE, BIO ASSET SUBCONTRACTED TO THE US SECRET SERVICE!
I AM SORRY, WHAT WAS THAT NAME AGAIN?
SIGH
IT'S BRAIN BOY.
OH, YES, OF COURSE, MR. PRICE. HELLO, NICE TO MEET YOU.
HOW CAN I BE OF SERVICE TODAY? (THIS CONVERSATION MAY BE RECORDED FOR--)
THE ENTIRE SERVICE DETAIL IS DOWN! WAYFARER IS IN IMMINENT DANGER, AND THE CIVILIANS ARE ABOUT TO BE KILLED INDISCRIMINATELY!
I AM IN AN UNFAMILIAR COMBAT SITUATION. PLEASE ADVISE!
HOLD ON. LET ME CHECK THE COMPUTER.
ALL RIGHT, IT IS JUST COMING UP ON MY SCREEN NOW.
I AM SORRY. THE SYSTEM IS VERY SLOW TODAY.
WELL, HURRY!
BRAIN BOY
SCRIPT #48
1. DRUGS
Empathize with the
reaction is justified.
HERE WE ARE. FIRST, I UNDERSTAND YOU ARE VERY UPSET, MR. PRICE, AND RIGHTFULLY SO.
WHY DON'T YOU TAKE A YELLOW MOON AND CALM YOURSELF DOWN?
ALBRIGHT HAS BEEN FEEDING ME THE SAME BREAKFAST CEREAL SINCE I WAS THREE YEARS OLD.
I KNOW THEY'RE REALLY DRUGS.
I'M NOT AN IDIOT.

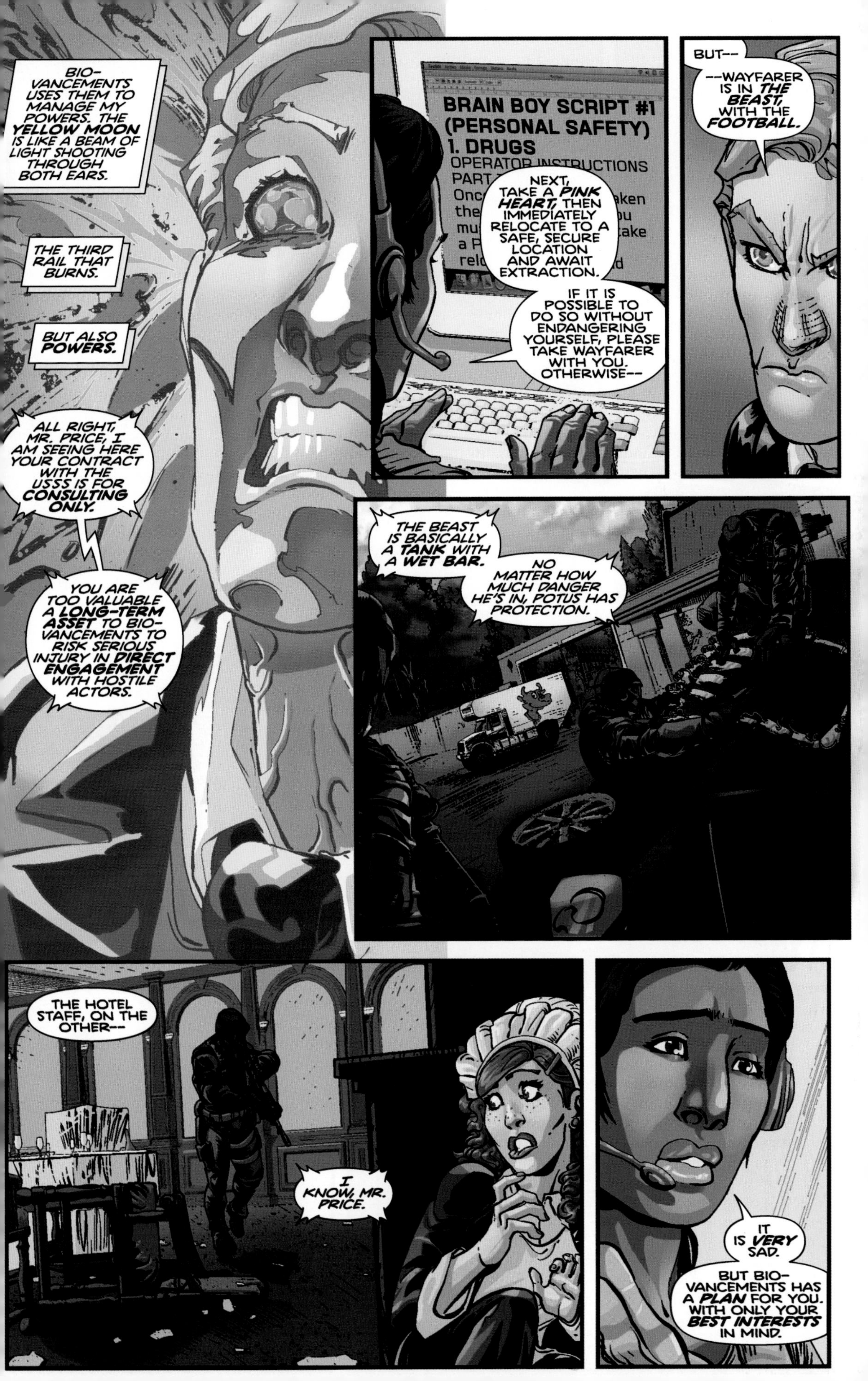
BIO-VANCEMENTS USES THEM TO MANAGE MY POWERS. THE YELLOW MOON IS LIKE A BEAM OF LIGHT SHOOTING THROUGH BOTH EARS.
THE THIRD RAIL THAT BURNS.
BUT ALSO POWERS.
ALL RIGHT, MR. PRICE, I AM SEEING HERE YOUR CONTRACT WITH THE USSS IS FOR CONSULTING ONLY.
YOU ARE TOO VALUABLE A LONG-TERM ASSET TO BIO-VANCEMENTS TO RISK SERIOUS INJURY IN DIRECT ENGAGEMENT WITH HOSTILE ACTORS.
BRAIN BOY SCRIPT #1
(PERSONAL SAFETY)
1. DRUGS
OPERATOR INSTRUCTIONS
NEXT, TAKE A PINK HEART, THEN IMMEDIATELY RELOCATE TO A SAFE, SECURE LOCATION AND AWAIT EXTRACTION.
IF IT IS POSSIBLE TO DO SO WITHOUT ENDANGERING YOURSELF, PLEASE TAKE WAYFARER WITH YOU. OTHERWISE--
BUT--
--WAYFARER IS IN THE BEAST, WITH THE FOOTBALL.
THE BEAST IS BASICALLY A TANK WITH A WET BAR.
NO MATTER HOW MUCH DANGER HE'S IN, POTUS HAS PROTECTION.
THE HOTEL STAFF, ON THE OTHER--
I KNOW, MR. PRICE.
IT IS VERY SAD.
BUT BIO-VANCEMENTS HAS A PLAN FOR YOU. WITH ONLY YOUR BEST INTERESTS IN MIND.

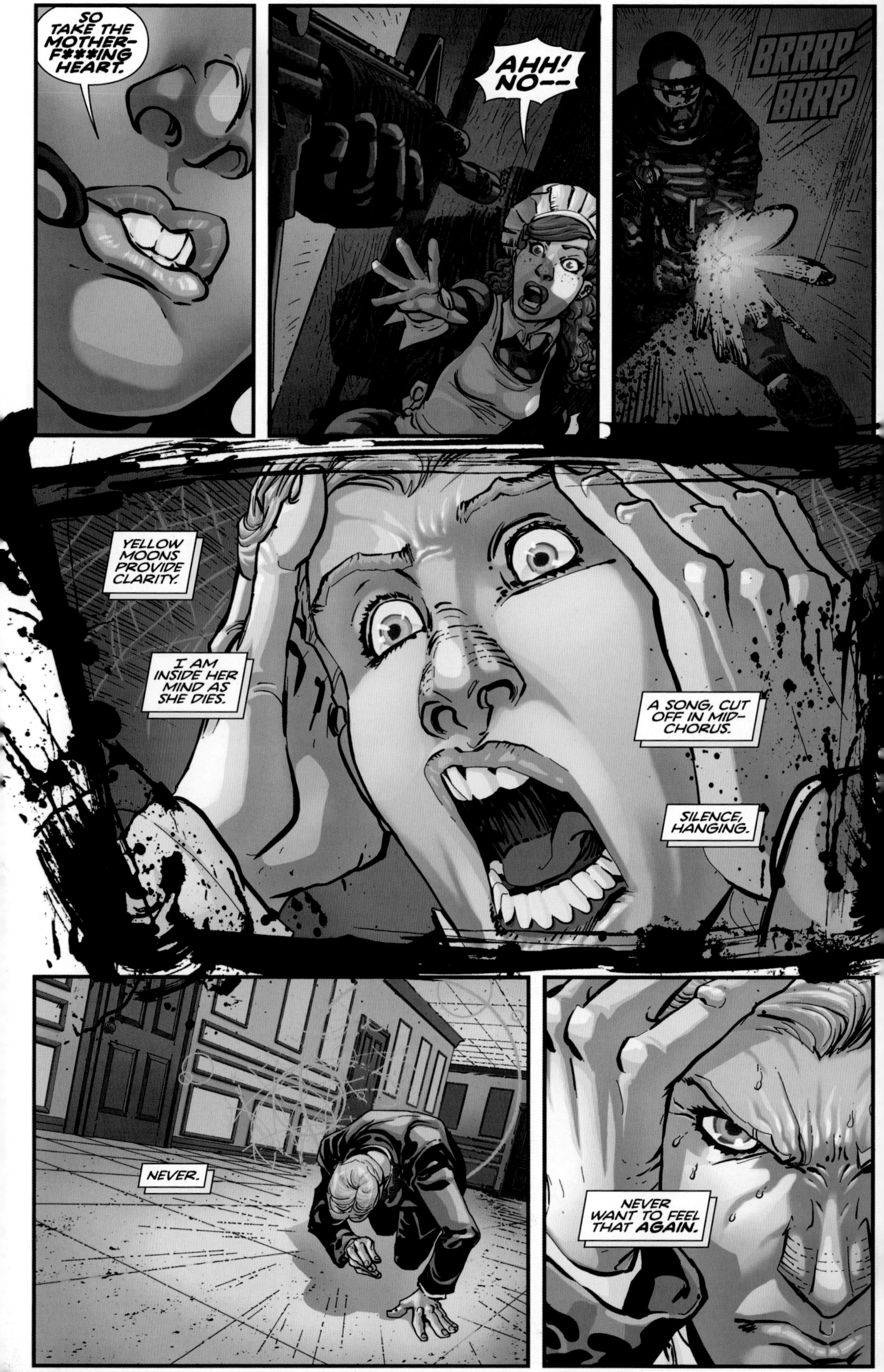
SO TAKE THE MOTHER-F***ING HEART.
AHH! NO--
BRRRP BRRP
YELLOW MOONS PROVIDE CLARITY.
I AM INSIDE HER MIND AS SHE DIES.
A SONG, CUT OFF IN MID-CHORUS.
SILENCE, HANGING.
NEVER.
NEVER WANT TO FEEL THAT AGAIN.

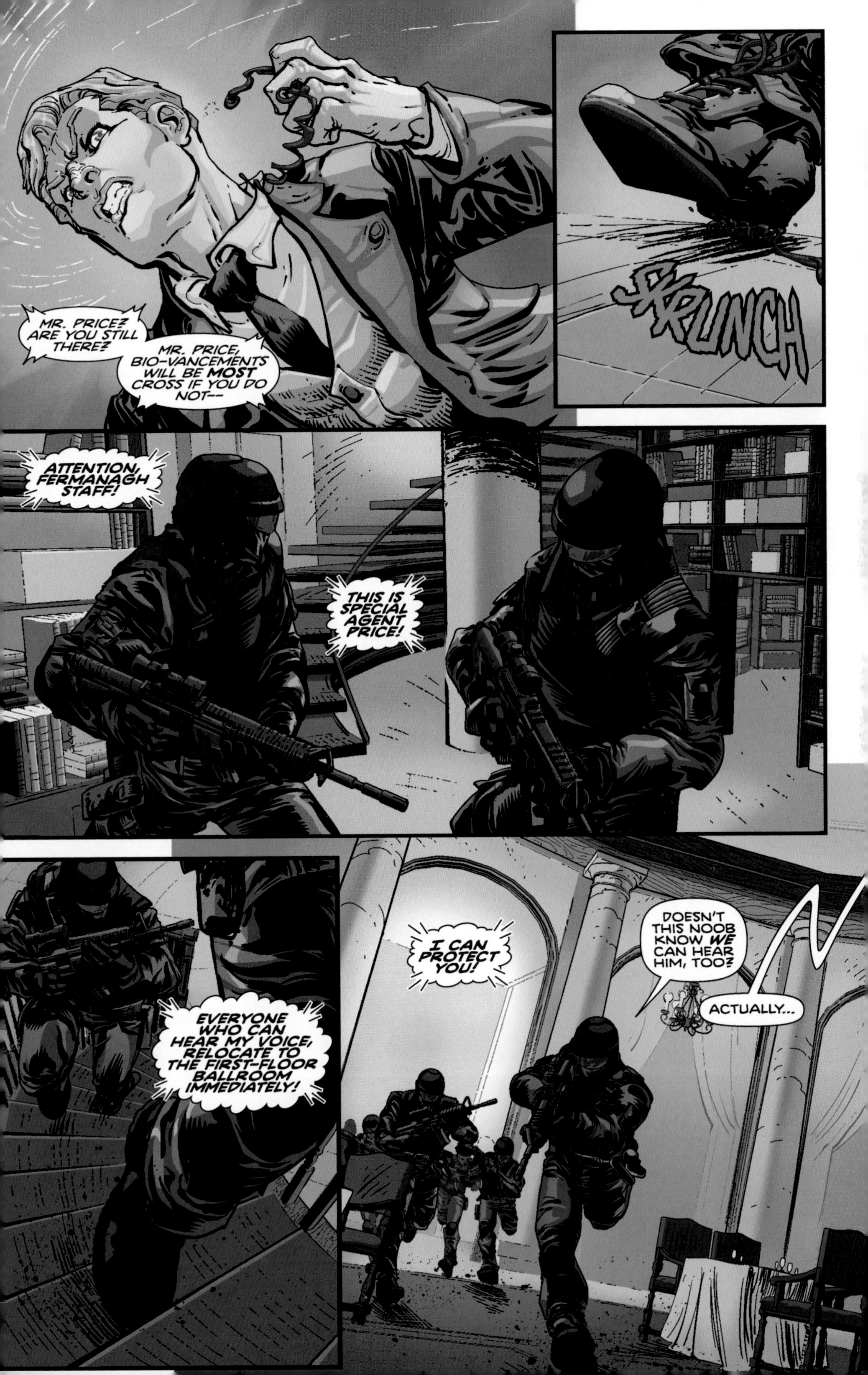
MR. PRICE? ARE YOU STILL THERE?
MR. PRICE, BIO-VANCEMENTS WILL BE MOST CROSS IF YOU DO NOT--
SKRUNCH
ATTENTION, FERMANAGH STAFF!
THIS IS SPECIAL AGENT PRICE!
I CAN PROTECT YOU!
DOESN'T THIS NOOB KNOW WE CAN HEAR HIM, TOO?
ACTUALLY...
EVERYONE WHO CAN HEAR MY VOICE, RELOCATE TO THE FIRST-FLOOR BALLROOM IMMEDIATELY!

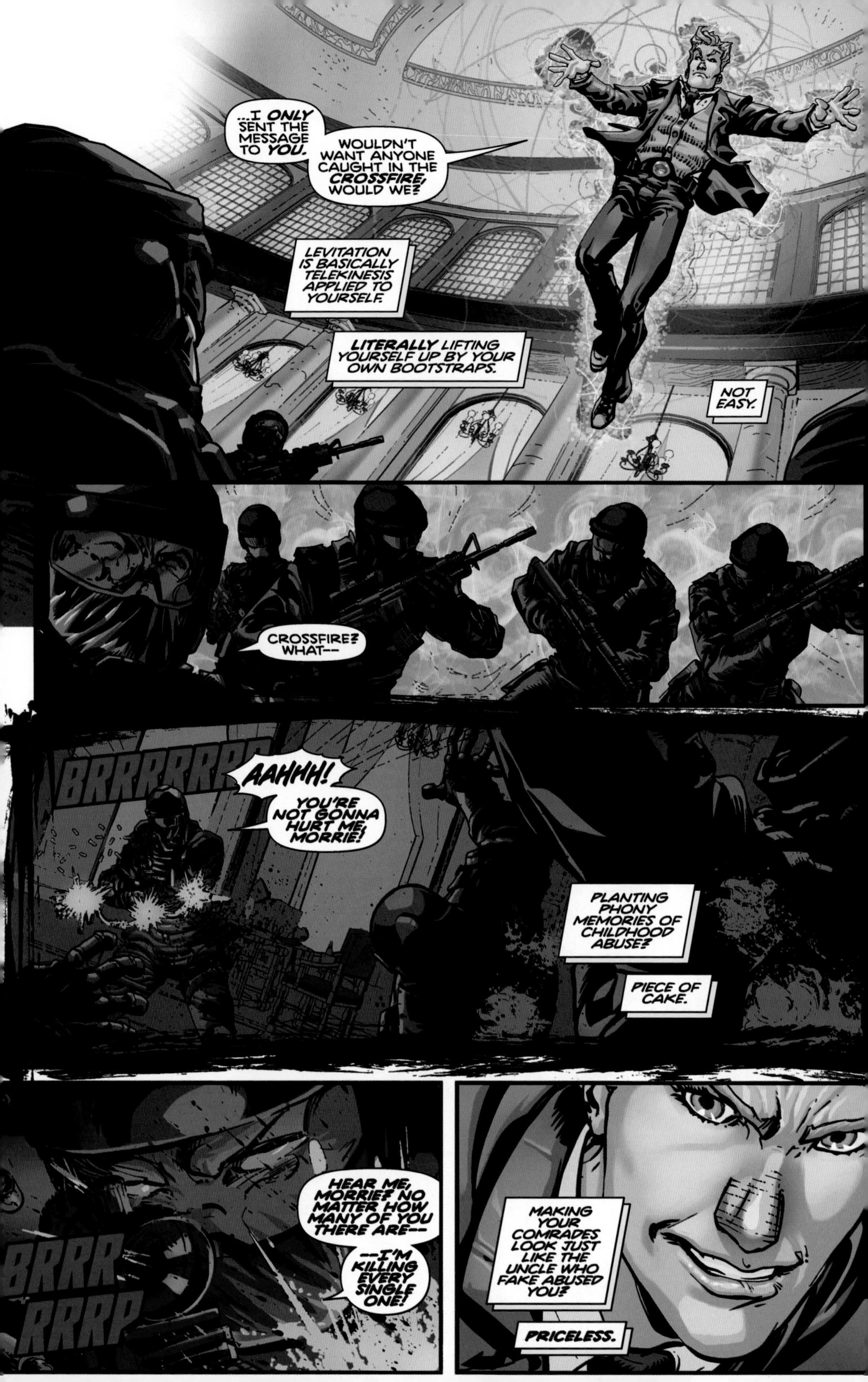
...I ONLY SENT THE MESSAGE TO YOU.
WOULDN'T WANT ANYONE CAUGHT IN THE CROSSFIRE, WOULD WE?
LEVITATION IS BASICALLY TELEKINESIS APPLIED TO YOURSELF.
LITERALLY LIFTING YOURSELF UP BY YOUR OWN BOOTSTRAPS.
NOT EASY.
CROSSFIRE? WHAT--
BRRRRRRP
AAHHH!
YOU'RE NOT GONNA HURT ME, MORRIE!
PLANTING PHONY MEMORIES OF CHILDHOOD ABUSE?
PIECE OF CAKE.
BRRR RRRP
HEAR ME, MORRIE? NO MATTER HOW MANY OF YOU THERE ARE--
--I'M KILLING EVERY SINGLE ONE!
MAKING YOUR COMRADES LOOK JUST LIKE THE UNCLE WHO FAKE ABUSED YOU?
PRICELESS.

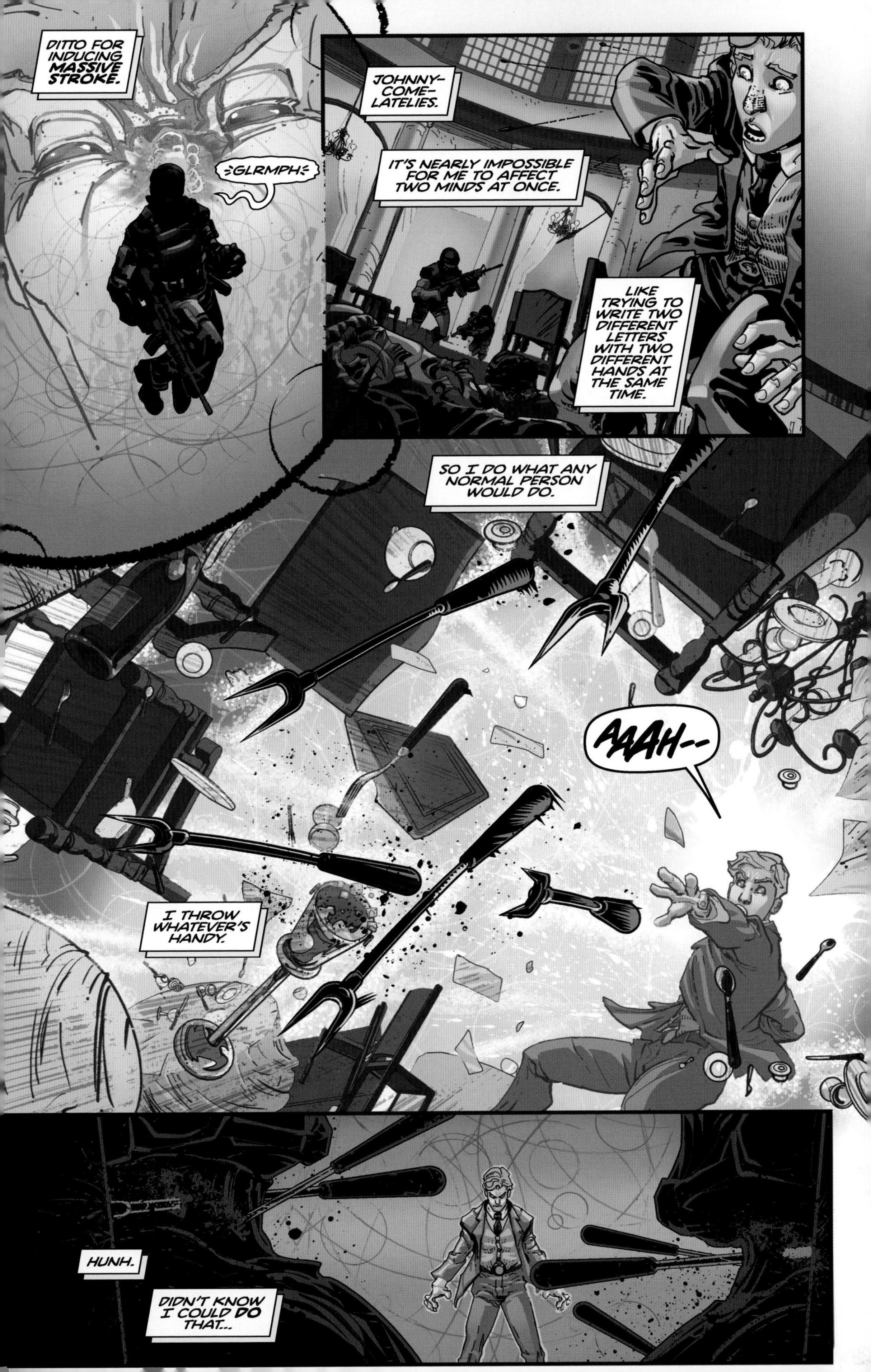
DITTO FOR INDUCING MASSIVE STROKE.
GLRMPH
JOHNNY-COME-LATELIES.
IT'S NEARLY IMPOSSIBLE FOR ME TO AFFECT TWO MINDS AT ONCE.
LIKE TRYING TO WRITE TWO DIFFERENT LETTERS WITH TWO DIFFERENT HANDS AT THE SAME TIME.
SO I DO WHAT ANY NORMAL PERSON WOULD DO.
AAAH--
I THROW WHATEVER'S HANDY.
HUNH.
DIDN'T KNOW I COULD DO THAT...

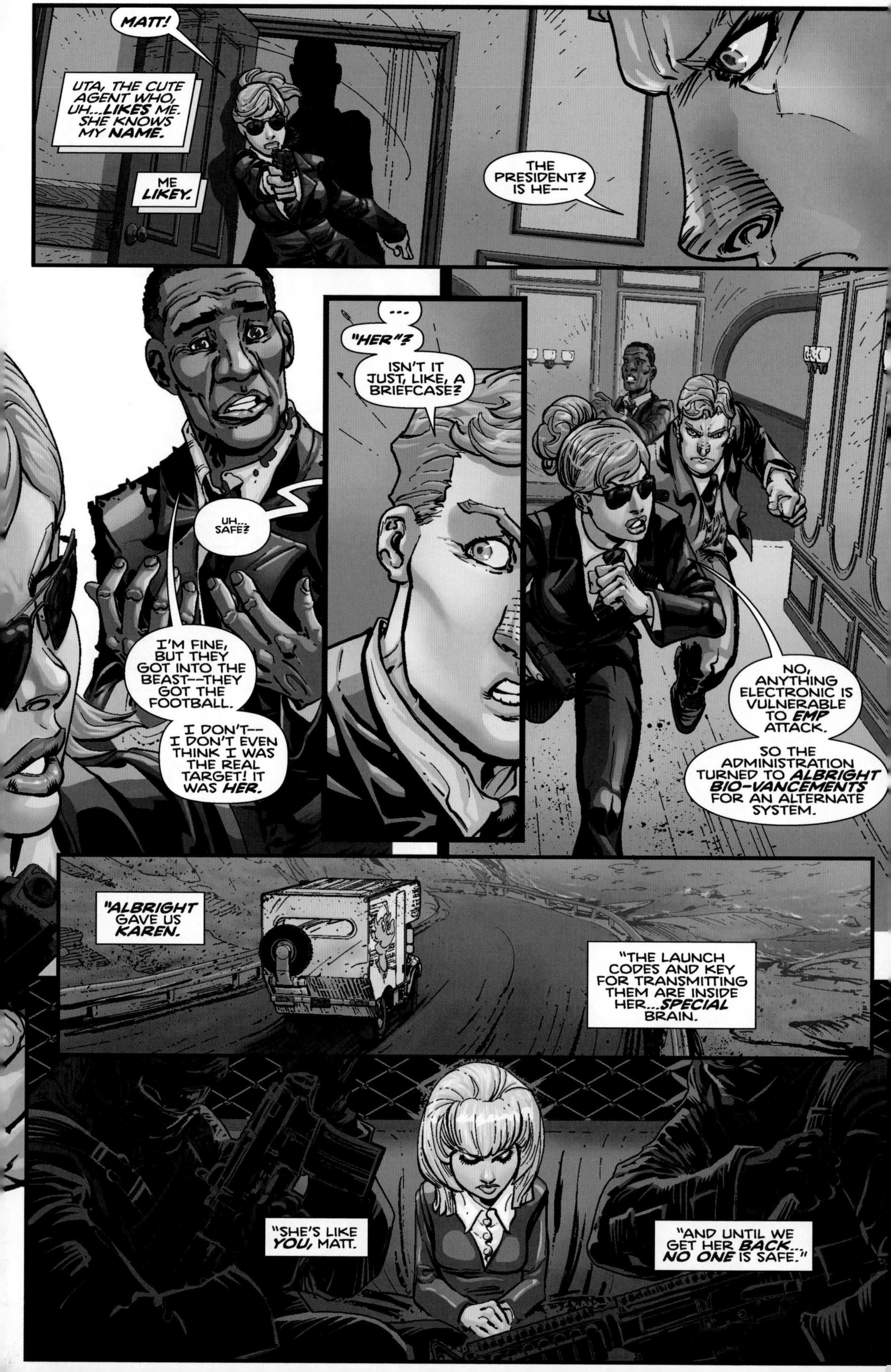
MATT!
UTA, THE CUTE AGENT WHO, UH...LIKES ME. SHE KNOWS MY NAME.
ME LIKEY.
THE PRESIDENT? IS HE--
UH... SAFE?
I'M FINE, BUT THEY GOT INTO THE BEAST--THEY GOT THE FOOTBALL.
I DON'T-- I DON'T EVEN THINK I WAS THE REAL TARGET! IT WAS HER.
...
"HER"?
ISN'T IT JUST, LIKE, A BRIEFCASE?
NO, ANYTHING ELECTRONIC IS VULNERABLE TO EMP ATTACK.
SO THE ADMINISTRATION TURNED TO ALBRIGHT BIO-VANCEMENTS FOR AN ALTERNATE SYSTEM.
"ALBRIGHT GAVE US KAREN.
"THE LAUNCH CODES AND KEY FOR TRANSMITTING THEM ARE INSIDE HER...SPECIAL BRAIN.
"SHE'S LIKE YOU, MATT.
"AND UNTIL WE GET HER BACK... NO ONE IS SAFE."

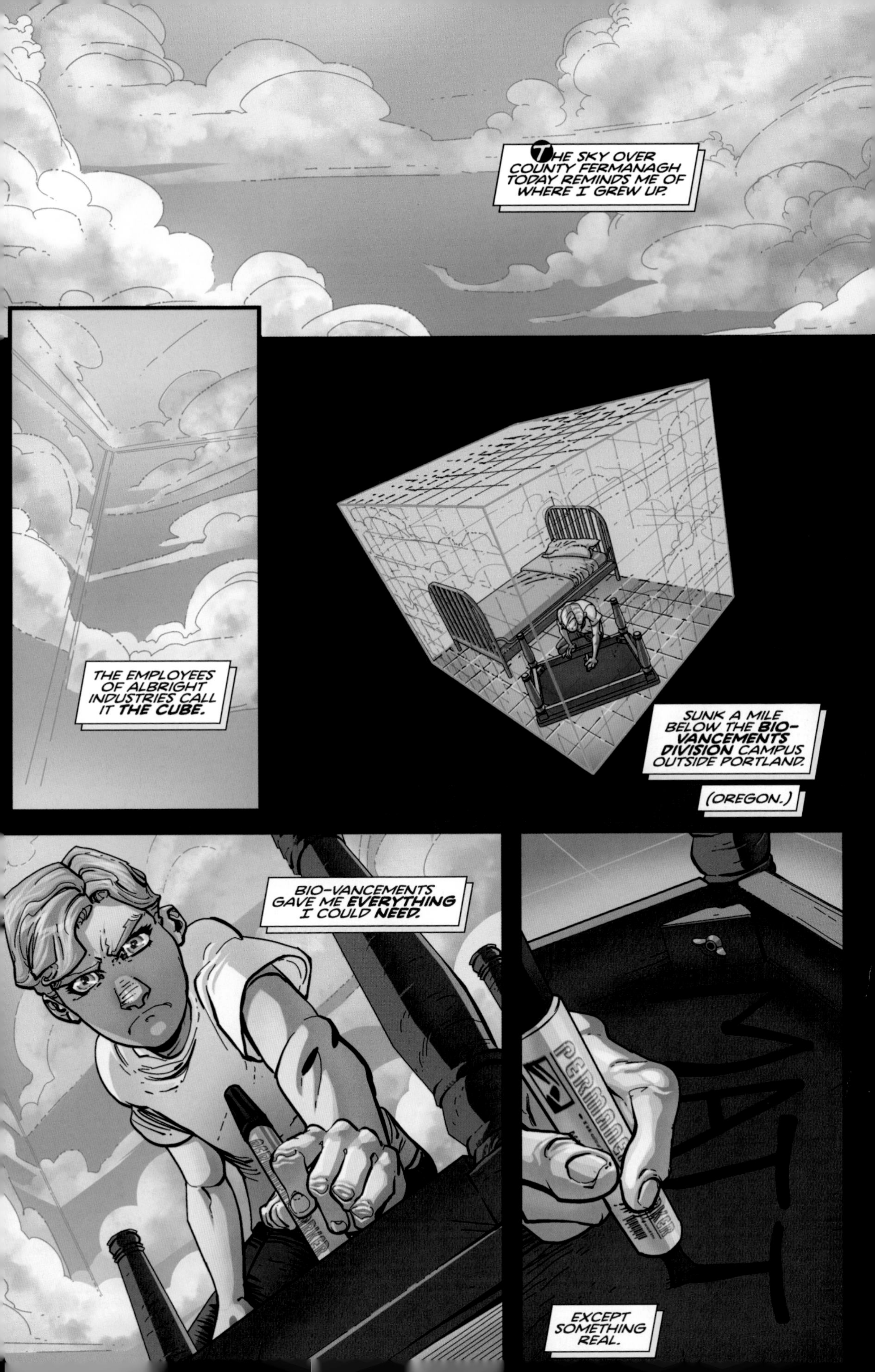
THE SKY OVER COUNTY FERMANAGH TODAY REMINDS ME OF WHERE I GREW UP.
THE EMPLOYEES OF ALBRIGHT INDUSTRIES CALL IT THE CUBE.
SUNK A MILE BELOW THE BIO-VANCEMENTS DIVISION CAMPUS OUTSIDE PORTLAND.
(OREGON.)
BIO-VANCEMENTS GAVE ME EVERYTHING I COULD NEED.
PERMANENT MARKER
EXCEPT SOMETHING REAL.

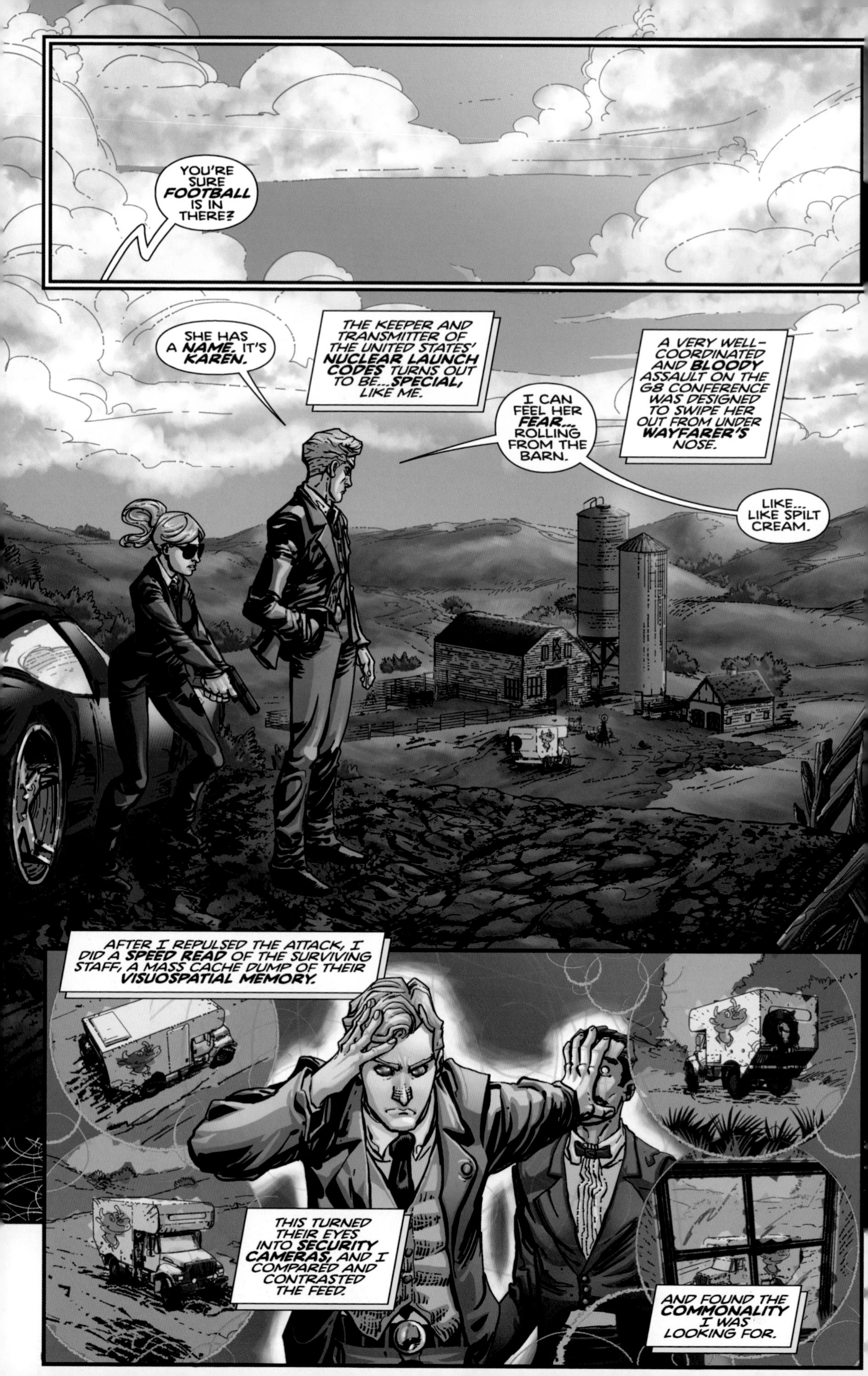

YOU'RE SURE **FOOTBALL** IS IN THERE?
SHE HAS A **NAME.** IT'S **KAREN.**
THE KEEPER AND TRANSMITTER OF THE UNITED STATES' **NUCLEAR LAUNCH CODES** TURNS OUT TO BE...**SPECIAL,** LIKE ME.
A VERY WELL-COORDINATED AND **BLOODY** ASSAULT ON THE G8 CONFERENCE WAS DESIGNED TO SWIPE HER OUT FROM UNDER **WAYFARER'S** NOSE.
I CAN FEEL HER **FEAR...** ROLLING FROM THE BARN.
LIKE... LIKE SPILT CREAM.
AFTER I REPULSED THE ATTACK, I DID A **SPEED READ** OF THE SURVIVING STAFF, A MASS CACHE DUMP OF THEIR **VISUOSPATIAL MEMORY.**
THIS TURNED THEIR EYES INTO **SECURITY CAMERAS,** AND I COMPARED AND CONTRASTED THE FEED.
AND FOUND THE **COMMONALITY** I WAS LOOKING FOR.

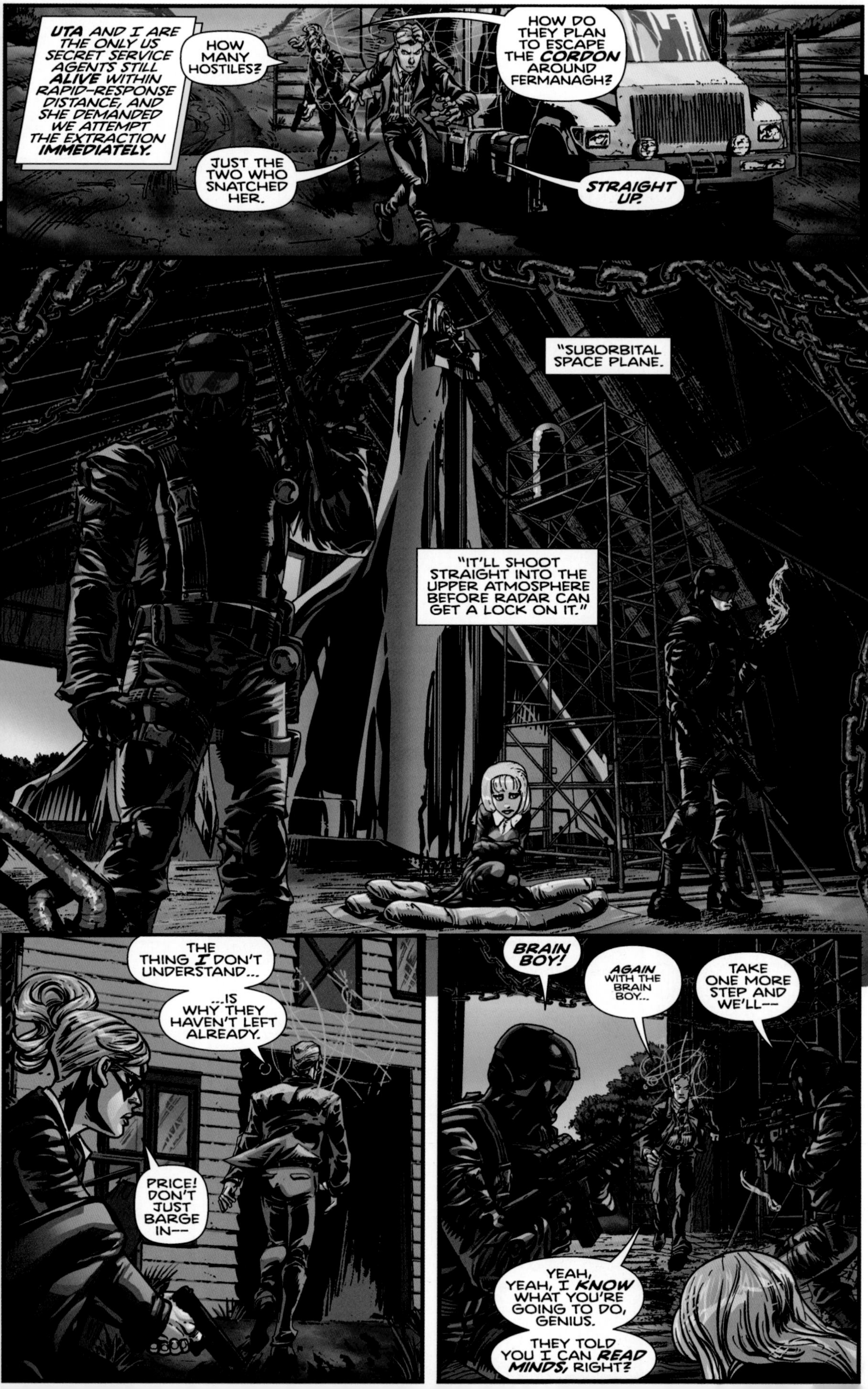
UTA AND I ARE THE ONLY US SECRET SERVICE AGENTS STILL ALIVE WITHIN RAPID-RESPONSE DISTANCE, AND SHE DEMANDED WE ATTEMPT THE EXTRACTION IMMEDIATELY.
HOW MANY HOSTILES?
JUST THE TWO WHO SNATCHED HER.
HOW DO THEY PLAN TO ESCAPE THE CORDON AROUND FERMANAGH?
STRAIGHT UP.
"SUBORBITAL SPACE PLANE.
"IT'LL SHOOT STRAIGHT INTO THE UPPER ATMOSPHERE BEFORE RADAR CAN GET A LOCK ON IT."
THE THING I DON'T UNDERSTAND...
...IS WHY THEY HAVEN'T LEFT ALREADY.
PRICE! DON'T JUST BARGE IN--
BRAIN BOY!
AGAIN WITH THE BRAIN BOY...
TAKE ONE MORE STEP AND WE'LL--
YEAH, YEAH, I KNOW WHAT YOU'RE GOING TO DO, GENIUS.
THEY TOLD YOU I CAN READ MINDS, RIGHT?

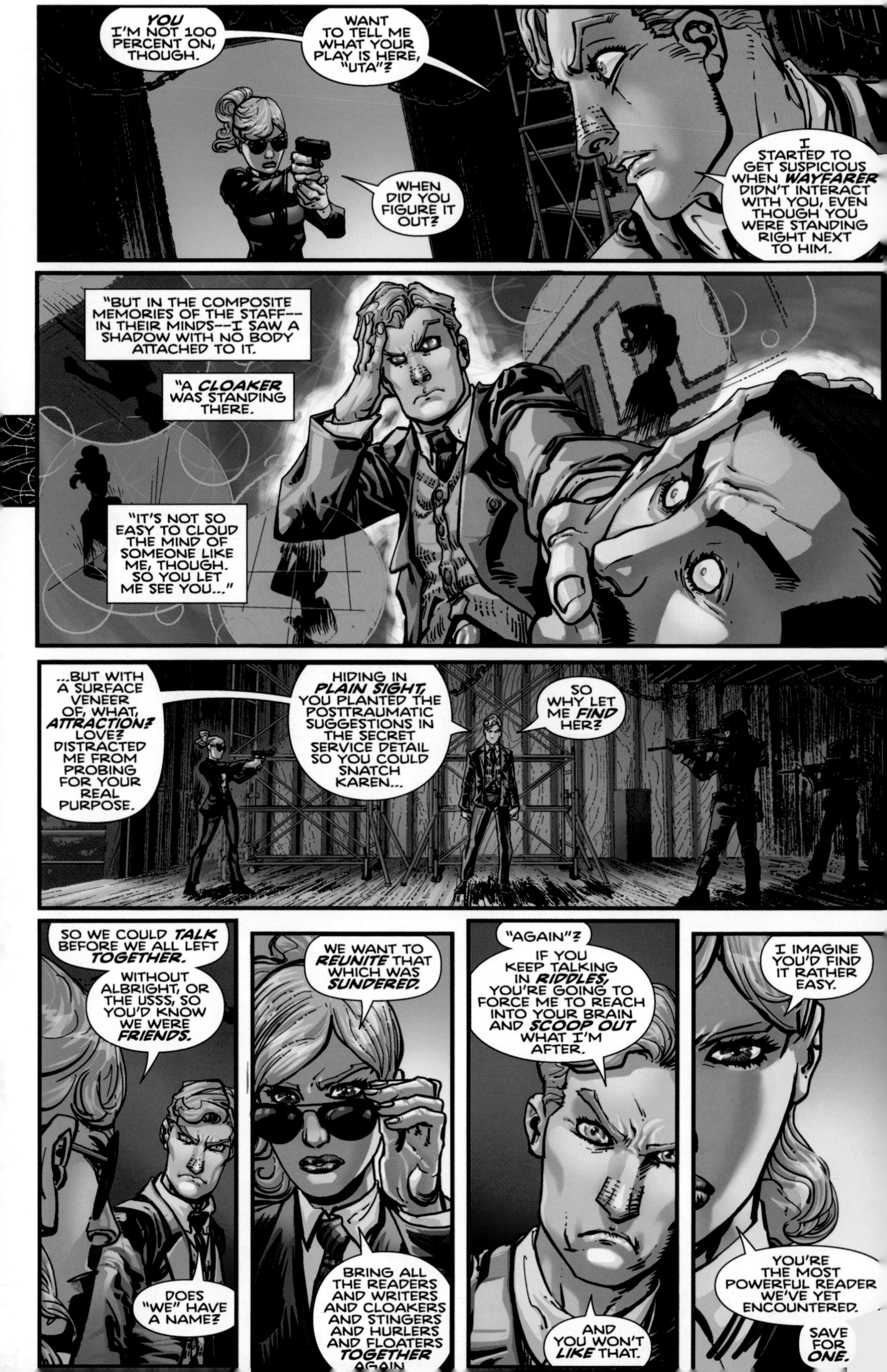
YOU I'M NOT 100 PERCENT ON, THOUGH.
WANT TO TELL ME WHAT YOUR PLAY IS HERE, "UTA"?
WHEN DID YOU FIGURE IT OUT?
I STARTED TO GET SUSPICIOUS WHEN WAYFARER DIDN'T INTERACT WITH YOU, EVEN THOUGH YOU WERE STANDING RIGHT NEXT TO HIM.
"BUT IN THE COMPOSITE MEMORIES OF THE STAFF-- IN THEIR MINDS--I SAW A SHADOW WITH NO BODY ATTACHED TO IT.
"A CLOAKER WAS STANDING THERE.
"IT'S NOT SO EASY TO CLOUD THE MIND OF SOMEONE LIKE ME, THOUGH. SO YOU LET ME SEE YOU..."
...BUT WITH A SURFACE VENEER OF, WHAT, ATTRACTION? LOVE? DISTRACTED ME FROM PROBING FOR YOUR REAL PURPOSE.
HIDING IN PLAIN SIGHT, YOU PLANTED THE POSTTRAUMATIC SUGGESTIONS IN THE SECRET SERVICE DETAIL SO YOU COULD SNATCH KAREN...
SO WHY LET ME FIND HER?
SO WE COULD TALK BEFORE WE ALL LEFT TOGETHER.
WITHOUT ALBRIGHT, OR THE USSS, SO YOU'D KNOW WE WERE FRIENDS.
DOES "WE" HAVE A NAME?
WE WANT TO REUNITE THAT WHICH WAS SUNDERED.
BRING ALL THE READERS AND WRITERS AND CLOAKERS AND STINGERS AND HURLERS AND FLOATERS TOGETHER AGAIN.
"AGAIN"?
IF YOU KEEP TALKING IN RIDDLES, YOU'RE GOING TO FORCE ME TO REACH INTO YOUR BRAIN AND SCOOP OUT WHAT I'M AFTER.
AND YOU WON'T LIKE THAT.
I IMAGINE YOU'D FIND IT RATHER EASY.
YOU'RE THE MOST POWERFUL READER WE'VE YET ENCOUNTERED.
SAVE FOR ONE.

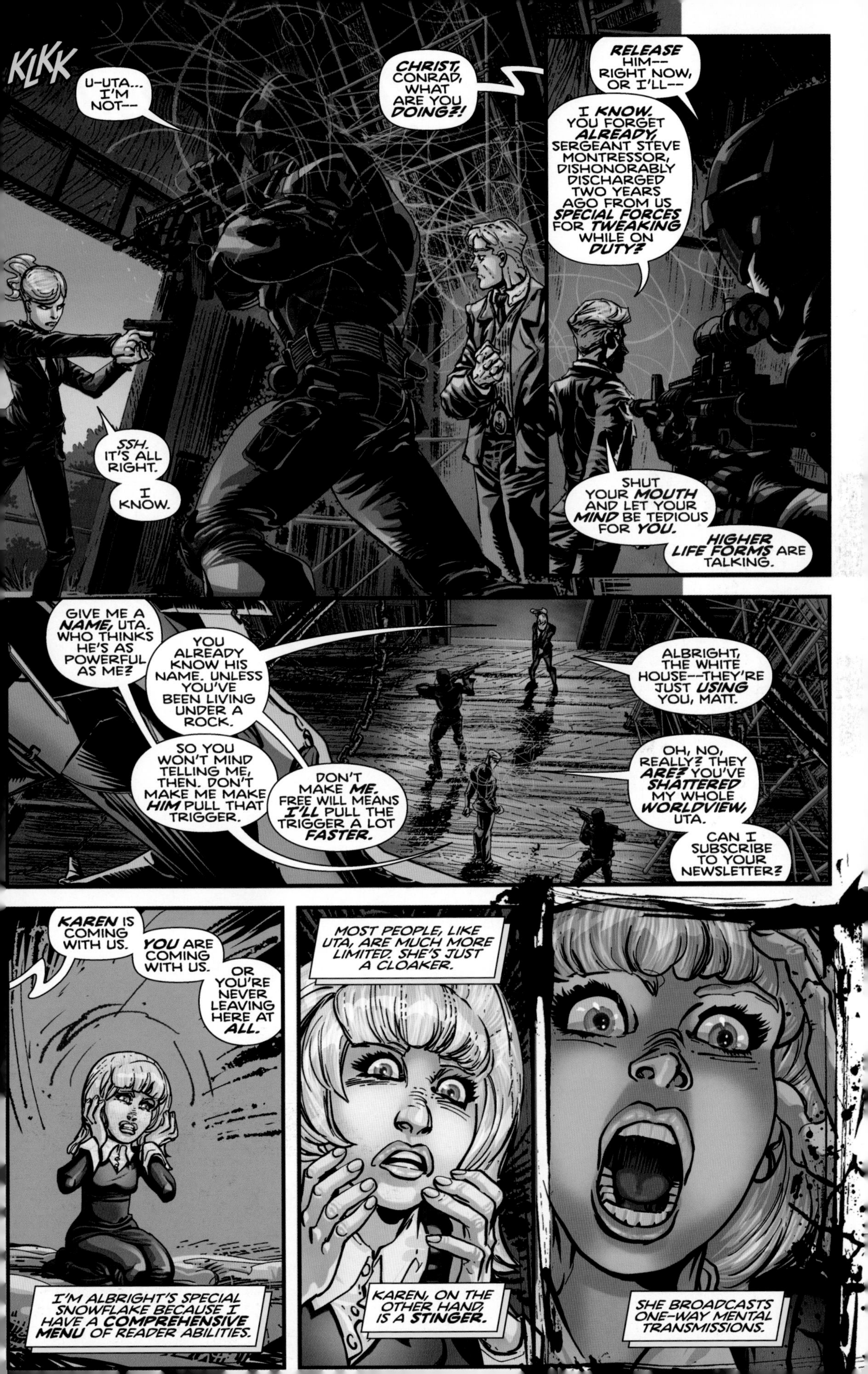
KLIKK
U-UTA... I'M NOT--
CHRIST, CONRAD, WHAT ARE YOU DOING?!
SSH. IT'S ALL RIGHT.
I KNOW.
RELEASE HIM-- RIGHT NOW, OR I'LL--
I KNOW. YOU FORGET ALREADY, SERGEANT STEVE MONTRESSOR, DISHONORABLY DISCHARGED TWO YEARS AGO FROM US SPECIAL FORCES FOR TWEAKING WHILE ON DUTY?
SHUT YOUR MOUTH AND LET YOUR MIND BE TEDIOUS FOR YOU.
HIGHER LIFE FORMS ARE TALKING.
GIVE ME A NAME, UTA. WHO THINKS HE'S AS POWERFUL AS ME?
YOU ALREADY KNOW HIS NAME. UNLESS YOU'VE BEEN LIVING UNDER A ROCK.
SO YOU WON'T MIND TELLING ME, THEN. DON'T MAKE ME MAKE HIM PULL THAT TRIGGER.
DON'T MAKE ME. FREE WILL MEANS I'LL PULL THE TRIGGER A LOT FASTER.
ALBRIGHT, THE WHITE HOUSE--THEY'RE JUST USING YOU, MATT.
OH, NO, REALLY? THEY ARE? YOU'VE SHATTERED MY WHOLE WORLDVIEW, UTA.
CAN I SUBSCRIBE TO YOUR NEWSLETTER?
KAREN IS COMING WITH US.
YOU ARE COMING WITH US.
OR YOU'RE NEVER LEAVING HERE AT ALL.
I'M ALBRIGHT'S SPECIAL SNOWFLAKE BECAUSE I HAVE A COMPREHENSIVE MENU OF READER ABILITIES.
MOST PEOPLE, LIKE UTA, ARE MUCH MORE LIMITED. SHE'S JUST A CLOAKER.
KAREN, ON THE OTHER HAND, IS A STINGER.
SHE BROADCASTS ONE-WAY MENTAL TRANSMISSIONS.

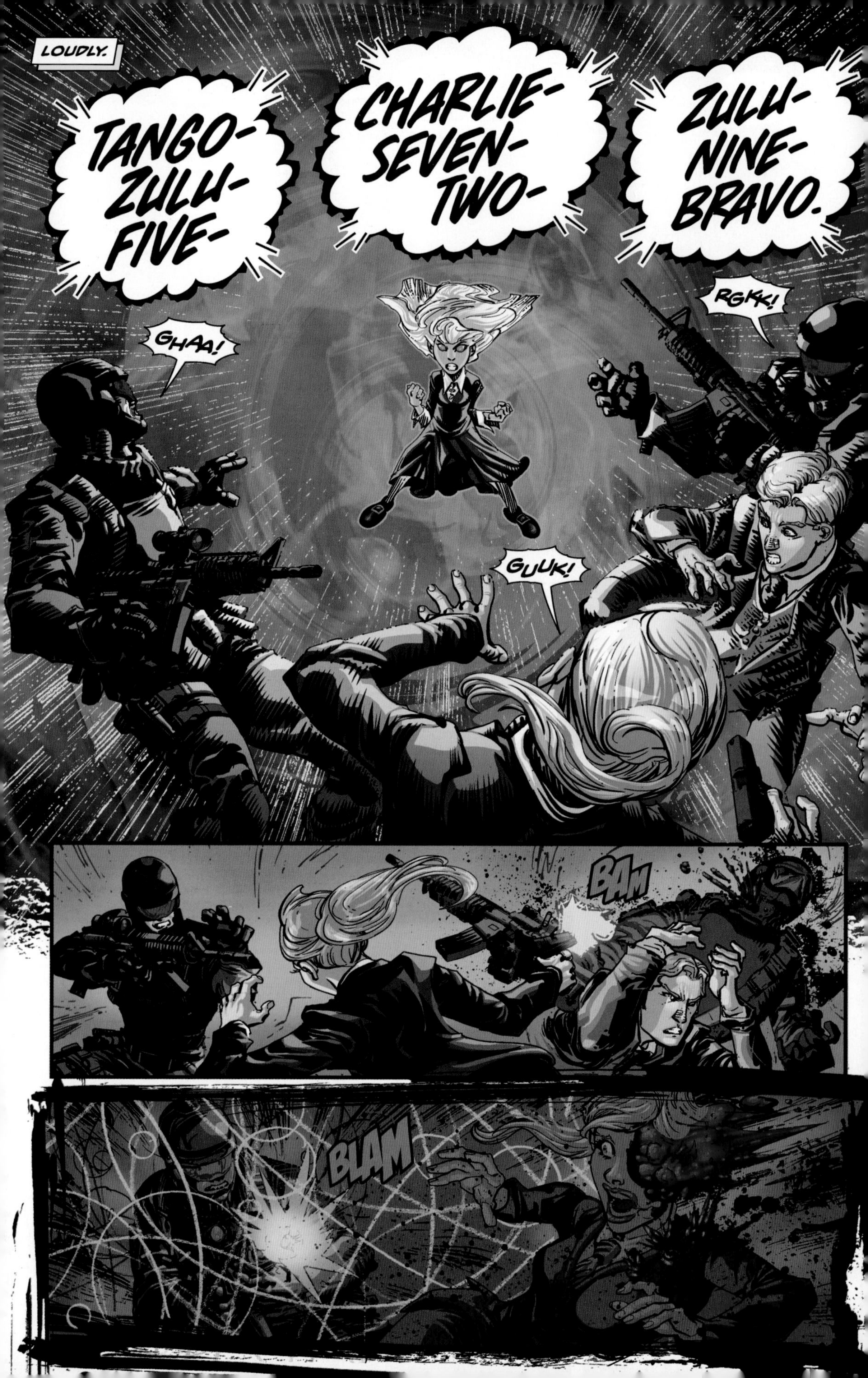

LOUDLY.
TANGO-ZULU-FIVE-
CHARLIE-SEVEN-TWO-
ZULU-NINE-BRAVO.
GHAA!
RGKK!
GUUK!
BAM
BLAM

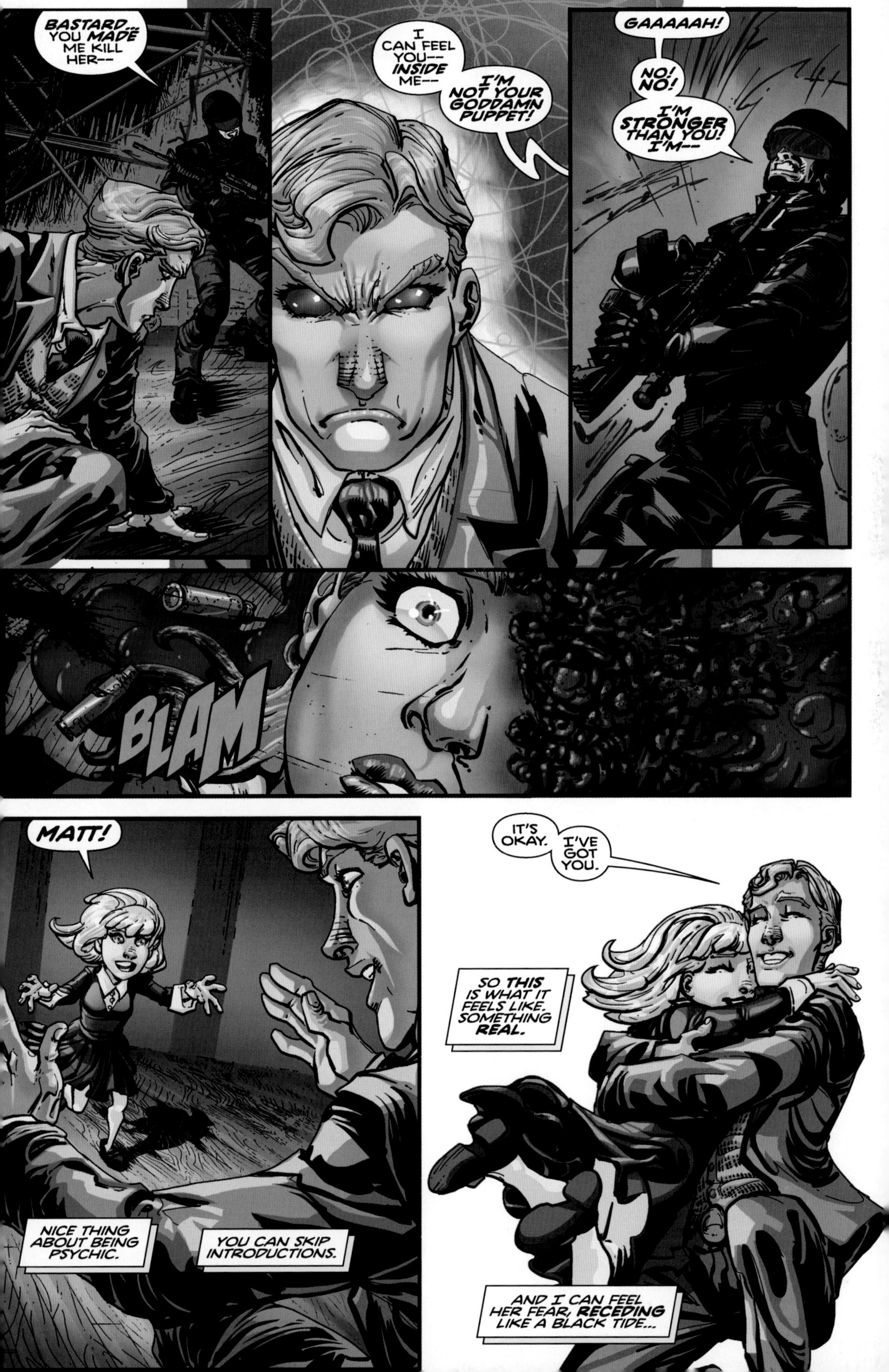
BASTARD... YOU MADE ME KILL HER--
I CAN FEEL YOU-- INSIDE ME--
I'M NOT YOUR GODDAMN PUPPET!
GAAAAAH!
NO! NO!
I'M STRONGER THAN YOU! I'M--
BLAM
MATT!
NICE THING ABOUT BEING PSYCHIC.
YOU CAN SKIP INTRODUCTIONS.
IT'S OKAY.
I'VE GOT YOU.
SO THIS IS WHAT IT FEELS LIKE. SOMETHING REAL.
AND I CAN FEEL HER FEAR, RECEDING LIKE A BLACK TIDE...

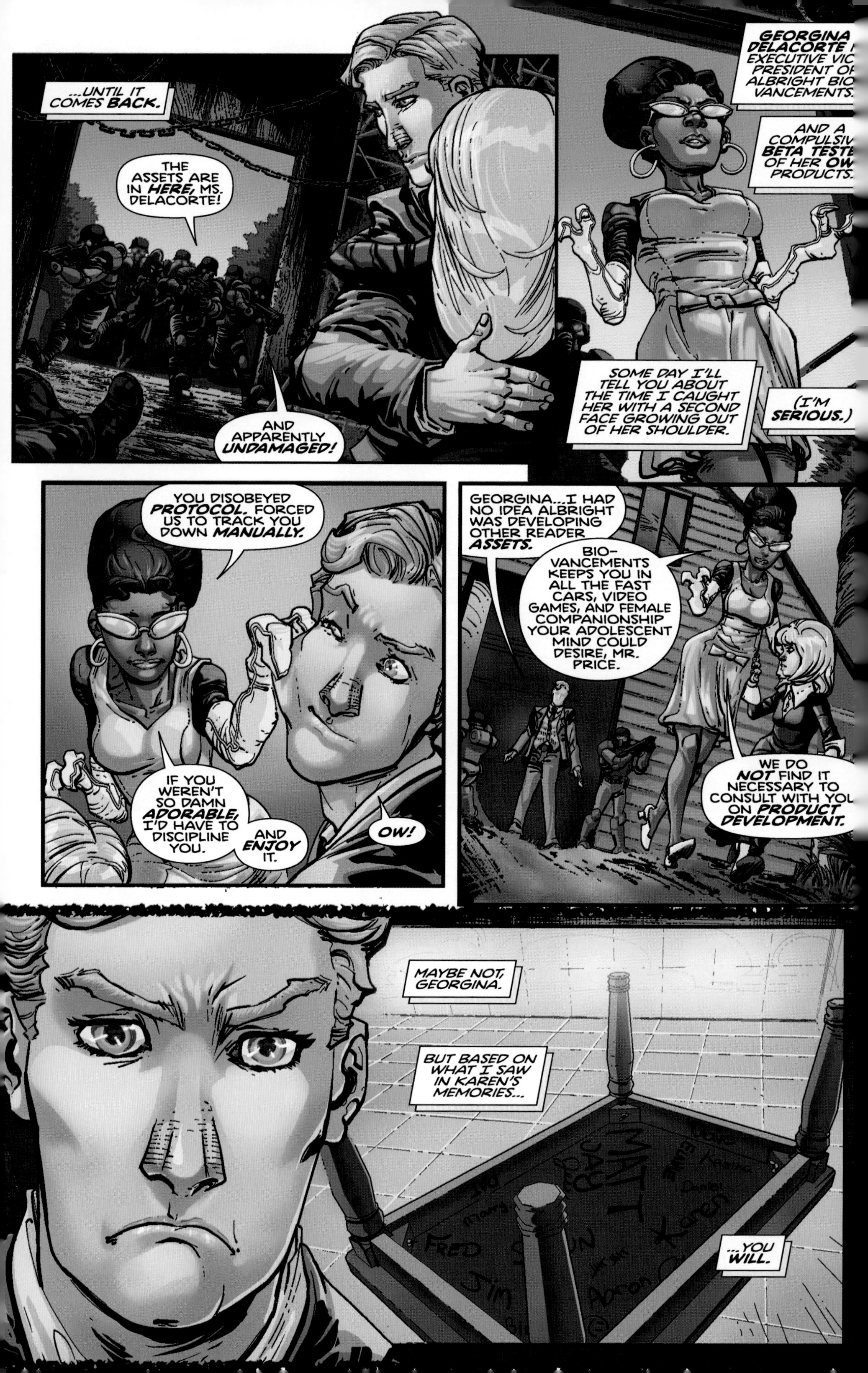

...UNTIL IT COMES BACK.
THE ASSETS ARE IN HERE, MS. DELACORTE!
AND APPARENTLY UNDAMAGED!
GEORGINA DELACORTE
EXECUTIVE VIC
PRESIDENT OF
ALBRIGHT BIO
VANCEMENTS.
AND A COMPULSIV
BETA TESTE
OF HER OW
PRODUCTS.
SOME DAY I'LL TELL YOU ABOUT THE TIME I CAUGHT HER WITH A SECOND FACE GROWING OUT OF HER SHOULDER.
(I'M SERIOUS.)
YOU DISOBEYED PROTOCOL. FORCED US TO TRACK YOU DOWN MANUALLY.
IF YOU WEREN'T SO DAMN ADORABLE, I'D HAVE TO DISCIPLINE YOU.
AND ENJOY IT.
OW!
GEORGINA...I HAD NO IDEA ALBRIGHT WAS DEVELOPING OTHER READER ASSETS.
BIO-VANCEMENTS KEEPS YOU IN ALL THE FAST CARS, VIDEO GAMES, AND FEMALE COMPANIONSHIP YOUR ADOLESCENT MIND COULD DESIRE, MR. PRICE.
WE DO NOT FIND IT NECESSARY TO CONSULT WITH YOU ON PRODUCT DEVELOPMENT.
MAYBE NOT, GEORGINA.
BUT BASED ON WHAT I SAW IN KAREN'S MEMORIES...
...YOU WILL.

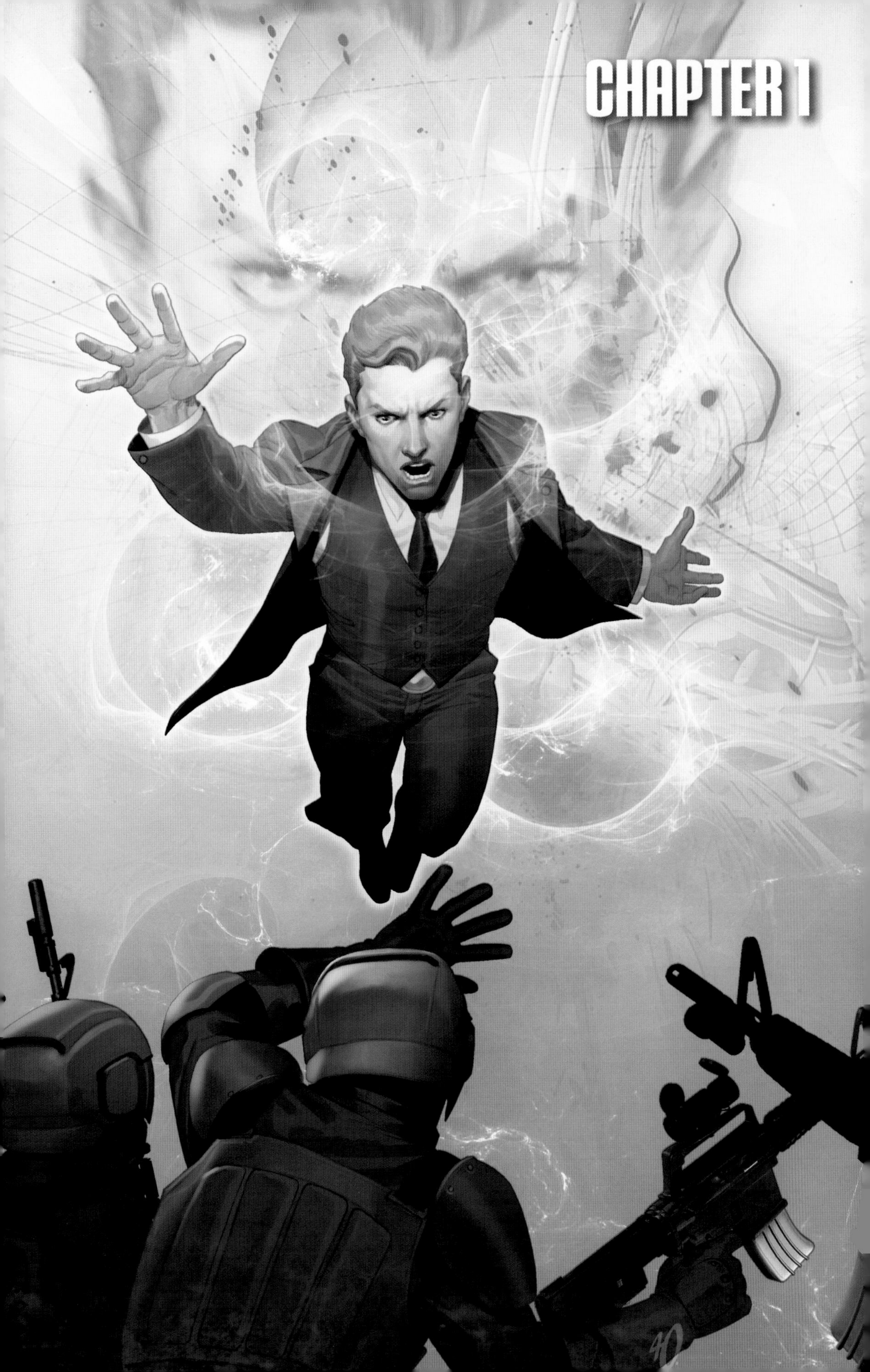
CHAPTER 1

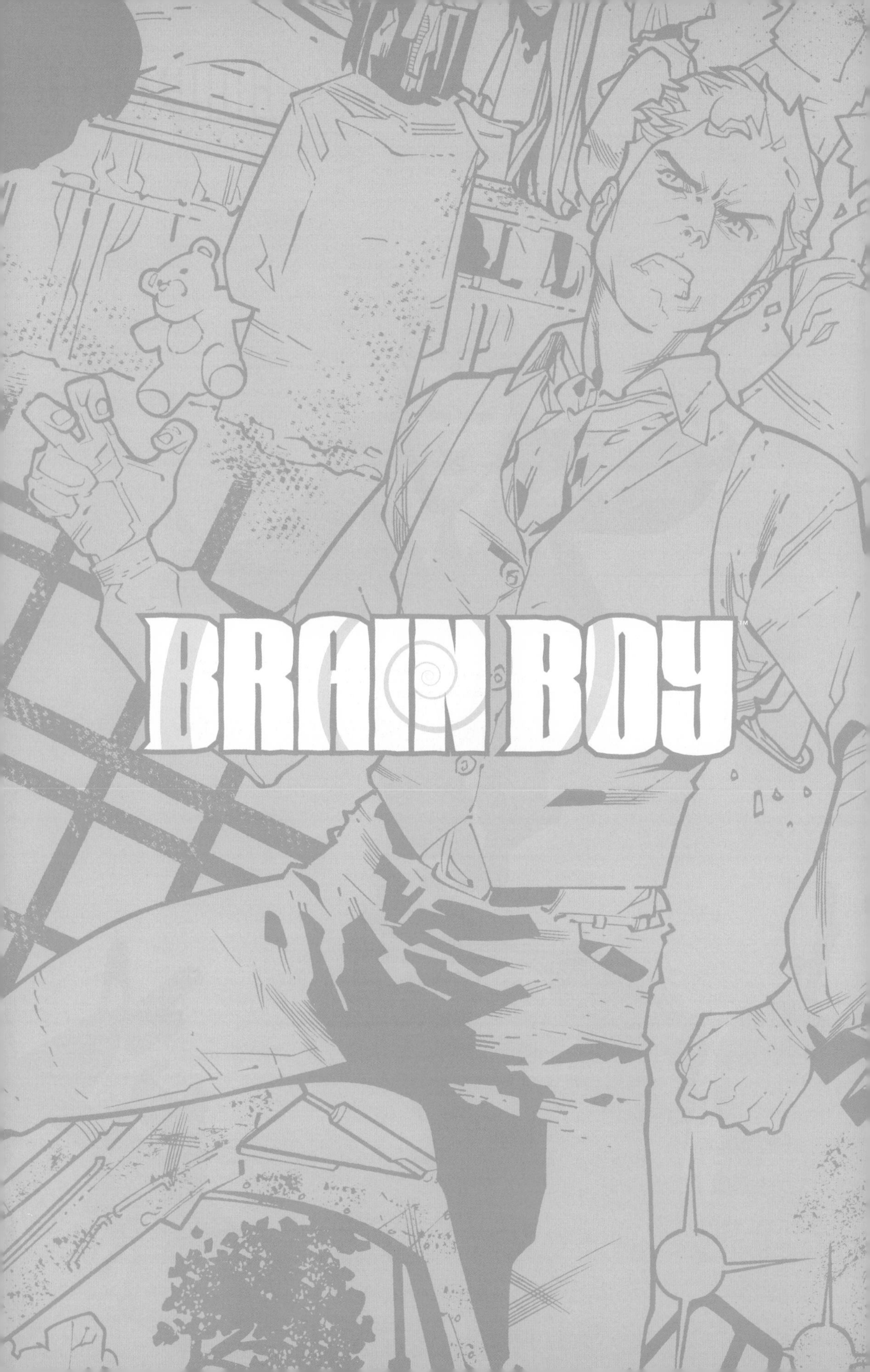
BRAIN BOY™

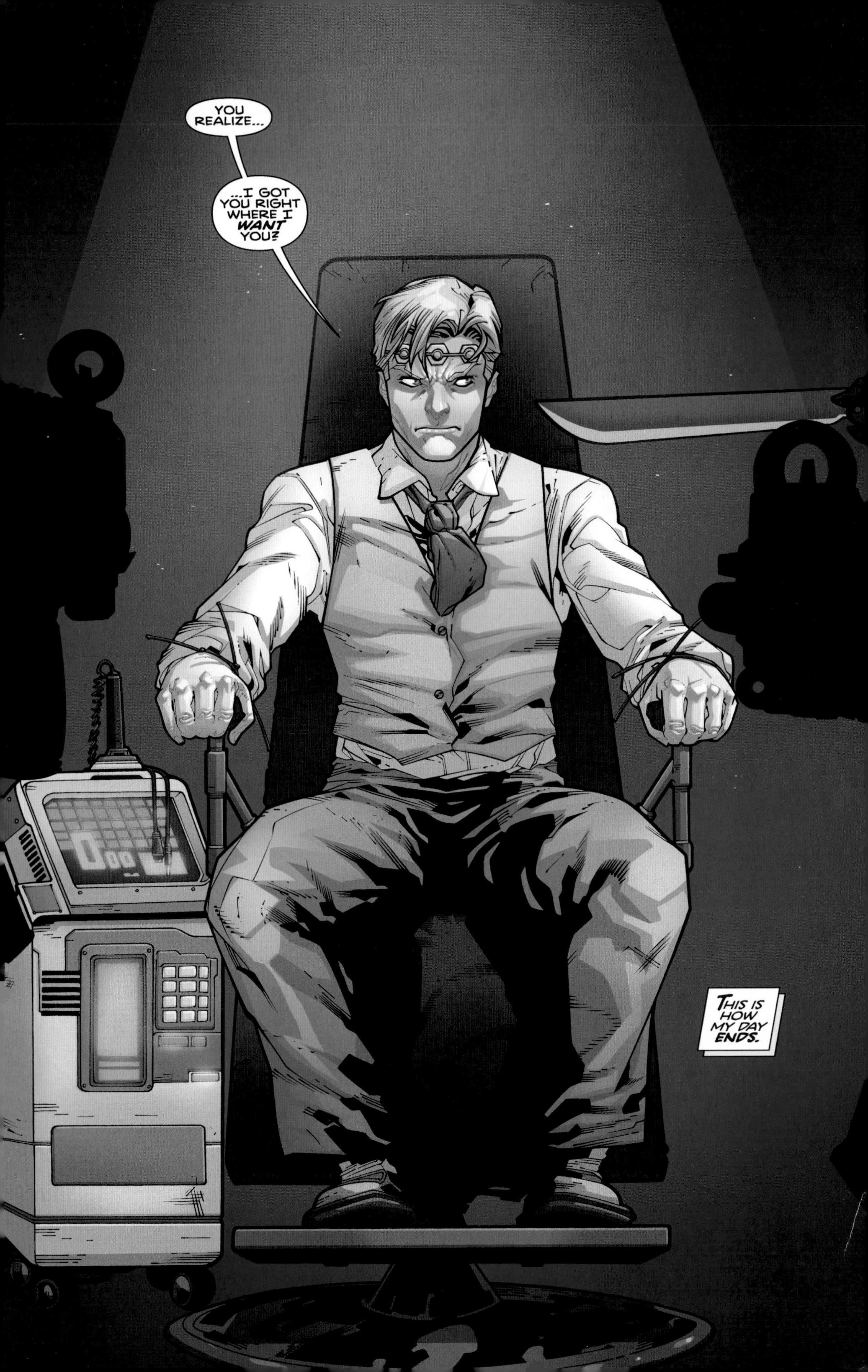
YOU REALIZE...
...I GOT YOU RIGHT WHERE I WANT YOU?
THIS IS HOW MY DAY ENDS.

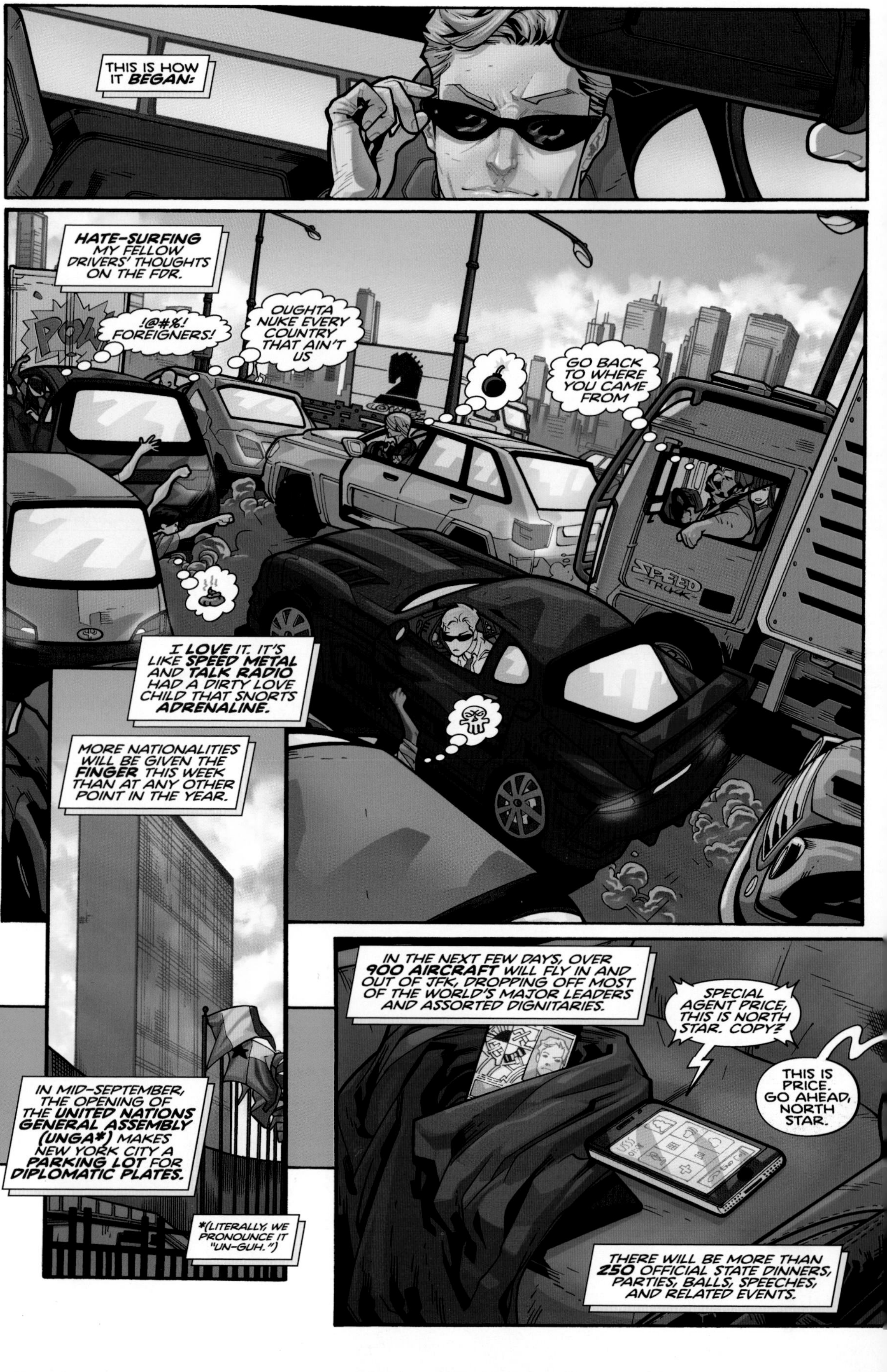

THIS IS HOW IT BEGAN:
HATE-SURFING MY FELLOW DRIVERS' THOUGHTS ON THE FDR.
POW
!@#%! FOREIGNERS!
OUGHTA NUKE EVERY COUNTRY THAT AIN'T US
GO BACK TO WHERE YOU CAME FROM
SPEED TRUKK
I LOVE IT. IT'S LIKE SPEED METAL AND TALK RADIO HAD A DIRTY LOVE CHILD THAT SNORTS ADRENALINE.
MORE NATIONALITIES WILL BE GIVEN THE FINGER THIS WEEK THAN AT ANY OTHER POINT IN THE YEAR.
IN MID-SEPTEMBER, THE OPENING OF THE UNITED NATIONS GENERAL ASSEMBLY (UNGA*) MAKES NEW YORK CITY A PARKING LOT FOR DIPLOMATIC PLATES.
*(LITERALLY, WE PRONOUNCE IT "UN-GUH.")
IN THE NEXT FEW DAYS, OVER 900 AIRCRAFT WILL FLY IN AND OUT OF JFK, DROPPING OFF MOST OF THE WORLD'S MAJOR LEADERS AND ASSORTED DIGNITARIES.
SPECIAL AGENT PRICE, THIS IS NORTH STAR. COPY?
THIS IS PRICE. GO AHEAD, NORTH STAR.
THERE WILL BE MORE THAN 250 OFFICIAL STATE DINNERS, PARTIES, BALLS, SPEECHES, AND RELATED EVENTS.

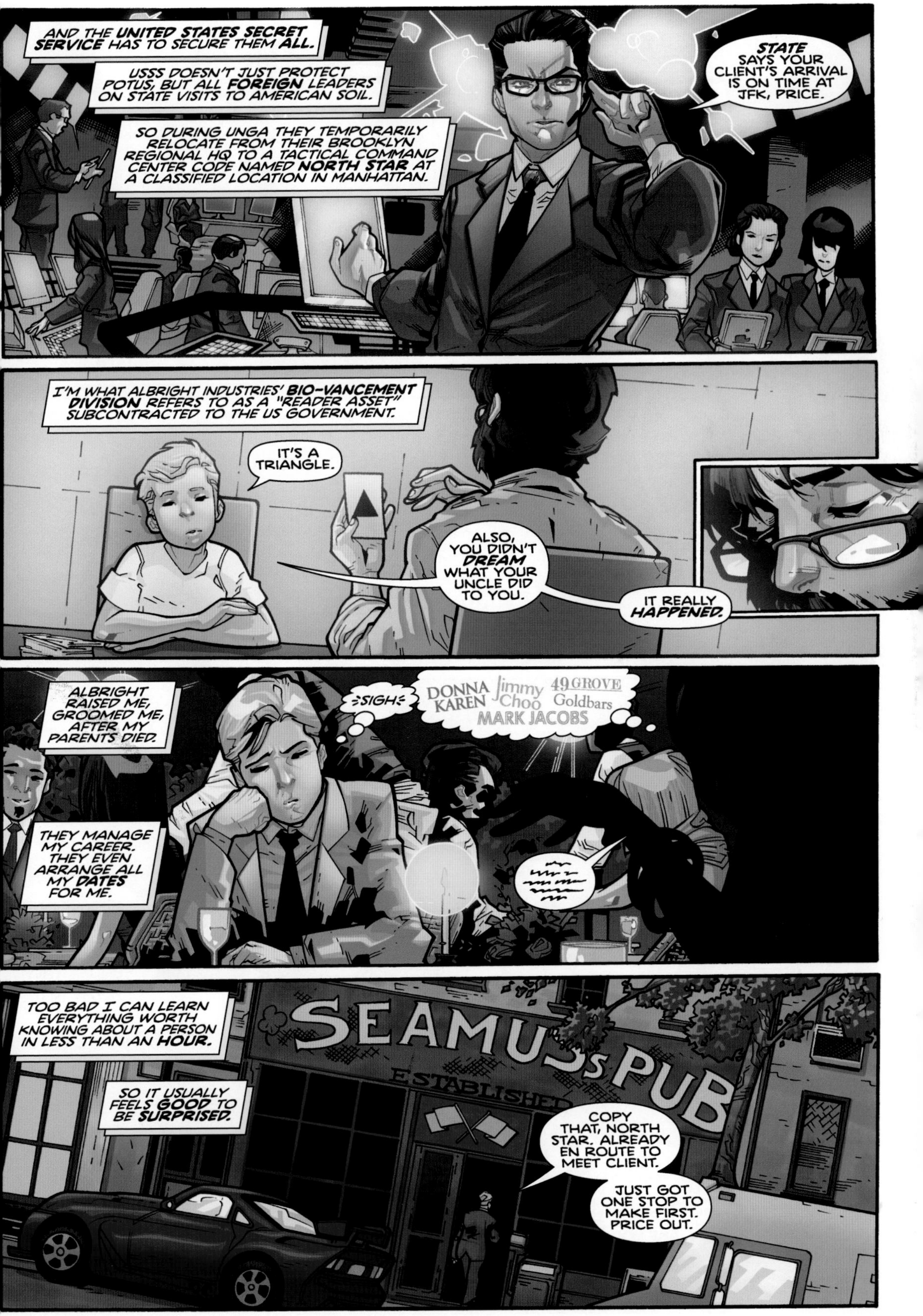
AND THE UNITED STATES SECRET SERVICE HAS TO SECURE THEM ALL.
USSS DOESN'T JUST PROTECT POTUS, BUT ALL FOREIGN LEADERS ON STATE VISITS TO AMERICAN SOIL.
SO DURING UNGA THEY TEMPORARILY RELOCATE FROM THEIR BROOKLYN REGIONAL HQ TO A TACTICAL COMMAND CENTER CODE NAMED NORTH STAR AT A CLASSIFIED LOCATION IN MANHATTAN.
STATE SAYS YOUR CLIENT'S ARRIVAL IS ON TIME AT JFK, PRICE.
I'M WHAT ALBRIGHT INDUSTRIES' BIO-VANCEMENT DIVISION REFERS TO AS A "READER ASSET" SUBCONTRACTED TO THE US GOVERNMENT.
IT'S A TRIANGLE.
ALSO, YOU DIDN'T DREAM WHAT YOUR UNCLE DID TO YOU.
IT REALLY HAPPENED.
ALBRIGHT RAISED ME, GROOMED ME, AFTER MY PARENTS DIED.
SIGH
DONNA KAREN
Jimmy Choo
49 GROVE
Goldbars
MARK JACOBS
THEY MANAGE MY CAREER. THEY EVEN ARRANGE ALL MY DATES FOR ME.
TOO BAD I CAN LEARN EVERYTHING WORTH KNOWING ABOUT A PERSON IN LESS THAN AN HOUR.
SEAMUS'S PUB
ESTABLISHED
SO IT USUALLY FEELS GOOD TO BE SURPRISED.
COPY THAT, NORTH STAR. ALREADY EN ROUTE TO MEET CLIENT.
JUST GOT ONE STOP TO MAKE FIRST. PRICE OUT.

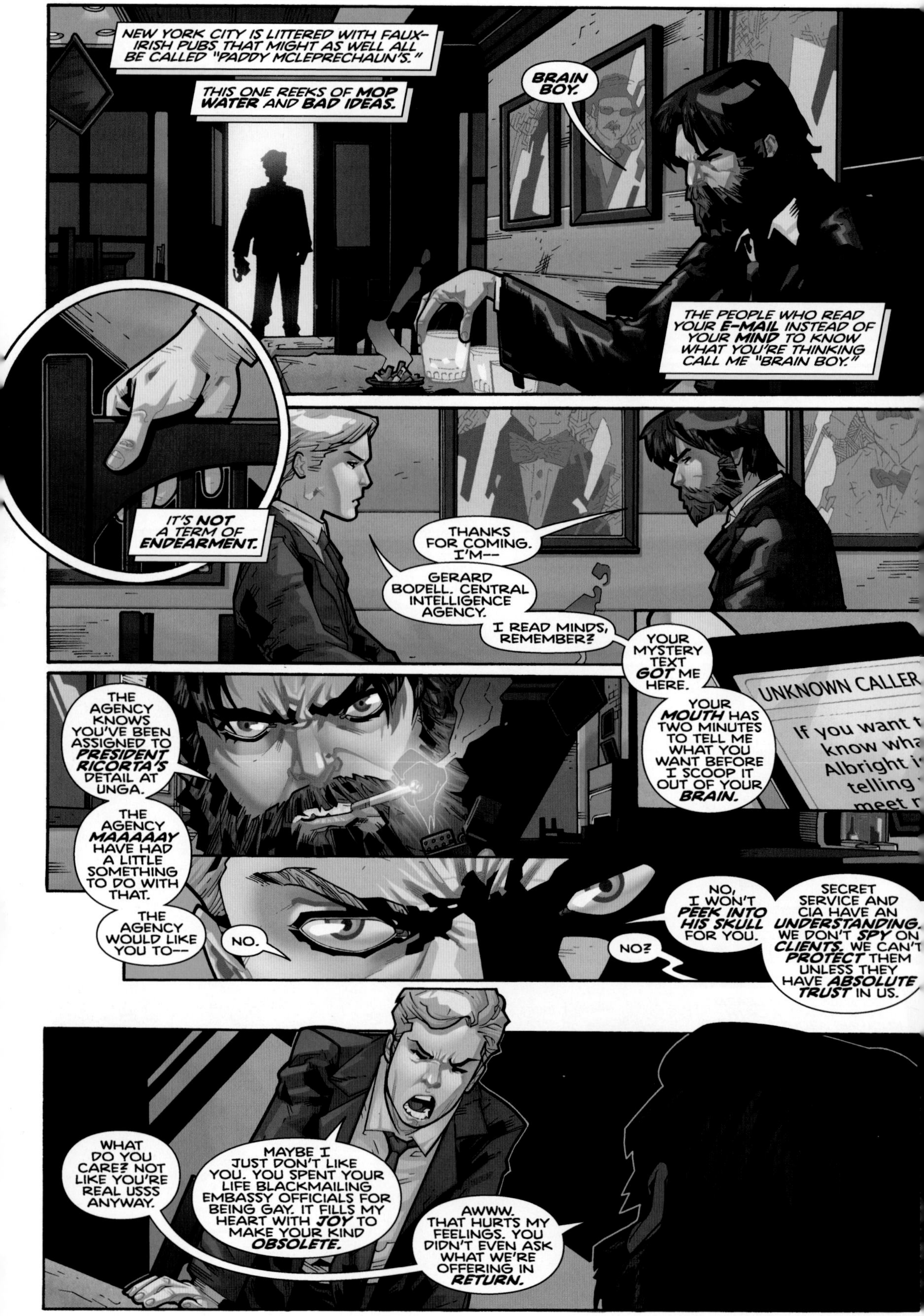

NEW YORK CITY IS LITTERED WITH FAUX-IRISH PUBS THAT MIGHT AS WELL ALL BE CALLED "PADDY MCLEPRECHAUN'S."
THIS ONE REEKS OF MOP WATER AND BAD IDEAS.
BRAIN BOY.
THE PEOPLE WHO READ YOUR E-MAIL INSTEAD OF YOUR MIND TO KNOW WHAT YOU'RE THINKING CALL ME "BRAIN BOY."
IT'S NOT A TERM OF ENDEARMENT.
THANKS FOR COMING. I'M--
GERARD BODELL. CENTRAL INTELLIGENCE AGENCY.
I READ MINDS, REMEMBER?
YOUR MYSTERY TEXT GOT ME HERE.
YOUR MOUTH HAS TWO MINUTES TO TELL ME WHAT YOU WANT BEFORE I SCOOP IT OUT OF YOUR BRAIN.
UNKNOWN CALLER
If you want t
know wha
Albright i
telling
meet m
THE AGENCY KNOWS YOU'VE BEEN ASSIGNED TO PRESIDENT RICORTA'S DETAIL AT UNGA.
THE AGENCY MAAAAAY HAVE HAD A LITTLE SOMETHING TO DO WITH THAT.
THE AGENCY WOULD LIKE YOU TO--
NO.
NO?
NO, I WON'T PEEK INTO HIS SKULL FOR YOU.
SECRET SERVICE AND CIA HAVE AN UNDERSTANDING. WE DON'T SPY ON CLIENTS. WE CAN'T PROTECT THEM UNLESS THEY HAVE ABSOLUTE TRUST IN US.
WHAT DO YOU CARE? NOT LIKE YOU'RE REAL USSS ANYWAY.
MAYBE I JUST DON'T LIKE YOU. YOU SPENT YOUR LIFE BLACKMAILING EMBASSY OFFICIALS FOR BEING GAY. IT FILLS MY HEART WITH JOY TO MAKE YOUR KIND OBSOLETE.
AWWW. THAT HURTS MY FEELINGS. YOU DIDN'T EVEN ASK WHAT WE'RE OFFERING IN RETURN.

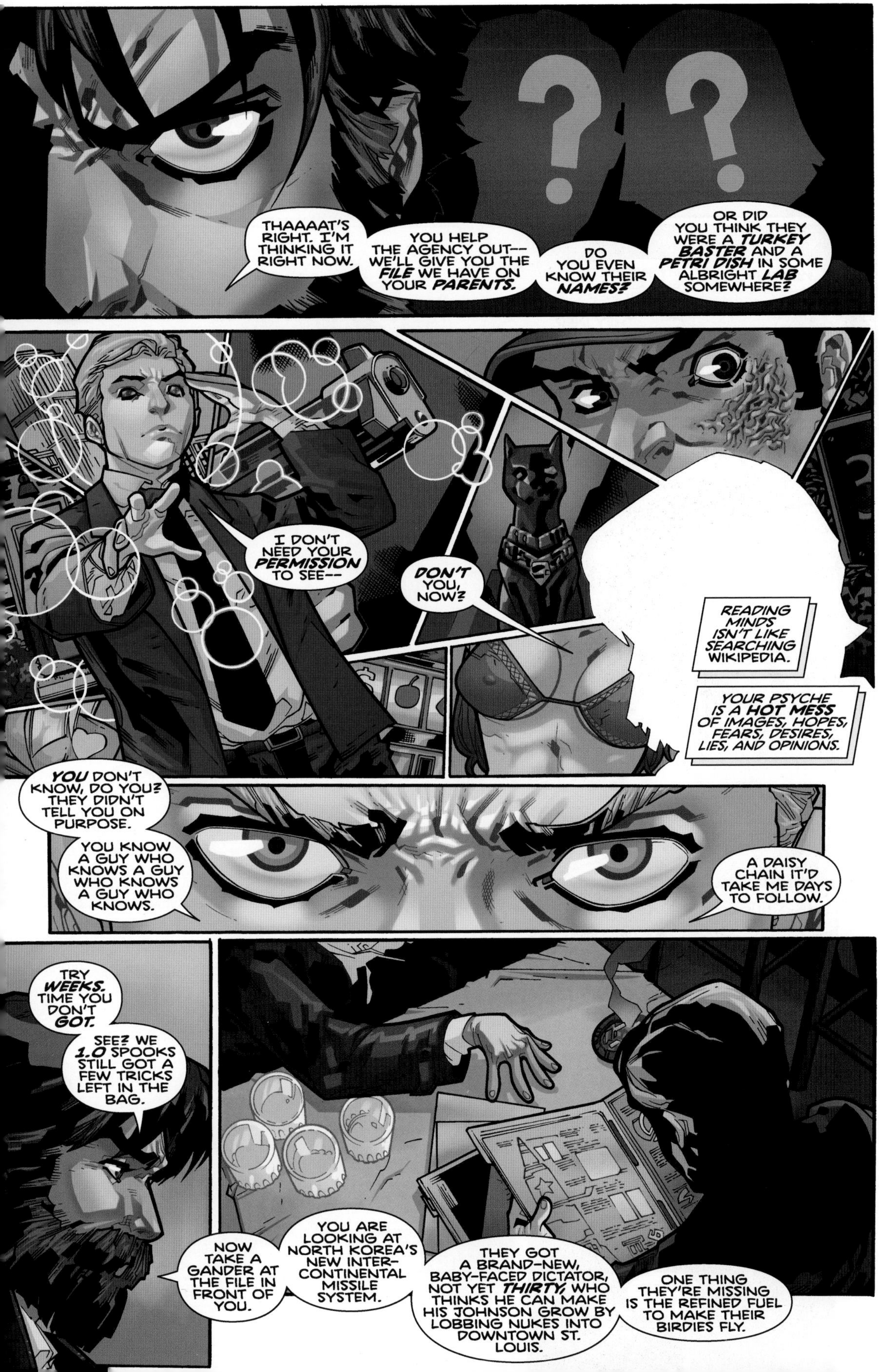
THAAAAT'S RIGHT. I'M THINKING IT RIGHT NOW.
YOU HELP THE AGENCY OUT-- WE'LL GIVE YOU THE FILE WE HAVE ON YOUR PARENTS.
DO YOU EVEN KNOW THEIR NAMES?
OR DID YOU THINK THEY WERE A TURKEY BASTER AND A PETRI DISH IN SOME ALBRIGHT LAB SOMEWHERE?
I DON'T NEED YOUR PERMISSION TO SEE--
DON'T YOU, NOW?
READING MINDS ISN'T LIKE SEARCHING WIKIPEDIA.
YOUR PSYCHE IS A HOT MESS OF IMAGES, HOPES, FEARS, DESIRES, LIES, AND OPINIONS.
YOU DON'T KNOW, DO YOU? THEY DIDN'T TELL YOU ON PURPOSE.
YOU KNOW A GUY WHO KNOWS A GUY WHO KNOWS A GUY WHO KNOWS.
A DAISY CHAIN IT'D TAKE ME DAYS TO FOLLOW.
TRY WEEKS. TIME YOU DON'T GOT.
SEE? WE 1.0 SPOOKS STILL GOT A FEW TRICKS LEFT IN THE BAG.
NOW TAKE A GANDER AT THE FILE IN FRONT OF YOU.
YOU ARE LOOKING AT NORTH KOREA'S NEW INTER-CONTINENTAL MISSILE SYSTEM.
THEY GOT A BRAND-NEW, BABY-FACED DICTATOR, NOT YET THIRTY, WHO THINKS HE CAN MAKE HIS JOHNSON GROW BY LOBBING NUKES INTO DOWNTOWN ST. LOUIS.
ONE THING THEY'RE MISSING IS THE REFINED FUEL TO MAKE THEIR BIRDIES FLY.

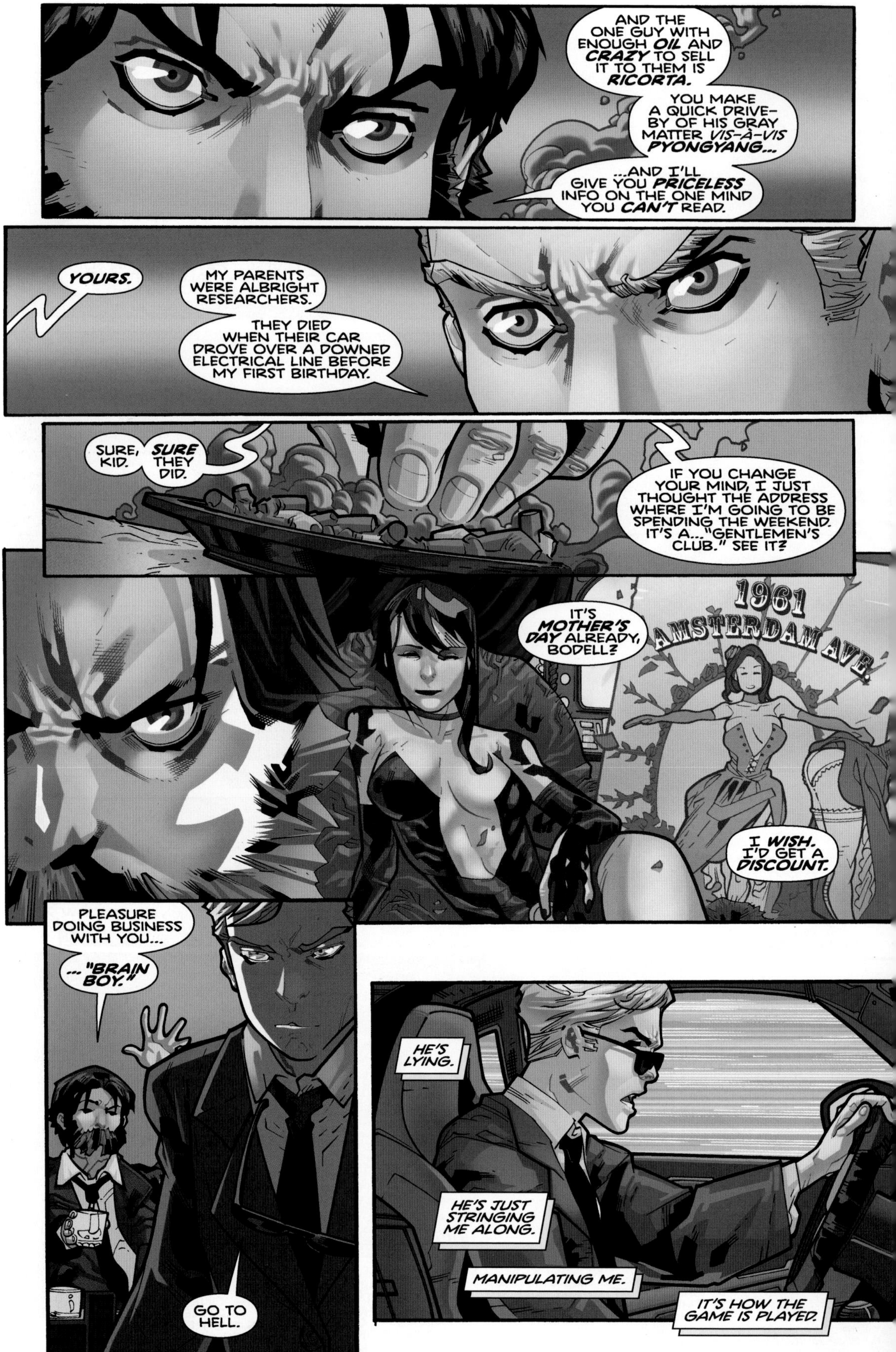
AND THE ONE GUY WITH ENOUGH OIL AND CRAZY TO SELL IT TO THEM IS RICORTA.
YOU MAKE A QUICK DRIVE-BY OF HIS GRAY MATTER VIS-À-VIS PYONGYANG...
...AND I'LL GIVE YOU PRICELESS INFO ON THE ONE MIND YOU CAN'T READ.
YOURS.
MY PARENTS WERE ALBRIGHT RESEARCHERS.
THEY DIED WHEN THEIR CAR DROVE OVER A DOWNED ELECTRICAL LINE BEFORE MY FIRST BIRTHDAY.
SURE, KID.
SURE THEY DID.
IF YOU CHANGE YOUR MIND, I JUST THOUGHT THE ADDRESS WHERE I'M GOING TO BE SPENDING THE WEEKEND. IT'S A..."GENTLEMEN'S CLUB." SEE IT?
1961 AMSTERDAM AVE.
IT'S MOTHER'S DAY ALREADY, BODELL?
I WISH. I'D GET A DISCOUNT.
PLEASURE DOING BUSINESS WITH YOU...
..."BRAIN BOY."
GO TO HELL.
HE'S LYING.
HE'S JUST STRINGING ME ALONG.
MANIPULATING ME.
IT'S HOW THE GAME IS PLAYED.

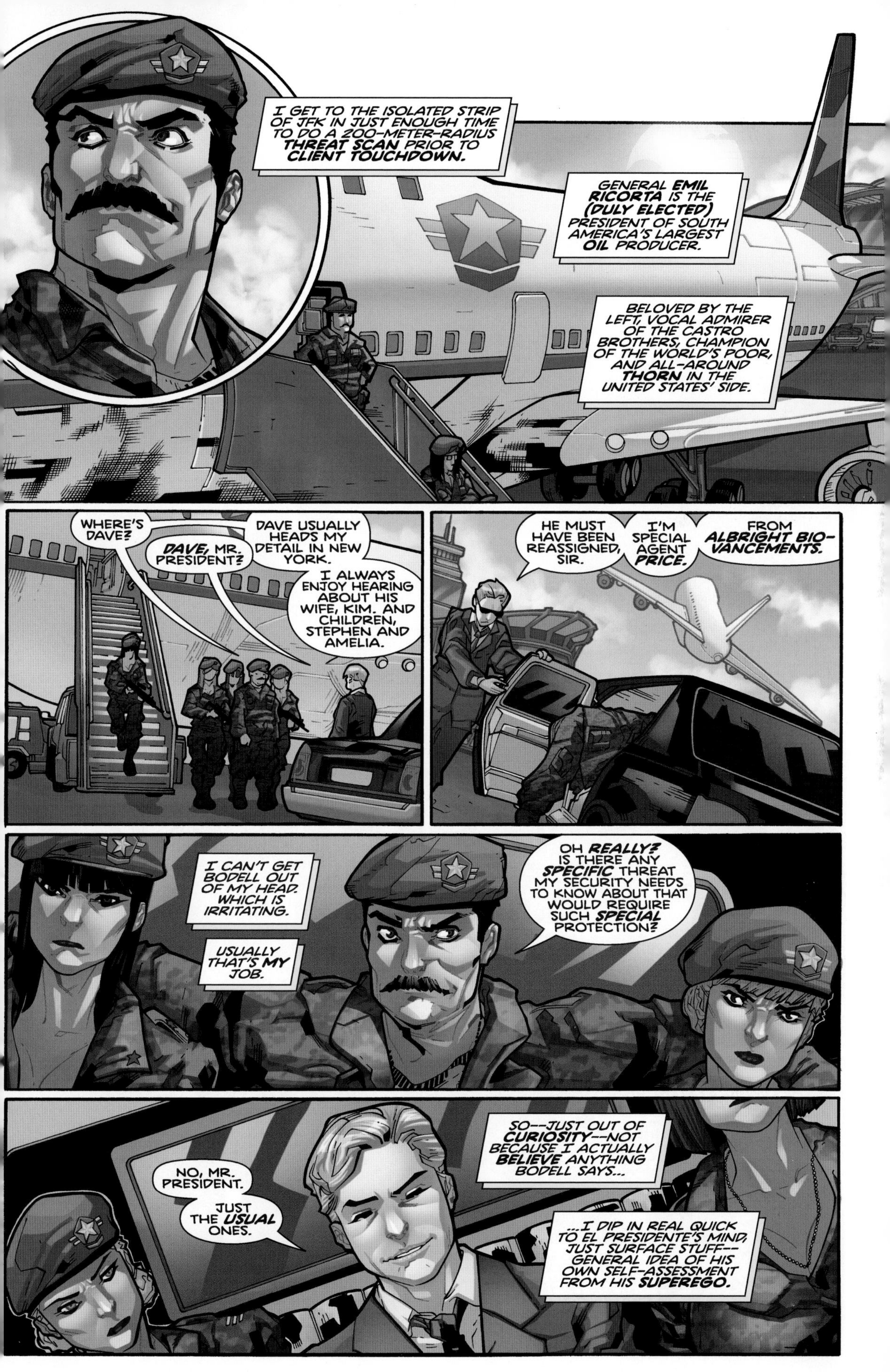
I GET TO THE ISOLATED STRIP OF JFK IN JUST ENOUGH TIME TO DO A 200-METER-RADIUS THREAT SCAN PRIOR TO CLIENT TOUCHDOWN.
GENERAL EMIL RICORTA IS THE (DULY ELECTED) PRESIDENT OF SOUTH AMERICA'S LARGEST OIL PRODUCER.
BELOVED BY THE LEFT, VOCAL ADMIRER OF THE CASTRO BROTHERS, CHAMPION OF THE WORLD'S POOR, AND ALL-AROUND THORN IN THE UNITED STATES' SIDE.
WHERE'S DAVE?
DAVE, MR. PRESIDENT?
DAVE USUALLY HEADS MY DETAIL IN NEW YORK.
I ALWAYS ENJOY HEARING ABOUT HIS WIFE, KIM, AND CHILDREN, STEPHEN AND AMELIA.
HE MUST HAVE BEEN REASSIGNED, SIR.
I'M SPECIAL AGENT PRICE.
FROM ALBRIGHT BIO-VANCEMENTS.
I CAN'T GET BODELL OUT OF MY HEAD. WHICH IS IRRITATING.
USUALLY THAT'S MY JOB.
OH REALLY? IS THERE ANY SPECIFIC THREAT MY SECURITY NEEDS TO KNOW ABOUT THAT WOULD REQUIRE SUCH SPECIAL PROTECTION?
SO--JUST OUT OF CURIOSITY--NOT BECAUSE I ACTUALLY BELIEVE ANYTHING BODELL SAYS...
NO, MR. PRESIDENT.
JUST THE USUAL ONES.
...I DIP IN REAL QUICK TO EL PRESIDENTE'S MIND, JUST SURFACE STUFF-- GENERAL IDEA OF HIS OWN SELF-ASSESSMENT FROM HIS SUPEREGO.

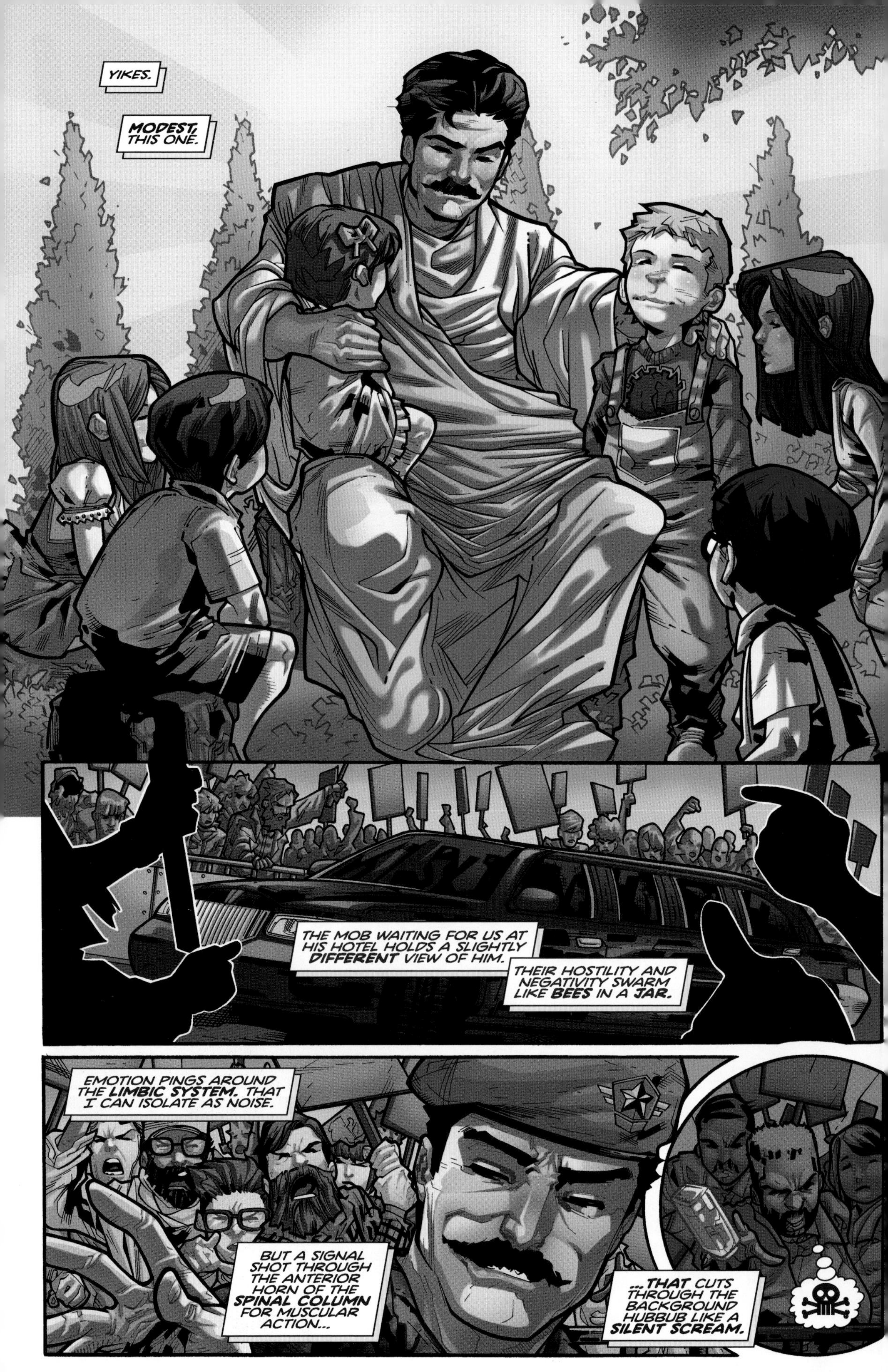
YIKES.
MODEST, THIS ONE.
THE MOB WAITING FOR US AT HIS HOTEL HOLDS A SLIGHTLY DIFFERENT VIEW OF HIM.
THEIR HOSTILITY AND NEGATIVITY SWARM LIKE BEES IN A JAR.
EMOTION PINGS AROUND THE LIMBIC SYSTEM. THAT I CAN ISOLATE AS NOISE.
BUT A SIGNAL SHOT THROUGH THE ANTERIOR HORN OF THE SPINAL COLUMN FOR MUSCULAR ACTION...
...THAT CUTS THROUGH THE BACKGROUND HUBBUB LIKE A SILENT SCREAM.

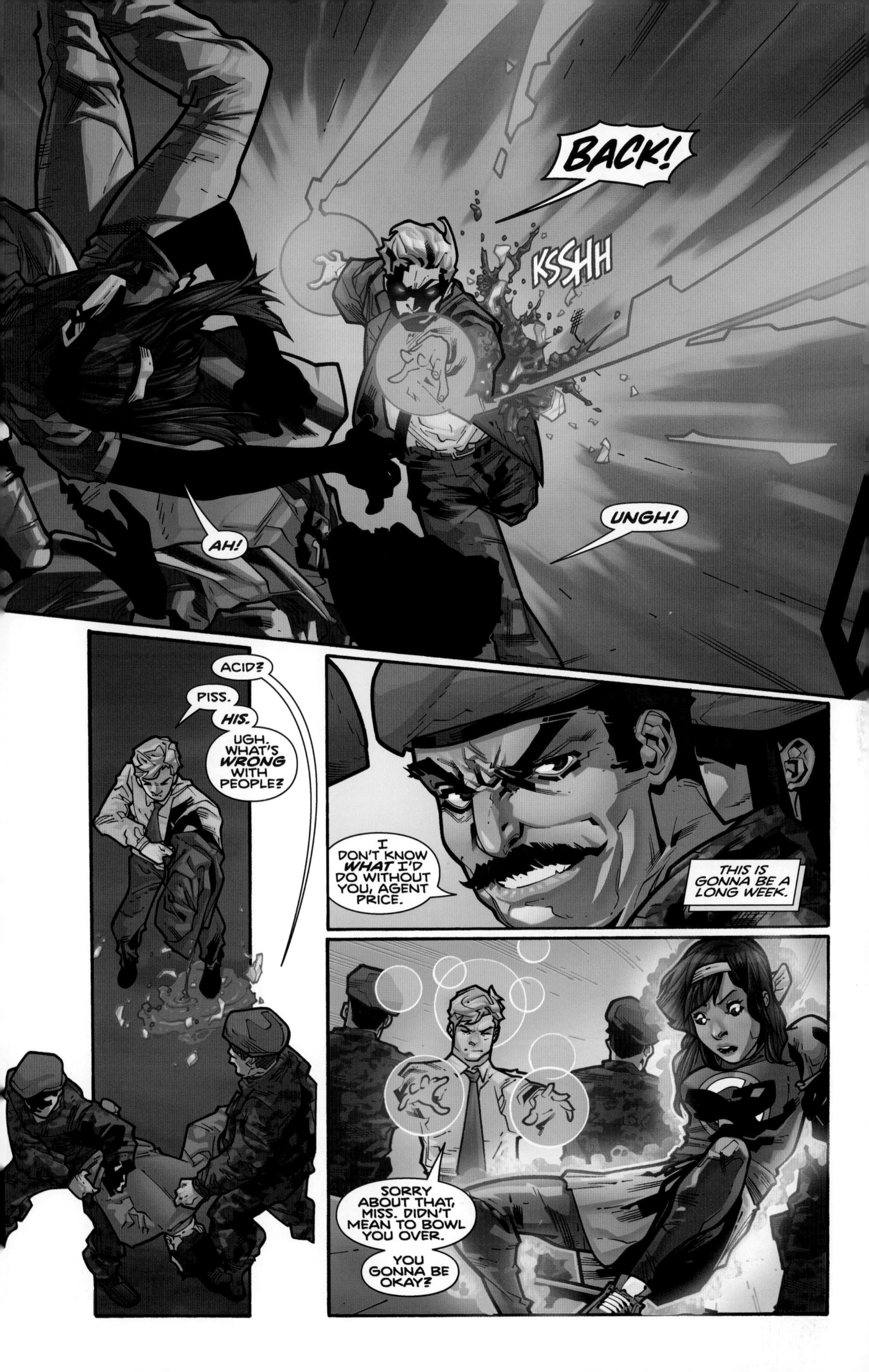
BACK!
KSSHH
AH!
UNGH!
ACID?
PISS.
HIS.
UGH. WHAT'S WRONG WITH PEOPLE?
I DON'T KNOW WHAT I'D DO WITHOUT YOU, AGENT PRICE.
THIS IS GONNA BE A LONG WEEK.
SORRY ABOUT THAT, MISS. DIDN'T MEAN TO BOWL YOU OVER.
YOU GONNA BE OKAY?

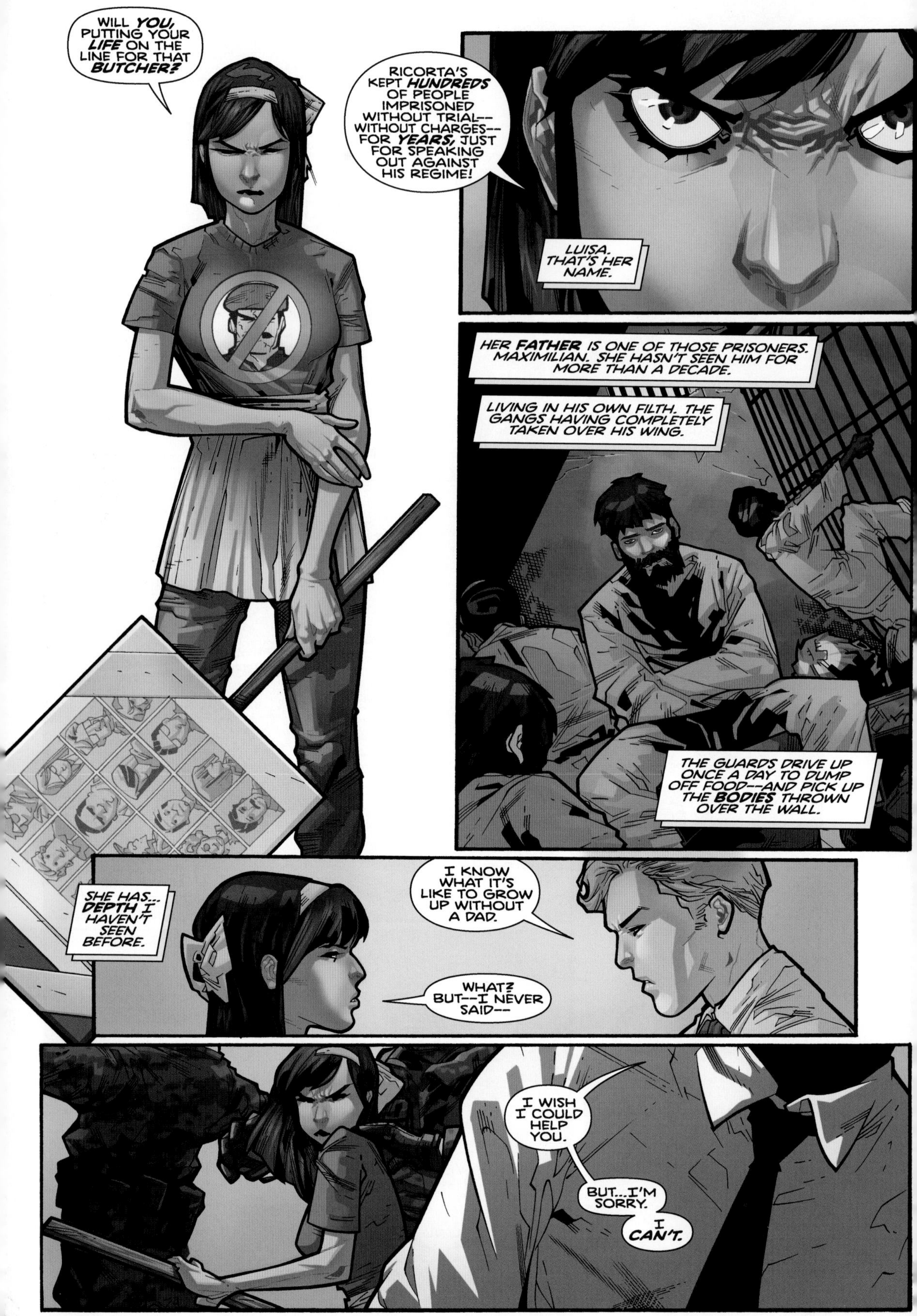
WILL YOU, PUTTING YOUR LIFE ON THE LINE FOR THAT BUTCHER?
RICORTA'S KEPT HUNDREDS OF PEOPLE IMPRISONED WITHOUT TRIAL-- WITHOUT CHARGES-- FOR YEARS, JUST FOR SPEAKING OUT AGAINST HIS REGIME!
LUISA. THAT'S HER NAME.
HER FATHER IS ONE OF THOSE PRISONERS. MAXIMILIAN. SHE HASN'T SEEN HIM FOR MORE THAN A DECADE.
LIVING IN HIS OWN FILTH. THE GANGS HAVING COMPLETELY TAKEN OVER HIS WING.
THE GUARDS DRIVE UP ONCE A DAY TO DUMP OFF FOOD--AND PICK UP THE BODIES THROWN OVER THE WALL.
SHE HAS... DEPTH I HAVEN'T SEEN BEFORE.
I KNOW WHAT IT'S LIKE TO GROW UP WITHOUT A DAD.
WHAT? BUT--I NEVER SAID--
I WISH I COULD HELP YOU.
BUT...I'M SORRY.
I CAN'T.

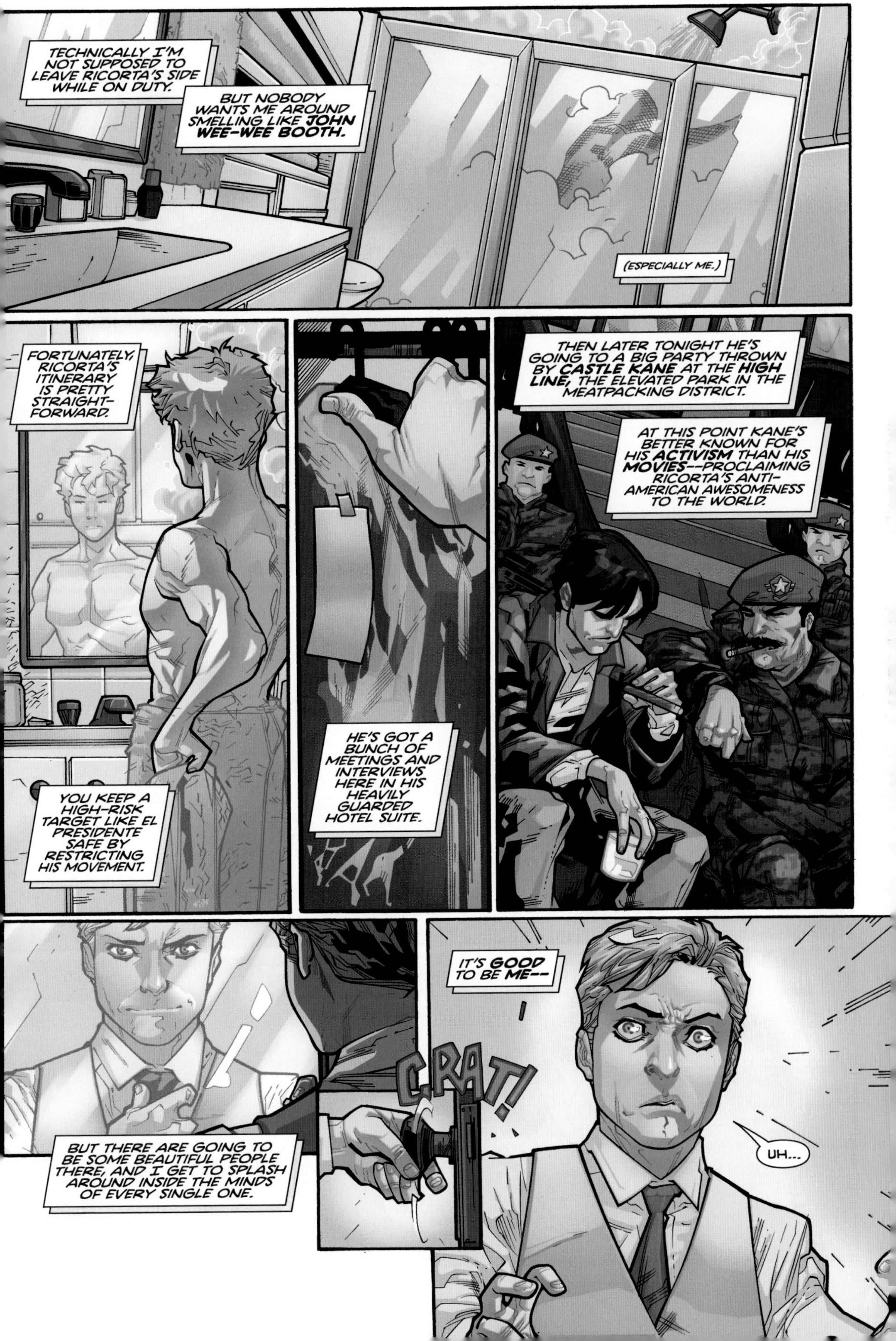

TECHNICALLY I'M NOT SUPPOSED TO LEAVE RICORTA'S SIDE WHILE ON DUTY.
BUT NOBODY WANTS ME AROUND SMELLING LIKE JOHN WEE-WEE BOOTH.
(ESPECIALLY ME.)
FORTUNATELY, RICORTA'S ITINERARY IS PRETTY STRAIGHT-FORWARD.
YOU KEEP A HIGH-RISK TARGET LIKE EL PRESIDENTE SAFE BY RESTRICTING HIS MOVEMENT.
HE'S GOT A BUNCH OF MEETINGS AND INTERVIEWS HERE IN HIS HEAVILY GUARDED HOTEL SUITE.
THEN LATER TONIGHT HE'S GOING TO A BIG PARTY THROWN BY CASTLE KANE AT THE HIGH LINE, THE ELEVATED PARK IN THE MEATPACKING DISTRICT.
AT THIS POINT KANE'S BETTER KNOWN FOR HIS ACTIVISM THAN HIS MOVIES--PROCLAIMING RICORTA'S ANTI-AMERICAN AWESOMENESS TO THE WORLD.
BUT THERE ARE GOING TO BE SOME BEAUTIFUL PEOPLE THERE, AND I GET TO SPLASH AROUND INSIDE THE MINDS OF EVERY SINGLE ONE.
IT'S GOOD TO BE ME--
CRAT!
UH...

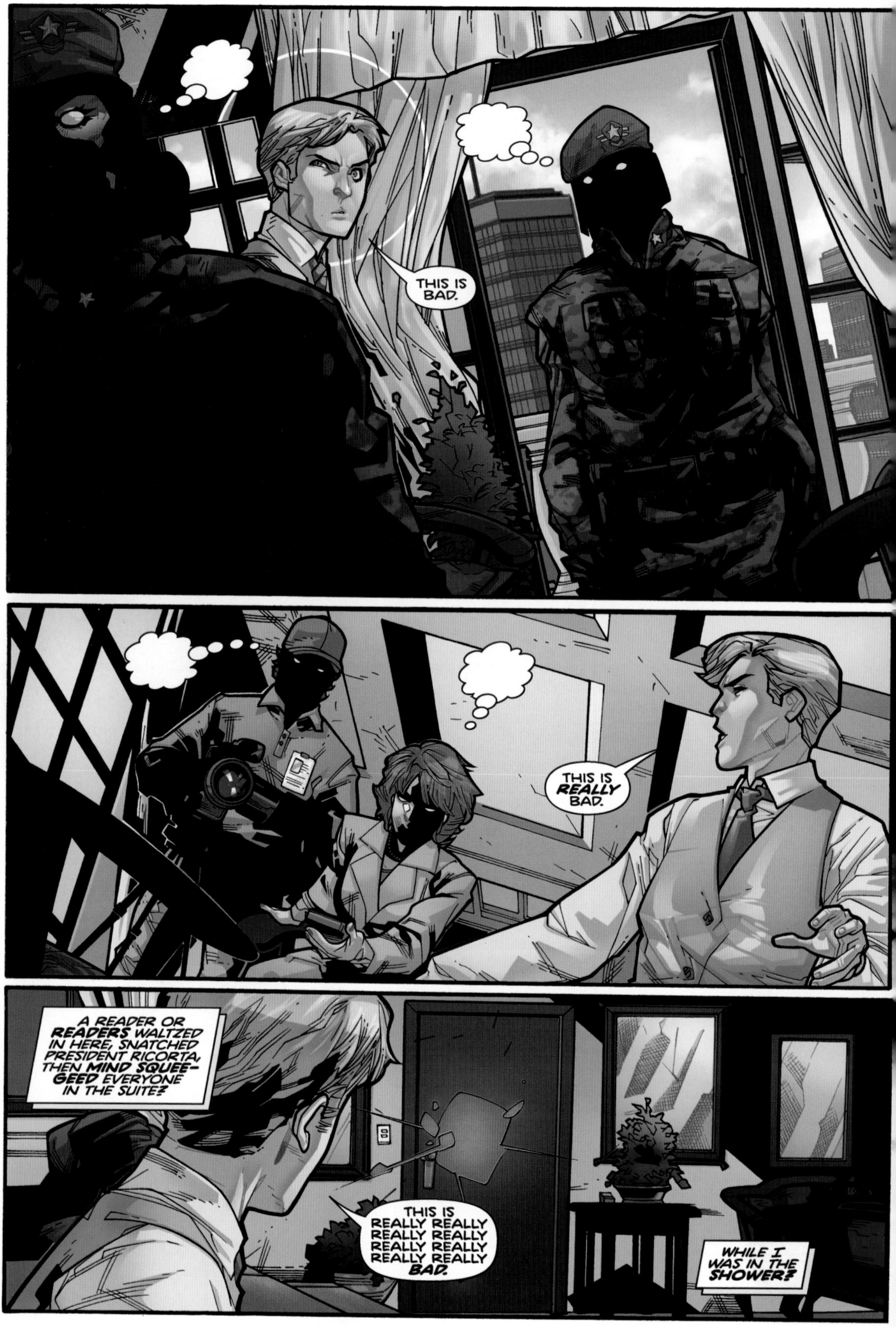
THIS IS BAD.
THIS IS REALLY BAD.
A READER OR READERS WALTZED IN HERE, SNATCHED PRESIDENT RICORTA, THEN MIND SQUEEGEED EVERYONE IN THE SUITE?
THIS IS REALLY REALLY REALLY REALLY REALLY REALLY REALLY REALLY BAD.
WHILE I WAS IN THE SHOWER?

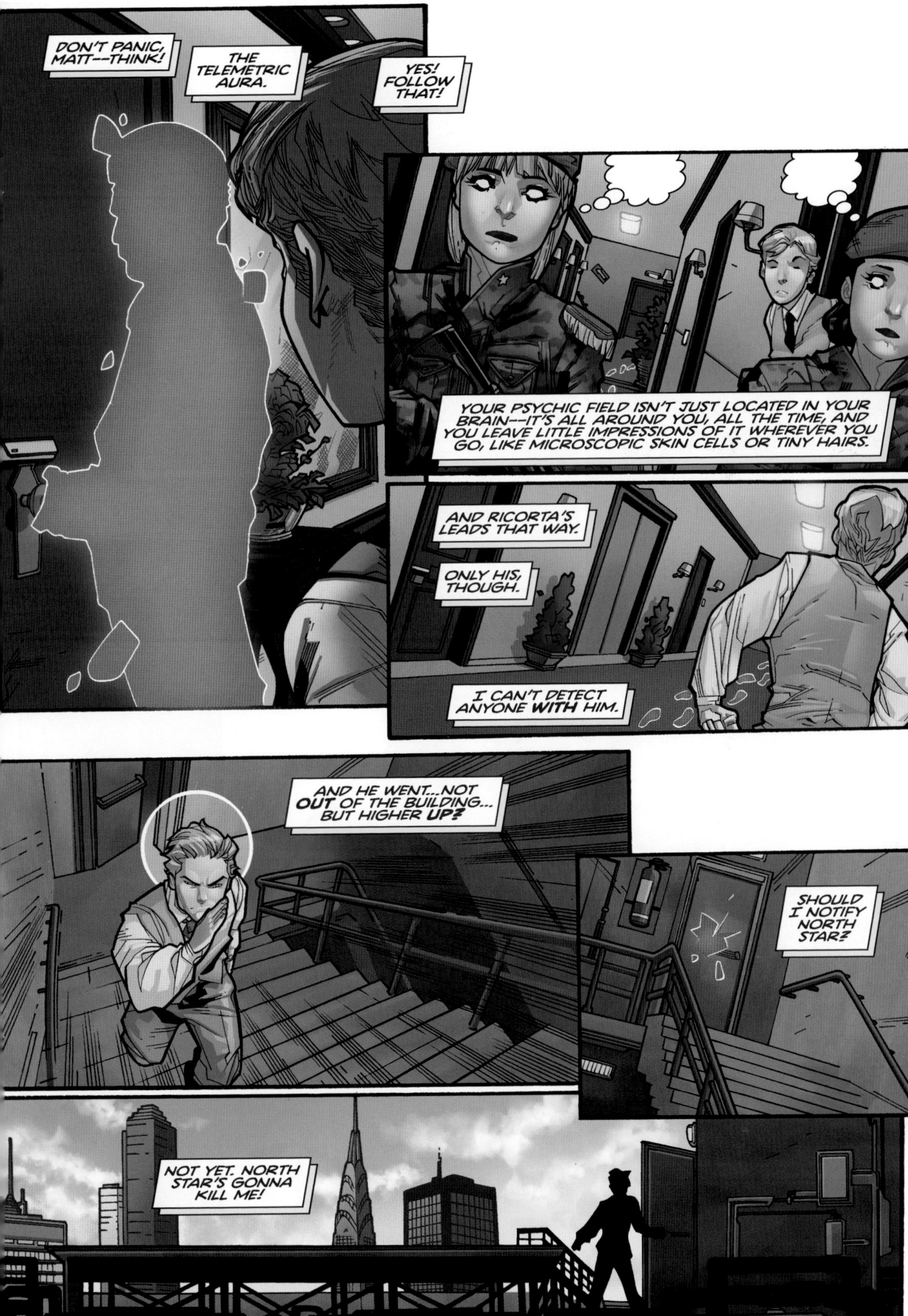

DON'T PANIC, MATT--THINK!
THE TELEMETRIC AURA.
YES! FOLLOW THAT!
YOUR PSYCHIC FIELD ISN'T JUST LOCATED IN YOUR BRAIN--IT'S ALL AROUND YOU, ALL THE TIME, AND YOU LEAVE LITTLE IMPRESSIONS OF IT WHEREVER YOU GO, LIKE MICROSCOPIC SKIN CELLS OR TINY HAIRS.
AND RICORTA'S LEADS THAT WAY.
ONLY HIS, THOUGH.
I CAN'T DETECT ANYONE WITH HIM.
AND HE WENT...NOT OUT OF THE BUILDING... BUT HIGHER UP?
SHOULD I NOTIFY NORTH STAR?
NOT YET. NORTH STAR'S GONNA KILL ME!

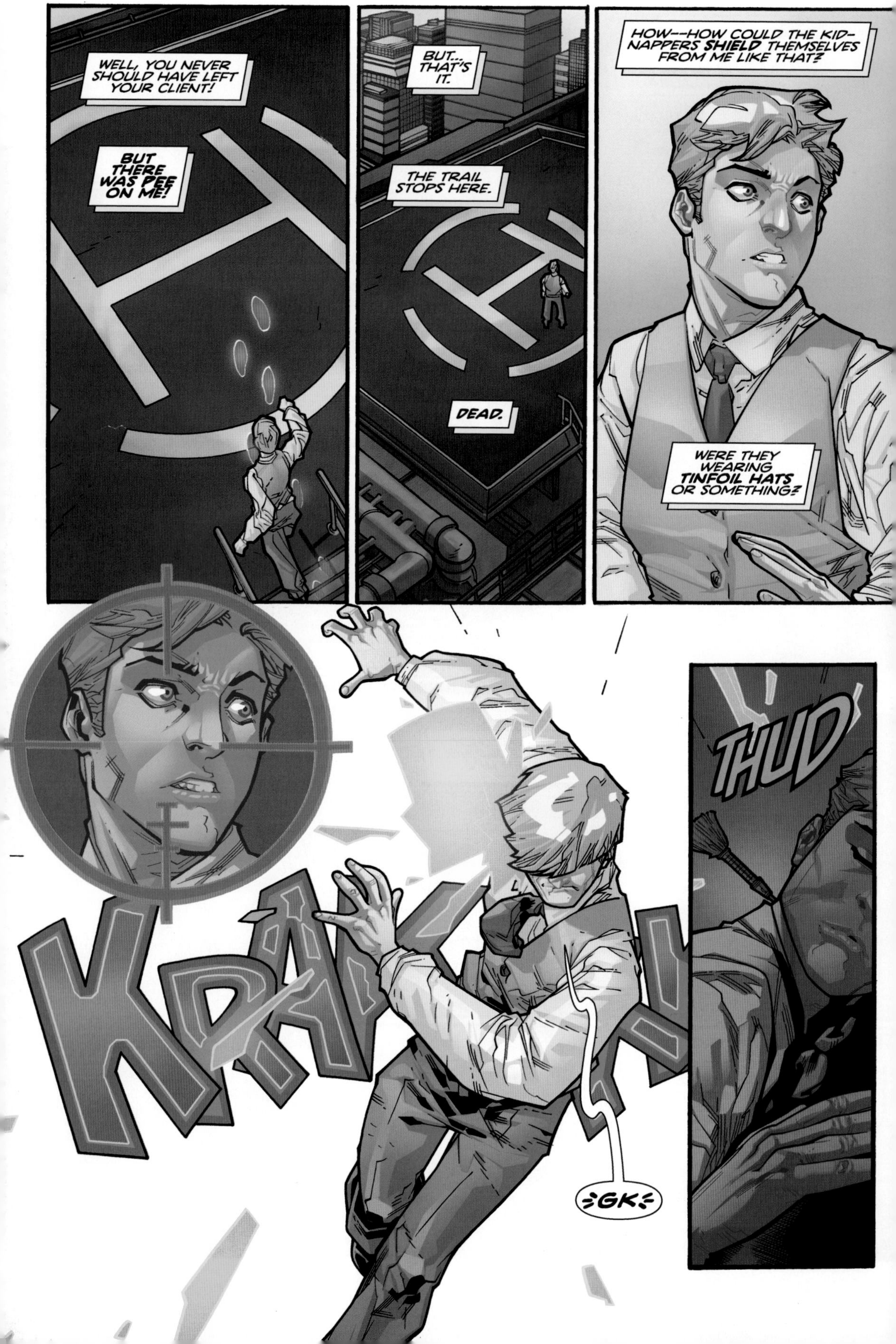

WELL, YOU NEVER SHOULD HAVE LEFT YOUR CLIENT!
BUT THERE WAS PEE ON ME!
BUT... THAT'S IT.
THE TRAIL STOPS HERE.
DEAD.
HOW--HOW COULD THE KID-NAPPERS SHIELD THEMSELVES FROM ME LIKE THAT?
WERE THEY WEARING TINFOIL HATS OR SOMETHING?
THUD
GK

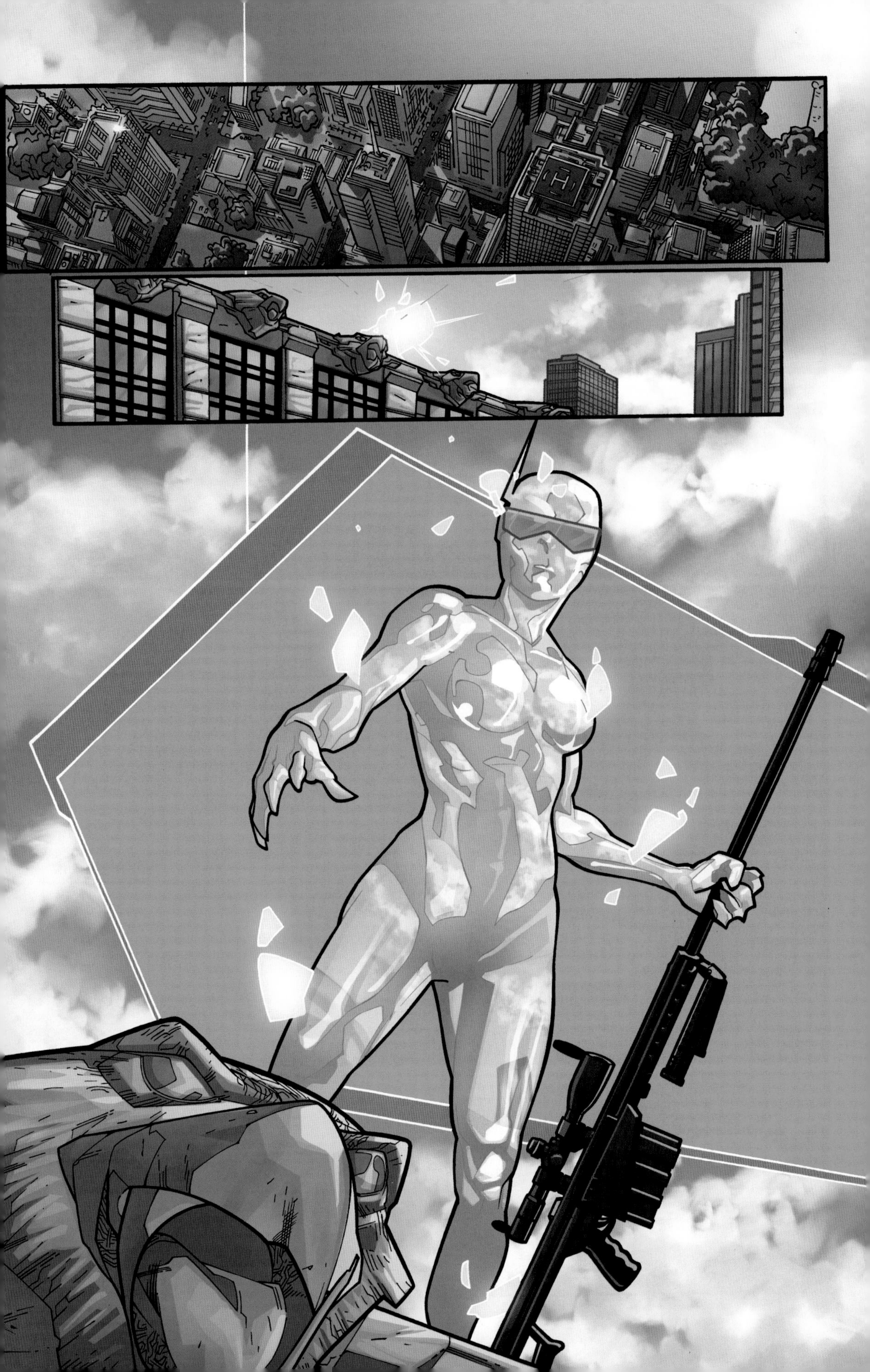

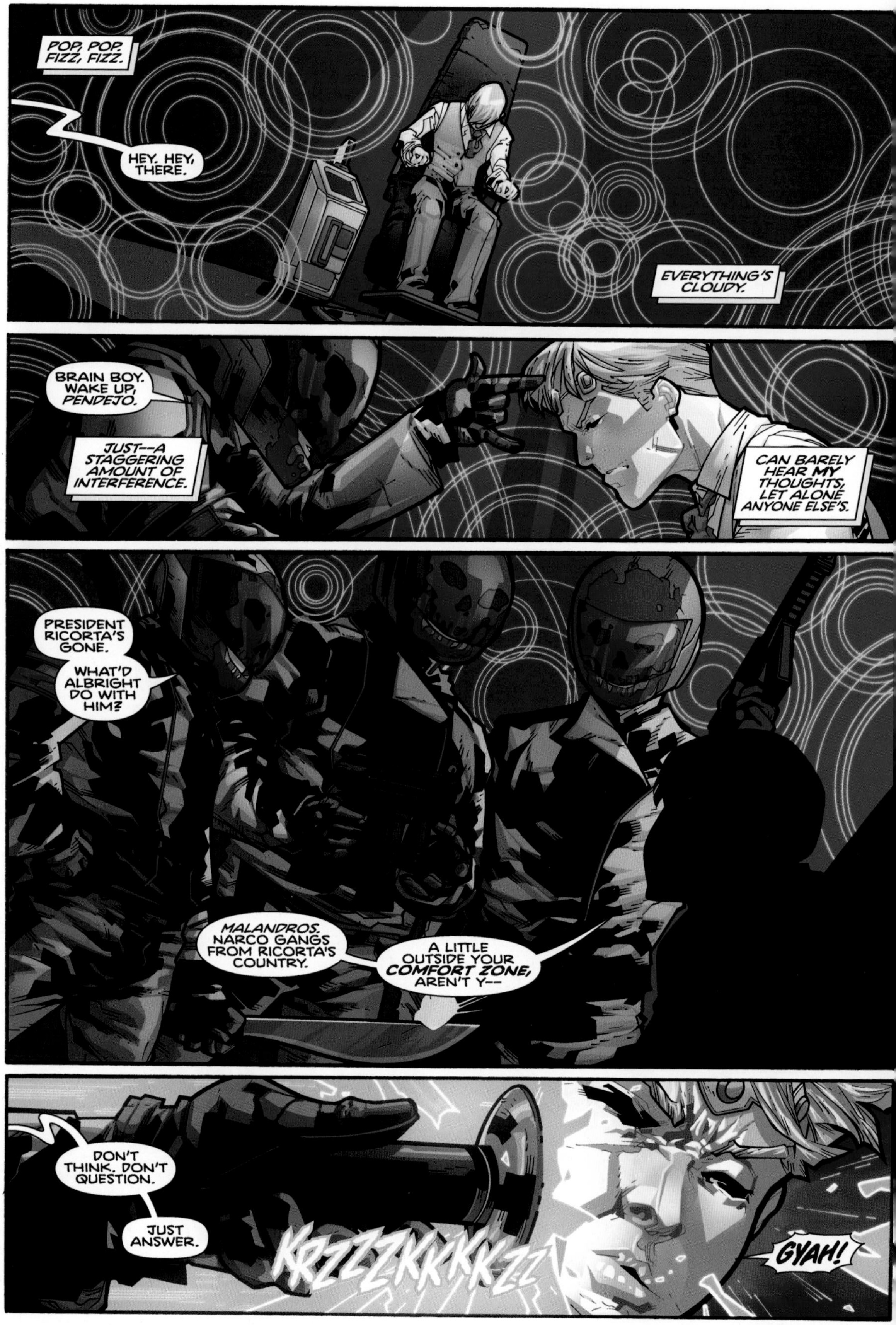
POP, POP. FIZZ, FIZZ.
HEY. HEY, THERE.
EVERYTHING'S CLOUDY.
BRAIN BOY. WAKE UP, PENDEJO.
JUST--A STAGGERING AMOUNT OF INTERFERENCE.
CAN BARELY HEAR MY THOUGHTS, LET ALONE ANYONE ELSE'S.
PRESIDENT RICORTA'S GONE.
WHAT'D ALBRIGHT DO WITH HIM?
MALANDROS. NARCO GANGS FROM RICORTA'S COUNTRY.
A LITTLE OUTSIDE YOUR COMFORT ZONE, AREN'T Y--
DON'T THINK. DON'T QUESTION.
JUST ANSWER.
KRZZZKKKKZZ
GYAH!

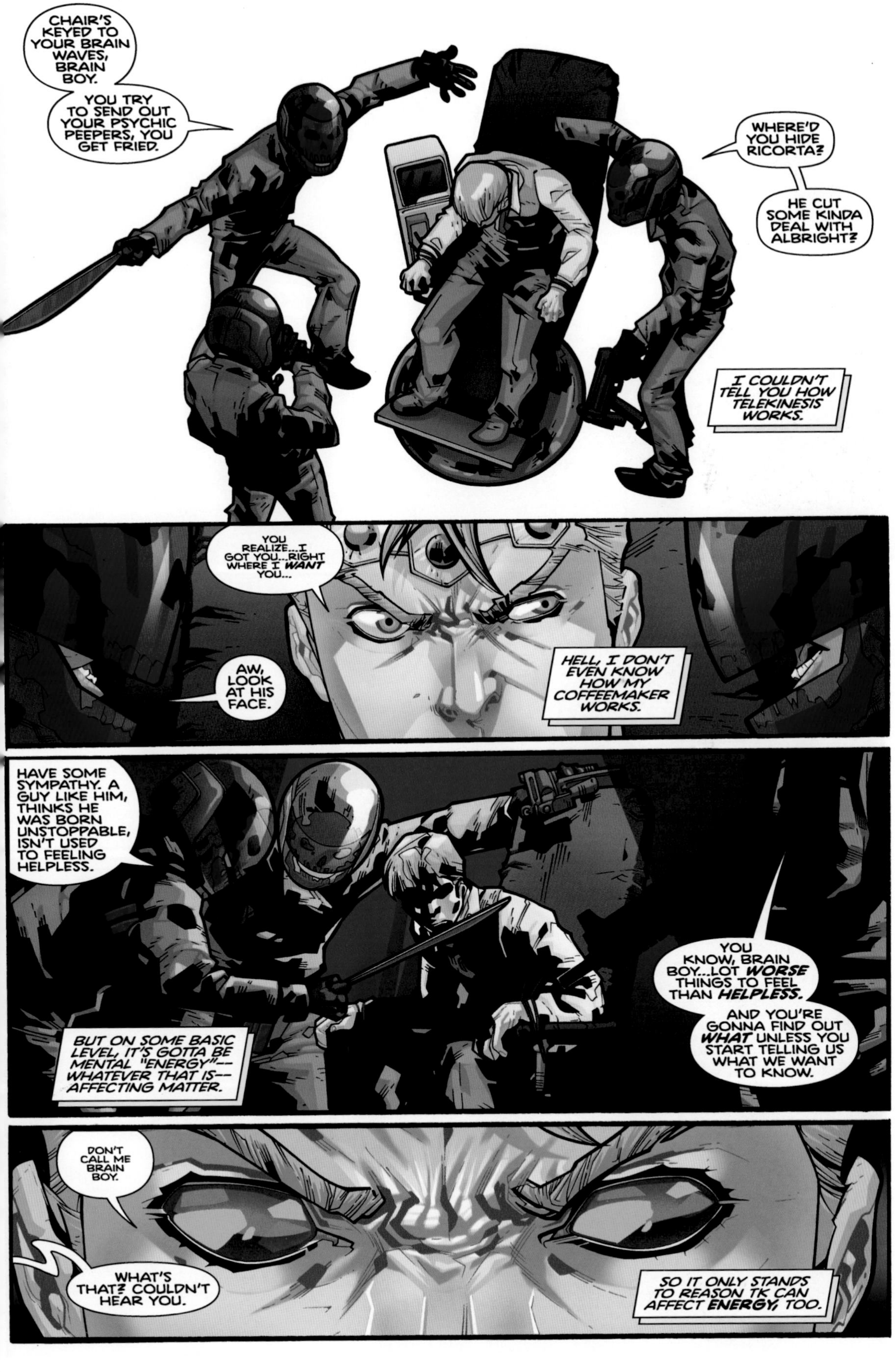
CHAIR'S KEYED TO YOUR BRAIN WAVES, BRAIN BOY.
YOU TRY TO SEND OUT YOUR PSYCHIC PEEPERS, YOU GET FRIED.
WHERE'D YOU HIDE RICORTA?
HE CUT SOME KINDA DEAL WITH ALBRIGHT?
I COULDN'T TELL YOU HOW TELEKINESIS WORKS.
YOU REALIZE...I GOT YOU...RIGHT WHERE I WANT YOU...
AW, LOOK AT HIS FACE.
HELL, I DON'T EVEN KNOW HOW MY COFFEEMAKER WORKS.
HAVE SOME SYMPATHY. A GUY LIKE HIM, THINKS HE WAS BORN UNSTOPPABLE, ISN'T USED TO FEELING HELPLESS.
YOU KNOW, BRAIN BOY...LOT WORSE THINGS TO FEEL THAN HELPLESS.
AND YOU'RE GONNA FIND OUT WHAT UNLESS YOU START TELLING US WHAT WE WANT TO KNOW.
BUT ON SOME BASIC LEVEL, IT'S GOTTA BE MENTAL "ENERGY"--WHATEVER THAT IS--AFFECTING MATTER.
DON'T CALL ME BRAIN BOY.
WHAT'S THAT? COULDN'T HEAR YOU.
SO IT ONLY STANDS TO REASON TK CAN AFFECT ENERGY, TOO.

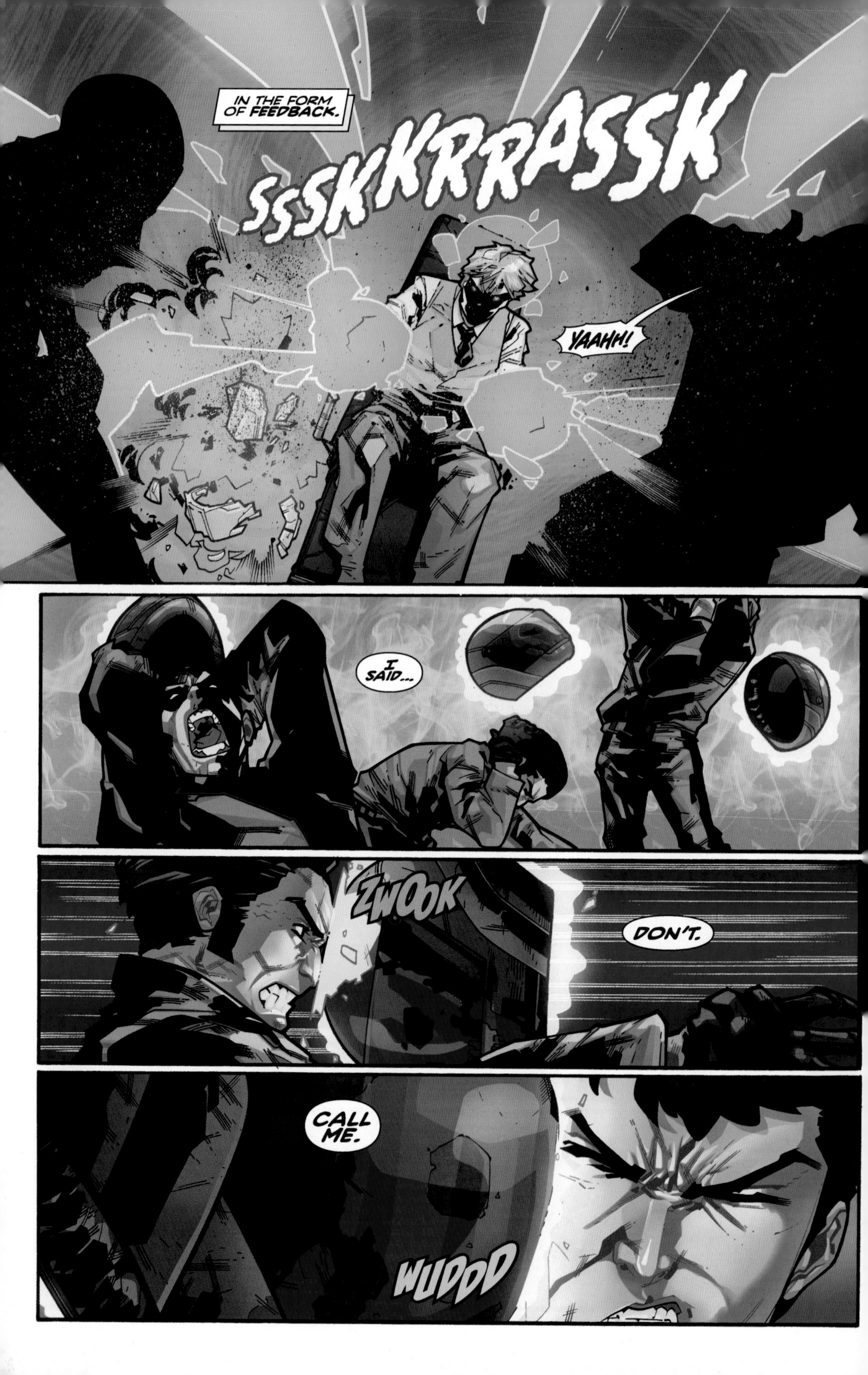
IN THE FORM OF FEEDBACK.
SSSKKRRASSK
YAAHH!
I SAID...
ZWOOK
DON'T.
CALL ME.
WUDDD

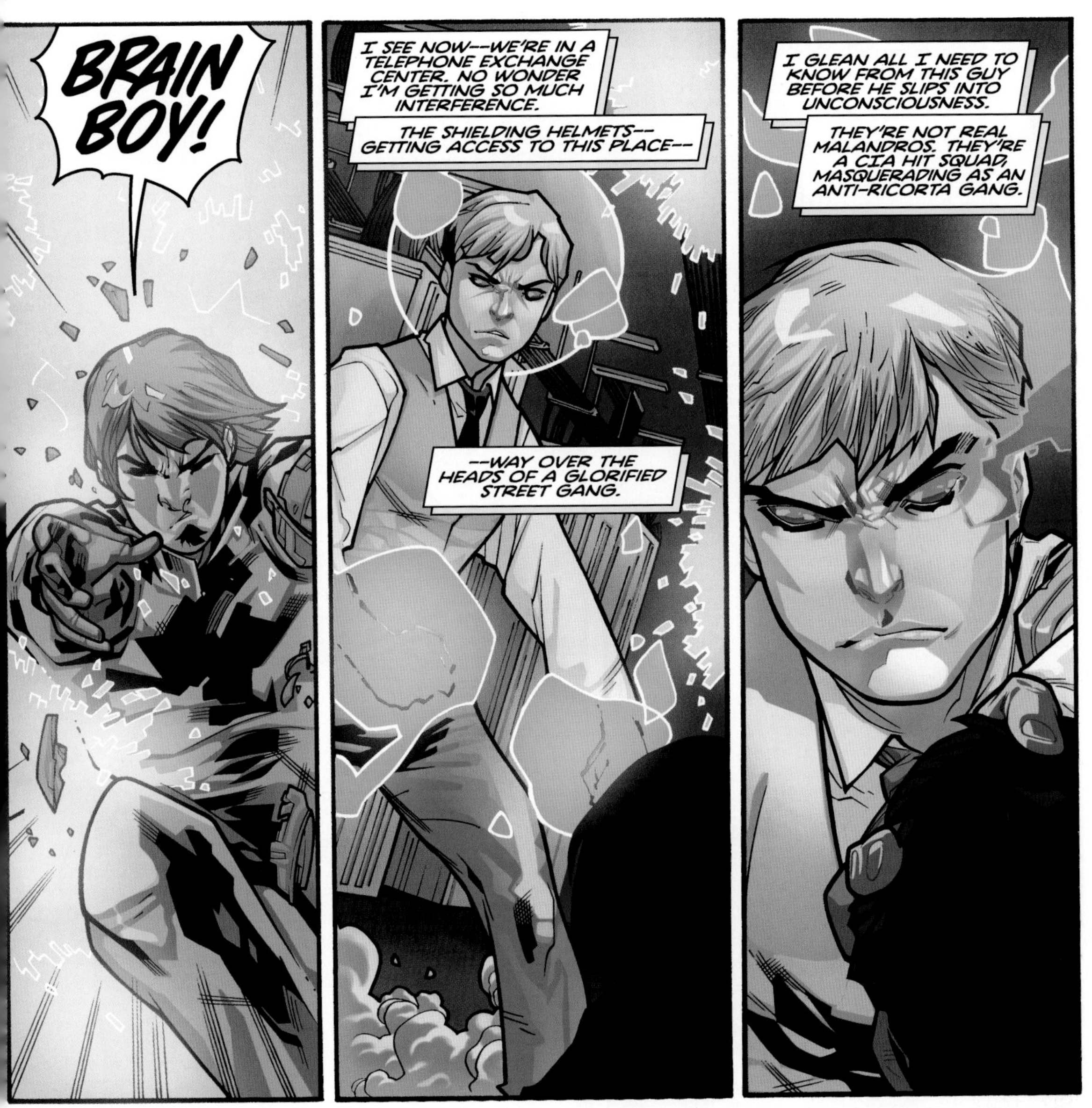
BRAIN BOY!
I SEE NOW--WE'RE IN A TELEPHONE EXCHANGE CENTER. NO WONDER I'M GETTING SO MUCH INTERFERENCE.
THE SHIELDING HELMETS-- GETTING ACCESS TO THIS PLACE--
--WAY OVER THE HEADS OF A GLORIFIED STREET GANG.
I GLEAN ALL I NEED TO KNOW FROM THIS GUY BEFORE HE SLIPS INTO UNCONSCIOUSNESS.
THEY'RE NOT REAL MALANDROS. THEY'RE A CIA HIT SQUAD, MASQUERADING AS AN ANTI-RICORTA GANG.

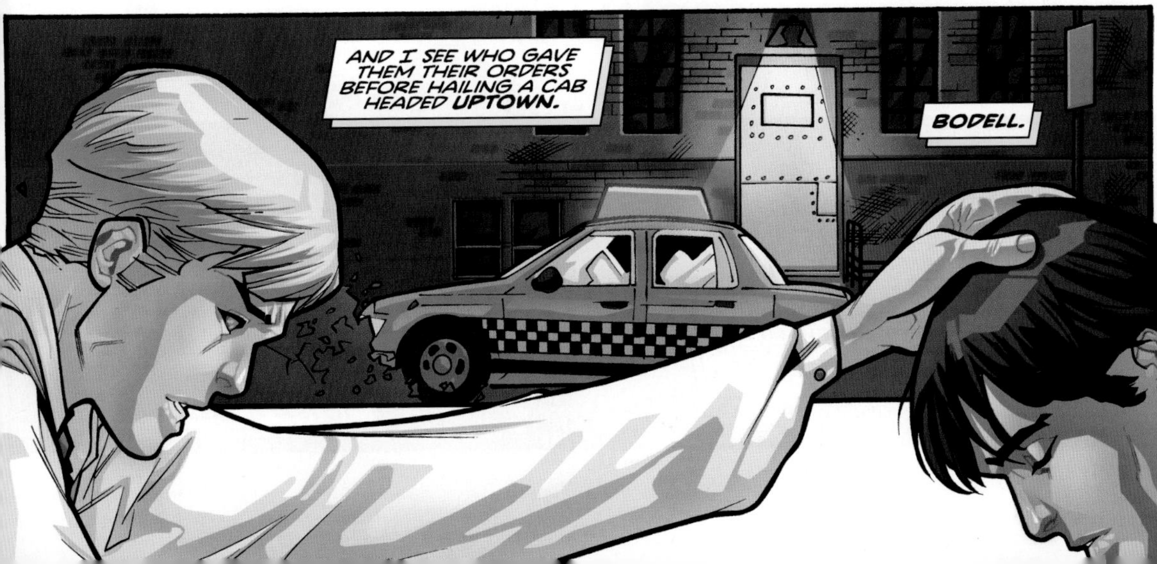
AND I SEE WHO GAVE THEM THEIR ORDERS BEFORE HAILING A CAB HEADED UPTOWN.
BODELL.

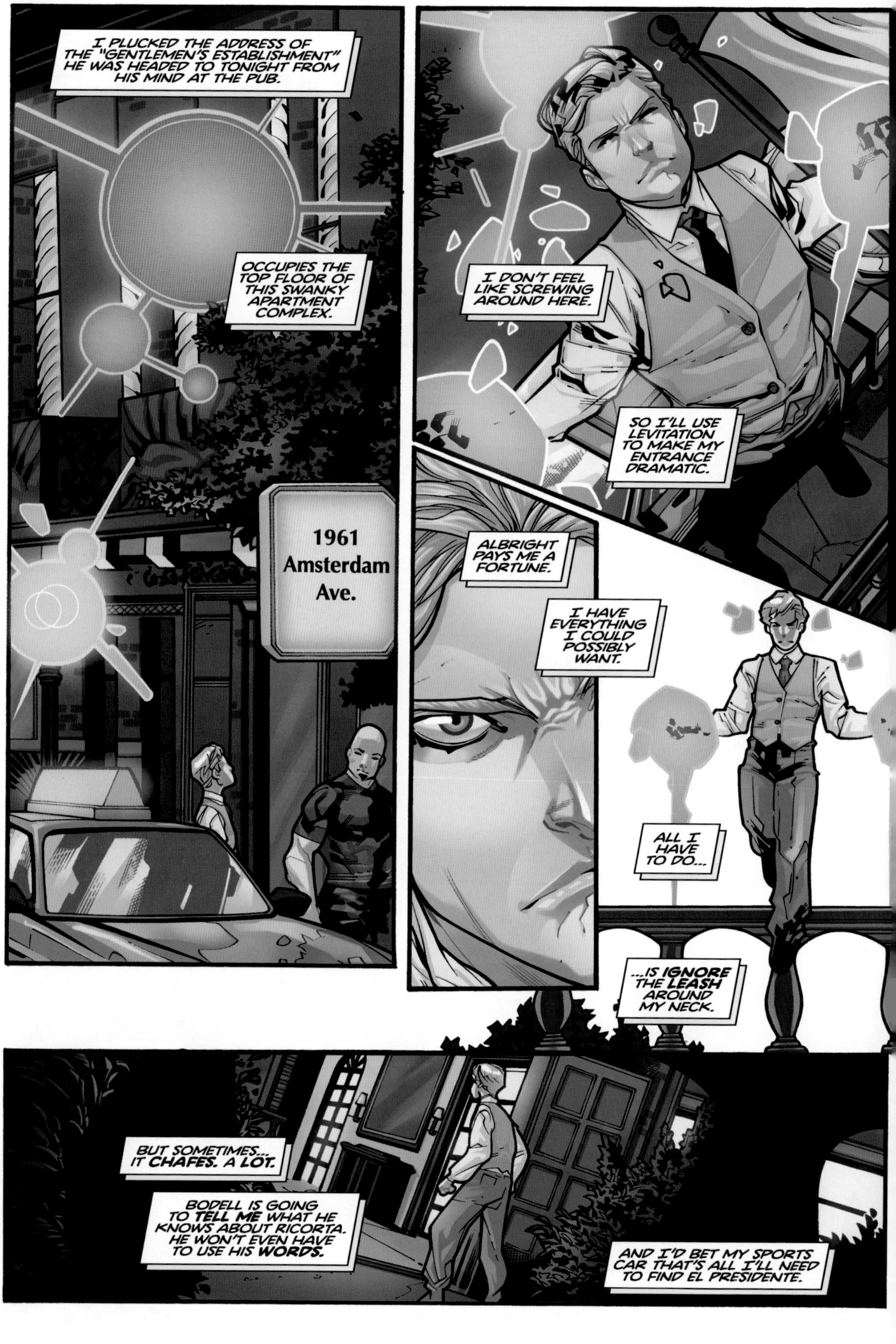
I PLUCKED THE ADDRESS OF THE "GENTLEMEN'S ESTABLISHMENT" HE WAS HEADED TO TONIGHT FROM HIS MIND AT THE PUB.
OCCUPIES THE TOP FLOOR OF THIS SWANKY APARTMENT COMPLEX.
1961 Amsterdam Ave.
I DON'T FEEL LIKE SCREWING AROUND HERE.
SO I'LL USE LEVITATION TO MAKE MY ENTRANCE DRAMATIC.
ALBRIGHT PAYS ME A FORTUNE.
I HAVE EVERYTHING I COULD POSSIBLY WANT.
ALL I HAVE TO DO...
...IS IGNORE THE LEASH AROUND MY NECK.
BUT SOMETIMES... IT CHAFES. A LOT.
BODELL IS GOING TO TELL ME WHAT HE KNOWS ABOUT RICORTA. HE WON'T EVEN HAVE TO USE HIS WORDS.
AND I'D BET MY SPORTS CAR THAT'S ALL I'LL NEED TO FIND EL PRESIDENTE.

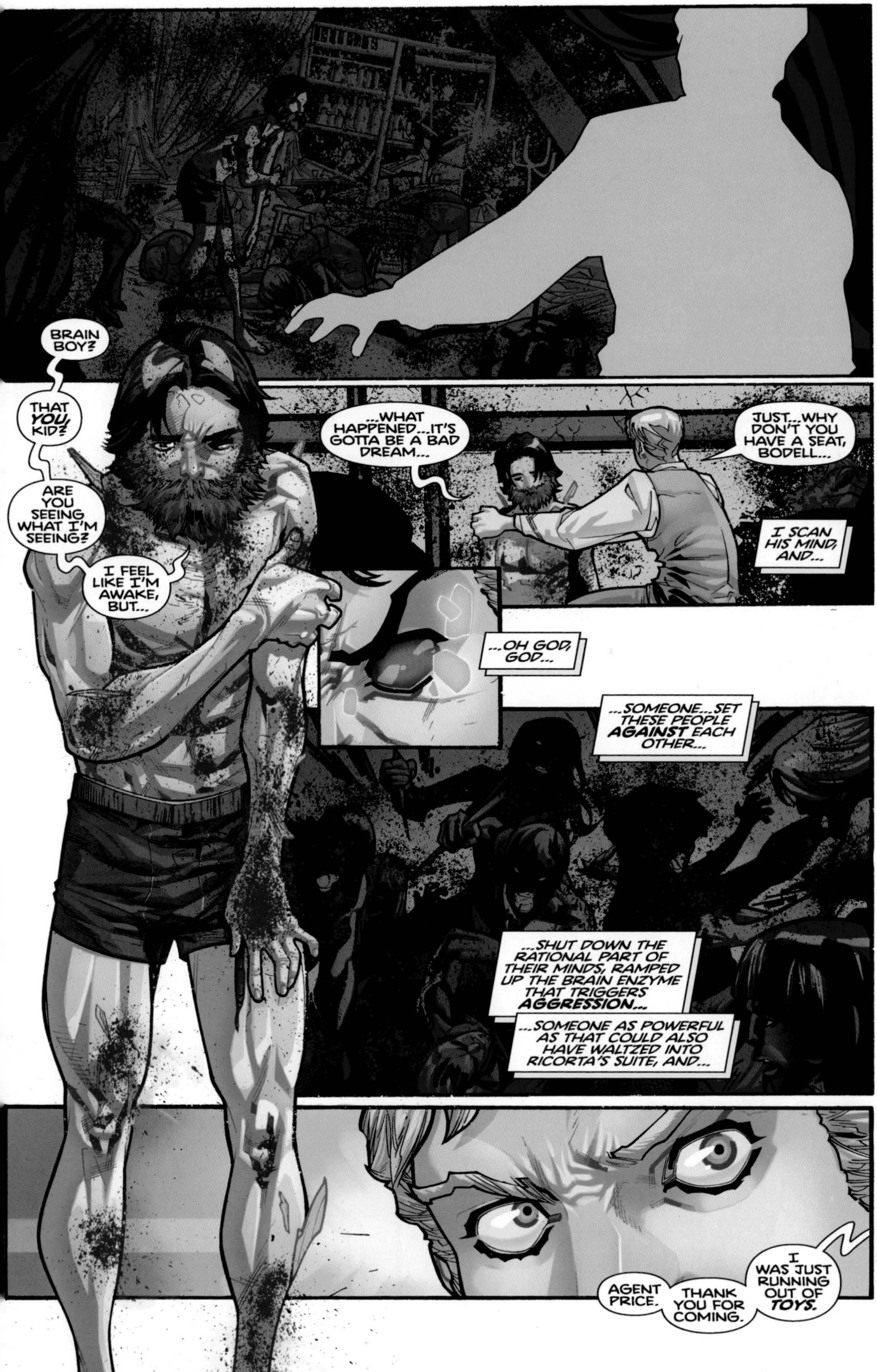
BRAIN BOY?
THAT YOU, KID?
ARE YOU SEEING WHAT I'M SEEING?
I FEEL LIKE I'M AWAKE, BUT...
...WHAT HAPPENED...IT'S GOTTA BE A BAD DREAM...
JUST...WHY DON'T YOU HAVE A SEAT, BODELL...
I SCAN HIS MIND, AND...
...OH GOD, GOD...
...SOMEONE...SET THESE PEOPLE AGAINST EACH OTHER...
...SHUT DOWN THE RATIONAL PART OF THEIR MINDS, RAMPED UP THE BRAIN ENZYME THAT TRIGGERS AGGRESSION...
...SOMEONE AS POWERFUL AS THAT COULD ALSO HAVE WALTZED INTO RICORTA'S SUITE, AND...
AGENT PRICE.
THANK YOU FOR COMING.
I WAS JUST RUNNING OUT OF TOYS.

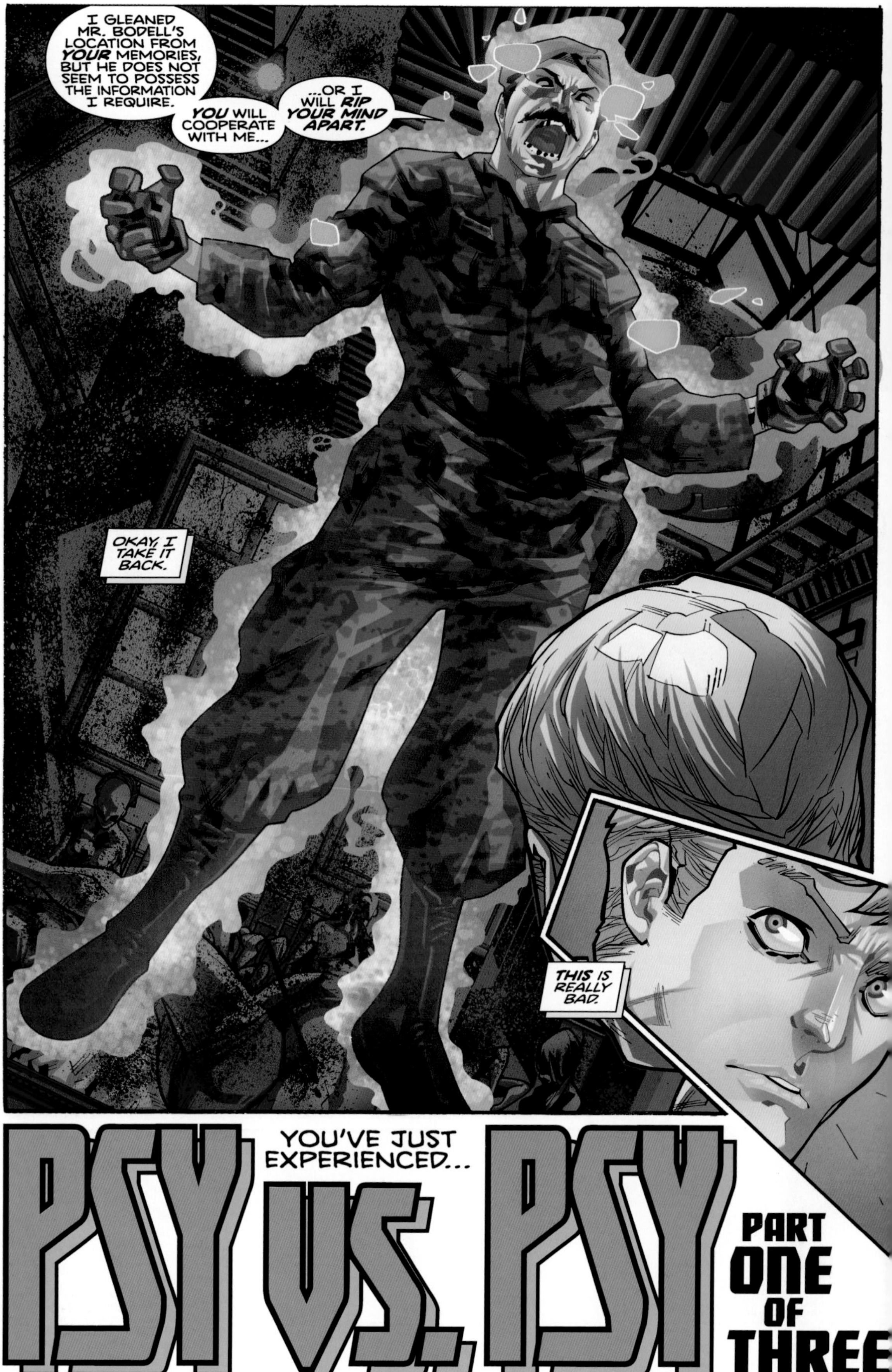

I GLEANED MR. BODELL'S LOCATION FROM YOUR MEMORIES, BUT HE DOES NOT SEEM TO POSSESS THE INFORMATION I REQUIRE.
YOU WILL COOPERATE WITH ME...
...OR I WILL RIP YOUR MIND APART.
OKAY, I TAKE IT BACK.
THIS IS REALLY BAD.
YOU'VE JUST EXPERIENCED...
PSY VS. PSY
PART ONE OF THREE

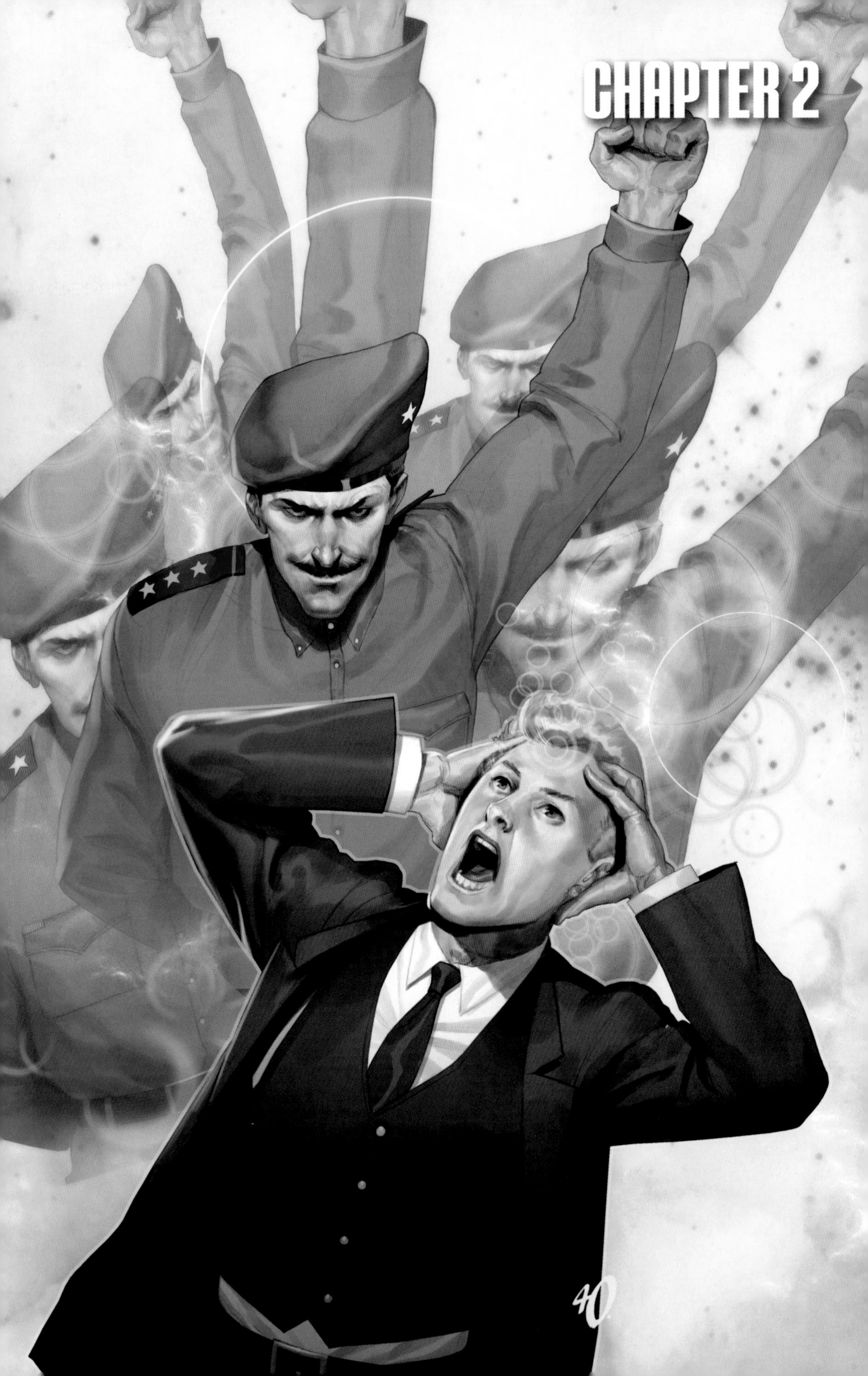
CHAPTER 2

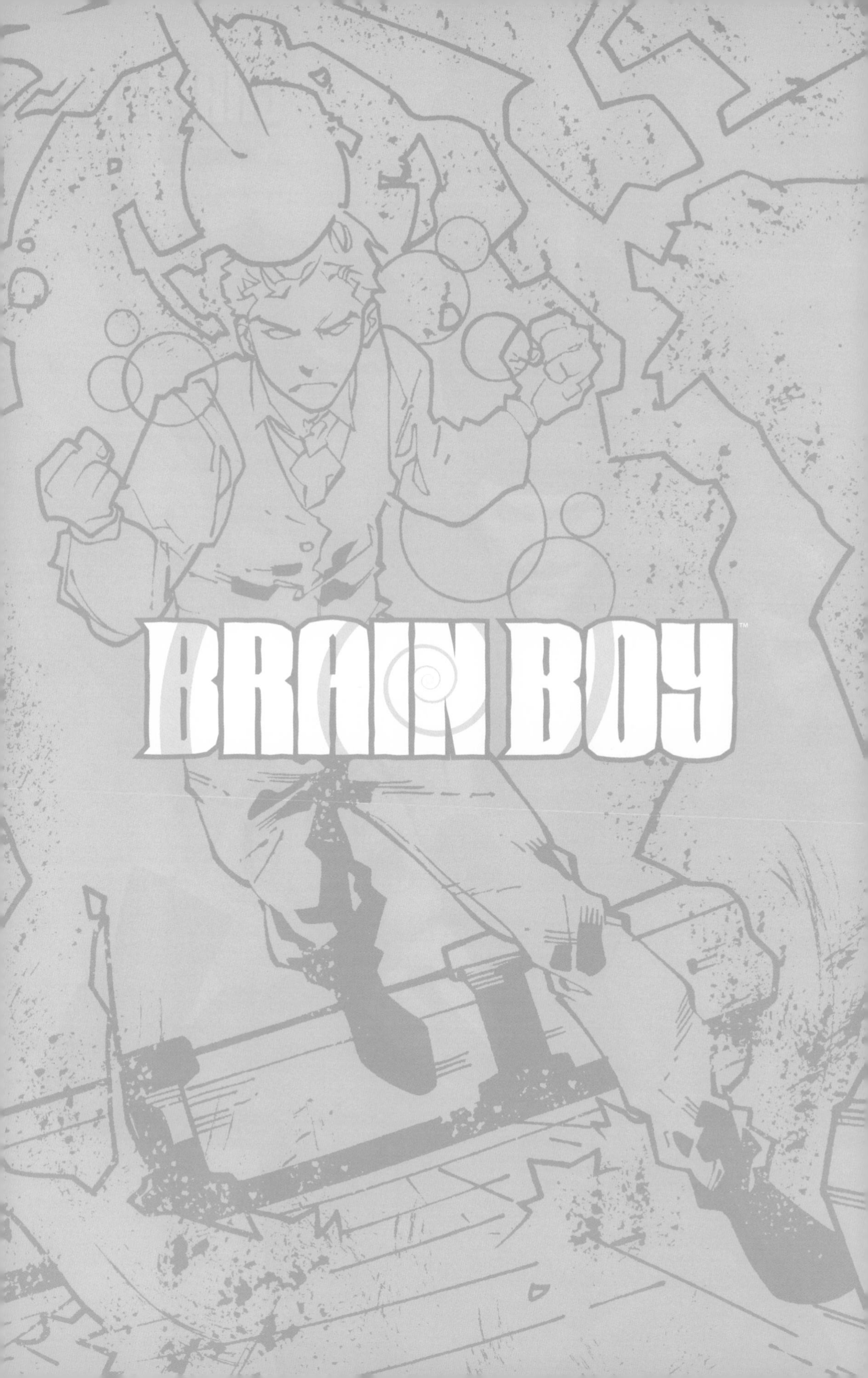
BRAIN BOY™

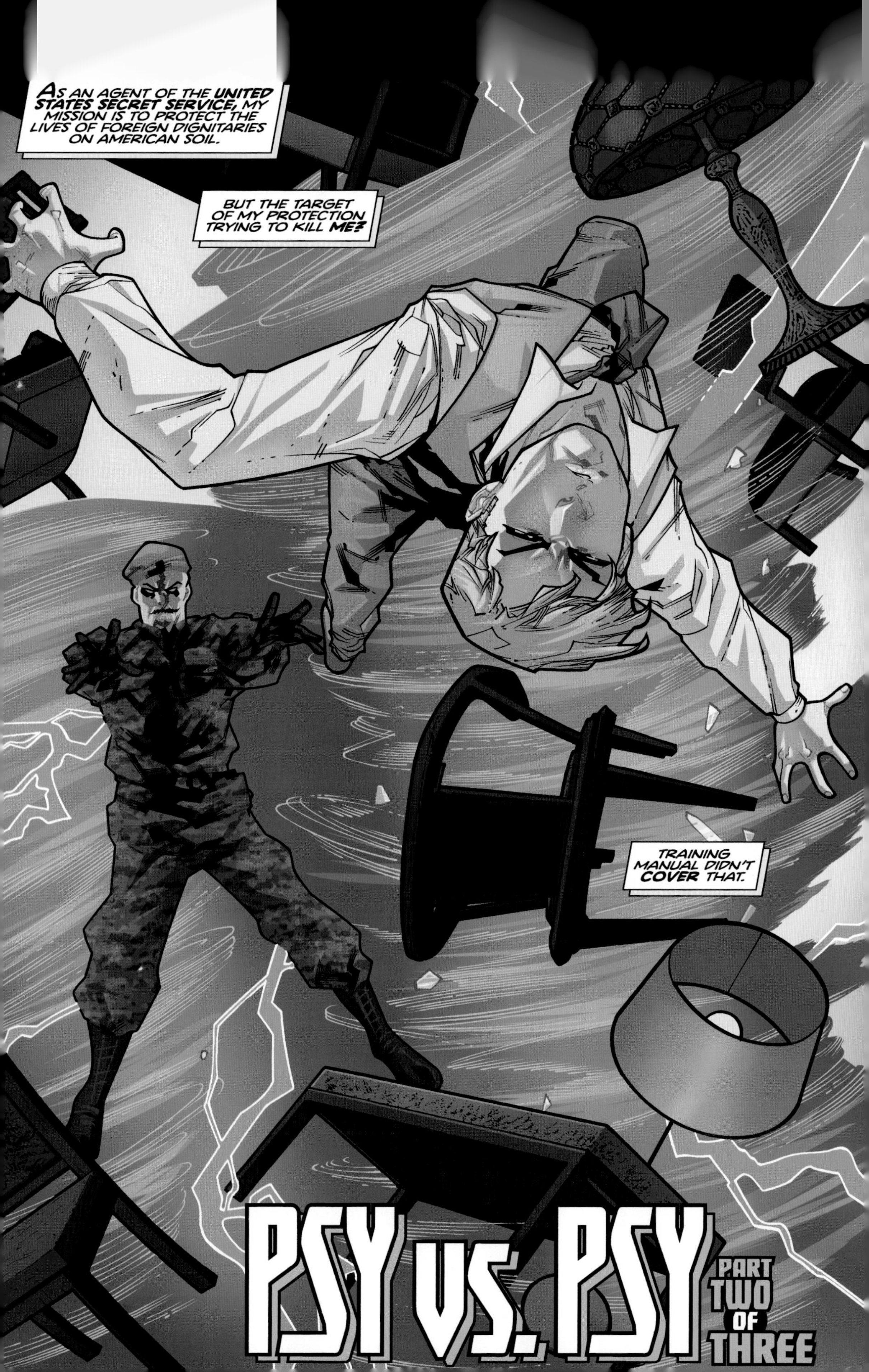
AS AN AGENT OF THE UNITED STATES SECRET SERVICE, MY MISSION IS TO PROTECT THE LIVES OF FOREIGN DIGNITARIES ON AMERICAN SOIL.
BUT THE TARGET OF MY PROTECTION TRYING TO KILL ME?
TRAINING MANUAL DIDN'T COVER THAT.
PSY VS. PSY
PART TWO OF THREE

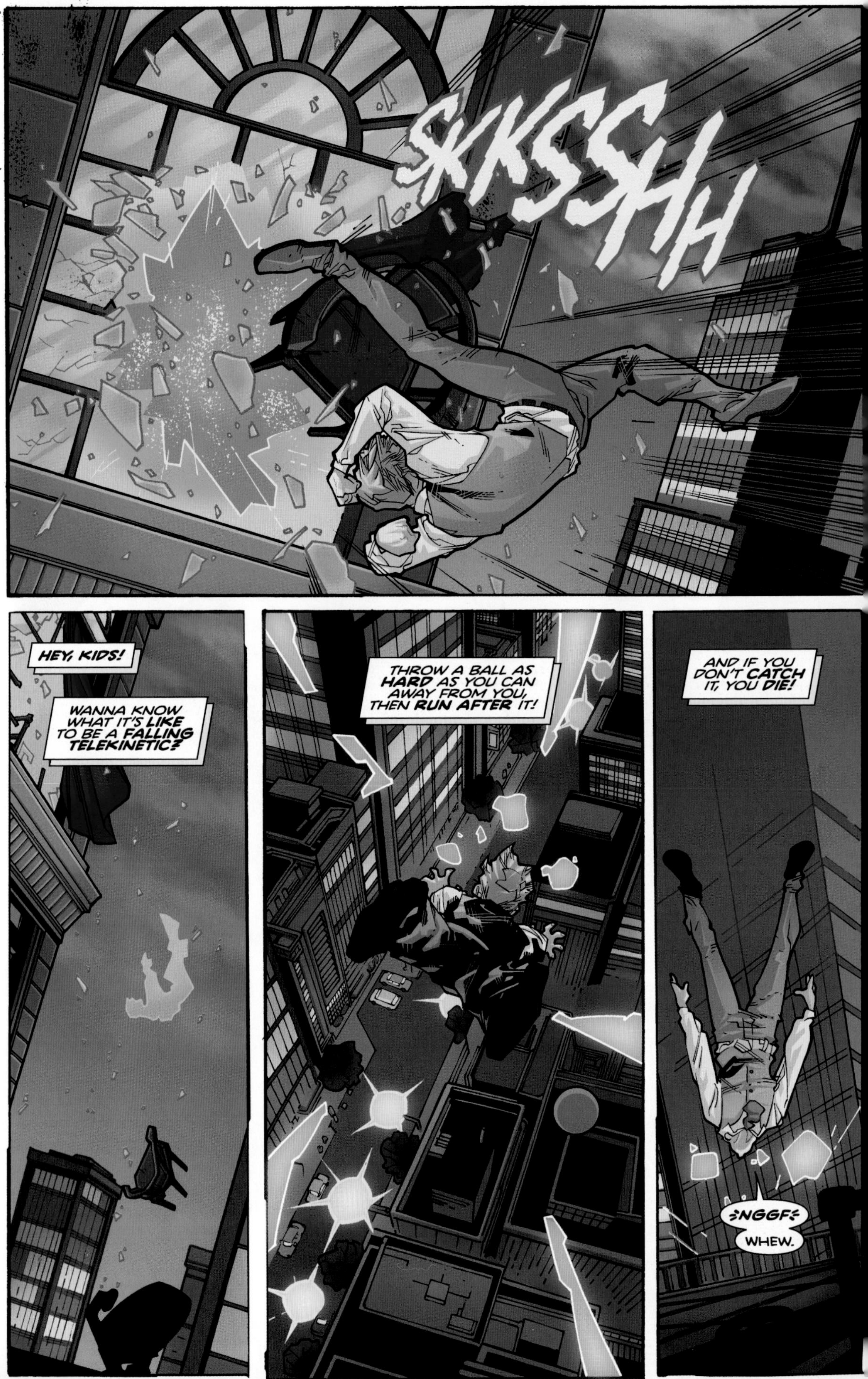
SKKSSHH
HEY, KIDS!
WANNA KNOW WHAT IT'S LIKE TO BE A FALLING TELEKINETIC?
THROW A BALL AS HARD AS YOU CAN AWAY FROM YOU, THEN RUN AFTER IT!
AND IF YOU DON'T CATCH IT, YOU DIE!
NGGF
WHEW.

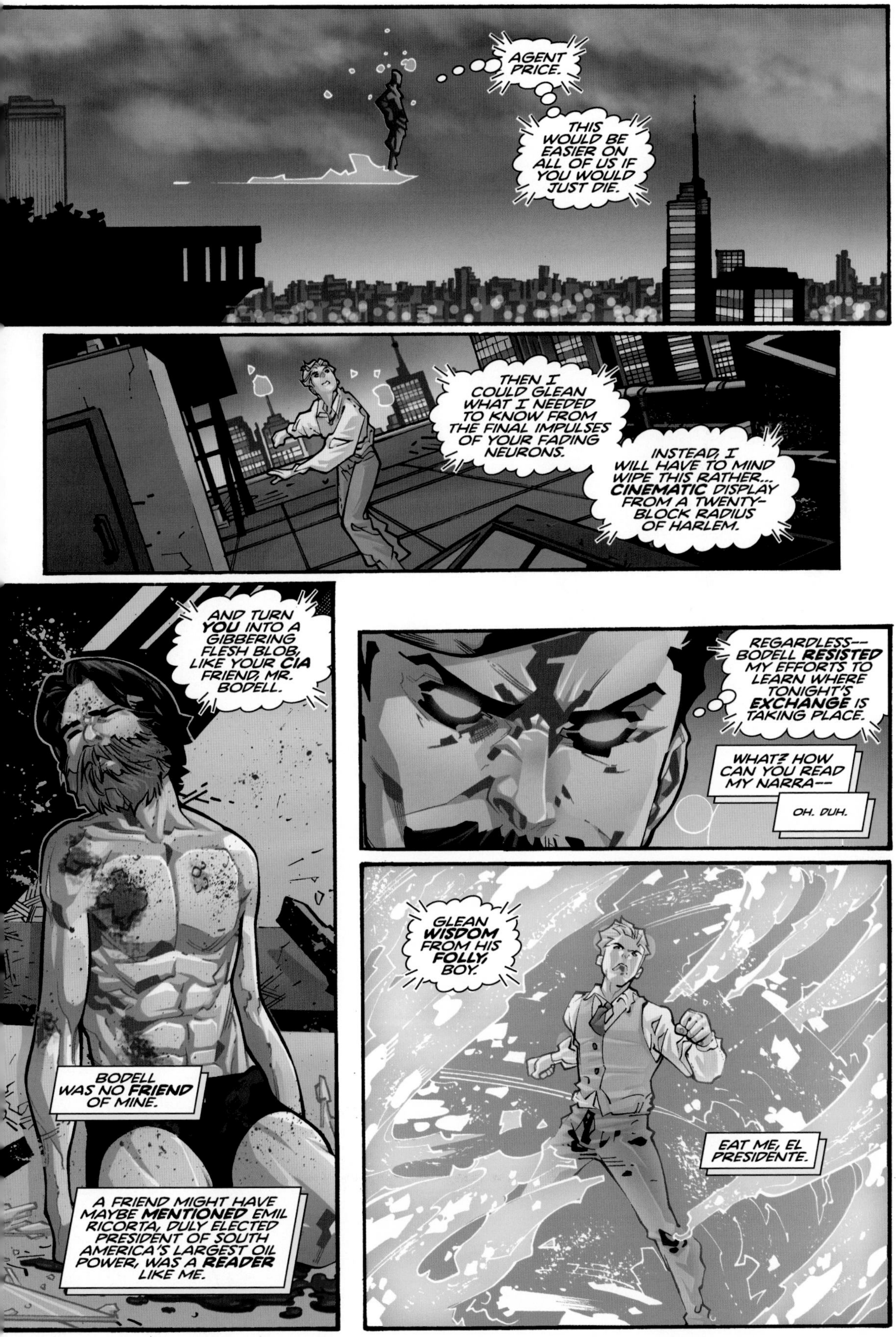
AGENT PRICE.
THIS WOULD BE EASIER ON ALL OF US IF YOU WOULD JUST DIE.
THEN I COULD GLEAN WHAT I NEEDED TO KNOW FROM THE FINAL IMPULSES OF YOUR FADING NEURONS.
INSTEAD, I WILL HAVE TO MIND WIPE THIS RATHER... CINEMATIC DISPLAY FROM A TWENTY-BLOCK RADIUS OF HARLEM.
AND TURN YOU INTO A GIBBERING FLESH BLOB, LIKE YOUR CIA FRIEND, MR. BODELL.
BODELL WAS NO FRIEND OF MINE.
A FRIEND MIGHT HAVE MAYBE MENTIONED EMIL RICORTA, DULY ELECTED PRESIDENT OF SOUTH AMERICA'S LARGEST OIL POWER, WAS A READER LIKE ME.
REGARDLESS-- BODELL RESISTED MY EFFORTS TO LEARN WHERE TONIGHT'S EXCHANGE IS TAKING PLACE.
WHAT? HOW CAN YOU READ MY NARRA--
OH. DUH.
GLEAN WISDOM FROM HIS FOLLY, BOY.
EAT ME, EL PRESIDENTE.

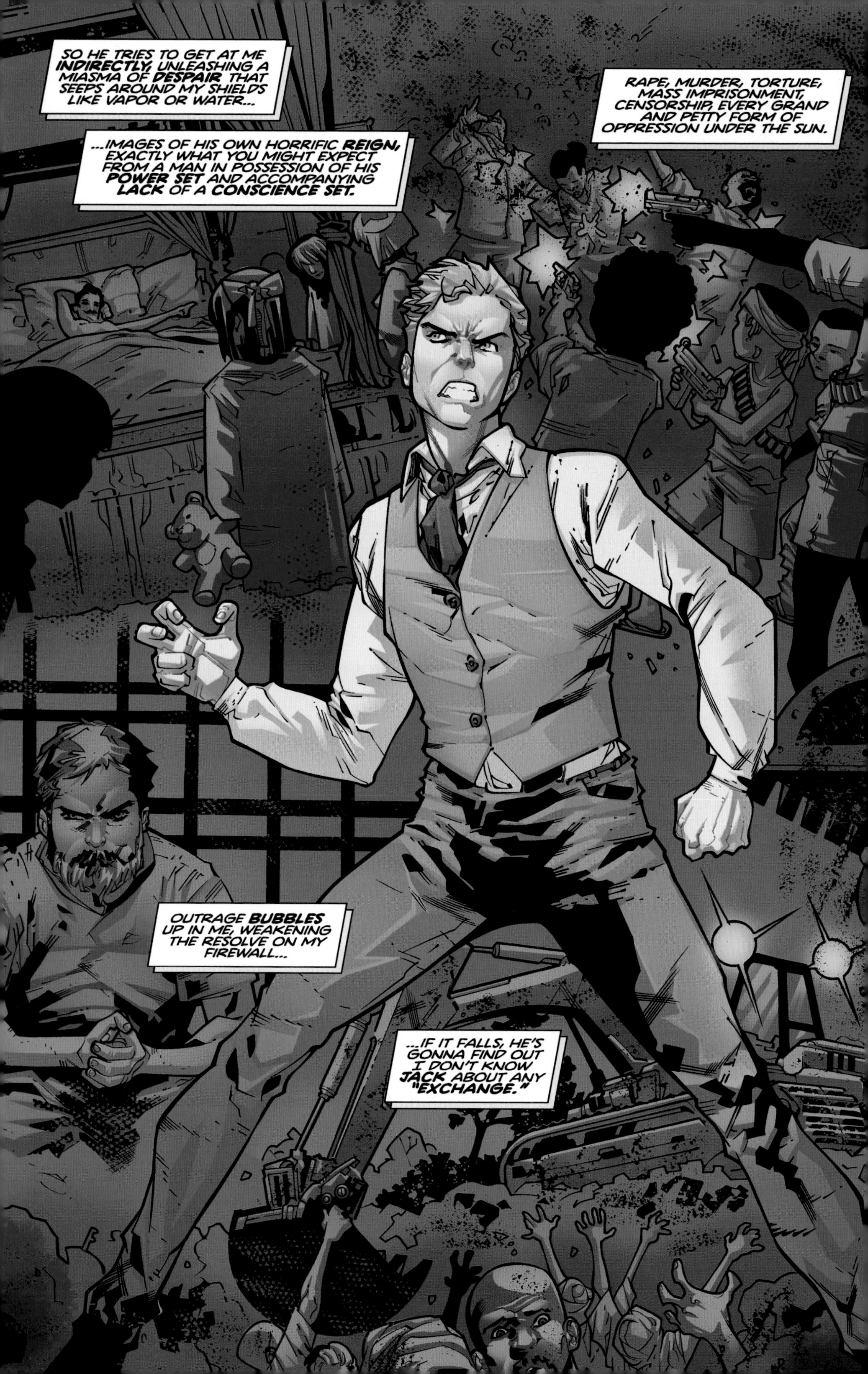
SO HE TRIES TO GET AT ME INDIRECTLY, UNLEASHING A MIASMA OF DESPAIR THAT SEEPS AROUND MY SHIELDS LIKE VAPOR OR WATER...
...IMAGES OF HIS OWN HORRIFIC REIGN, EXACTLY WHAT YOU MIGHT EXPECT FROM A MAN IN POSSESSION OF HIS POWER SET AND ACCOMPANYING LACK OF A CONSCIENCE SET.
RAPE, MURDER, TORTURE, MASS IMPRISONMENT, CENSORSHIP, EVERY GRAND AND PETTY FORM OF OPPRESSION UNDER THE SUN.
OUTRAGE BUBBLES UP IN ME, WEAKENING THE RESOLVE ON MY FIREWALL...
...IF IT FALLS, HE'S GONNA FIND OUT I DON'T KNOW JACK ABOUT ANY "EXCHANGE."

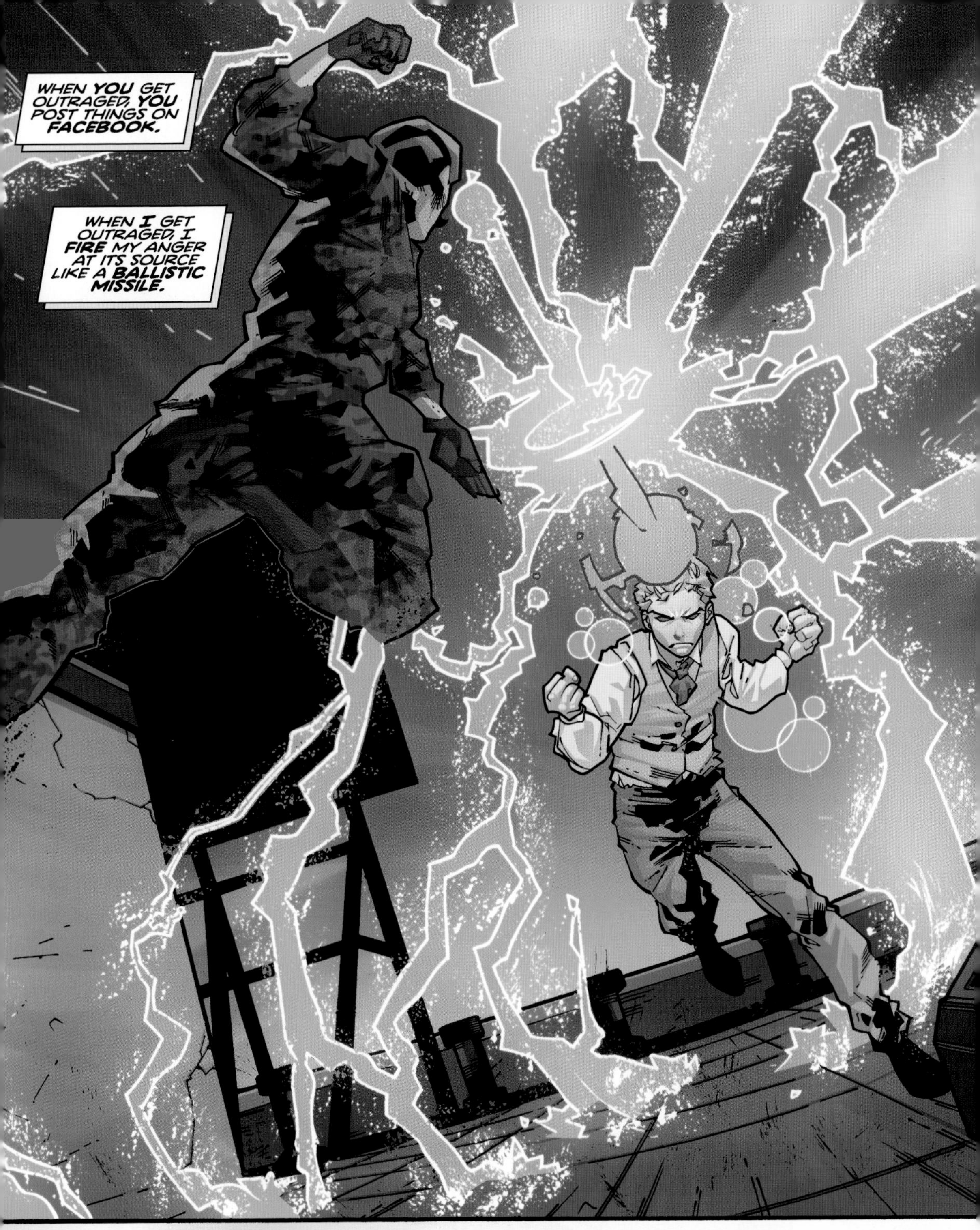
WHEN YOU GET OUTRAGED, YOU POST THINGS ON FACEBOOK.
WHEN I GET OUTRAGED, I FIRE MY ANGER AT ITS SOURCE LIKE A BALLISTIC MISSILE.

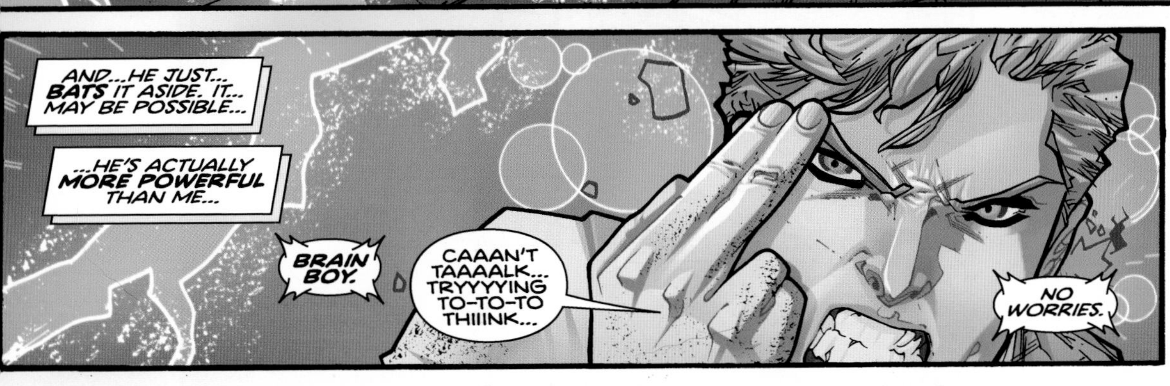
AND...HE JUST... BATS IT ASIDE. IT... MAY BE POSSIBLE...
...HE'S ACTUALLY MORE POWERFUL THAN ME...
BRAIN BOY.
CAAAN'T TAAAALK... TRYYYYING TO-TO-TO THIIINK...
NO WORRIES.

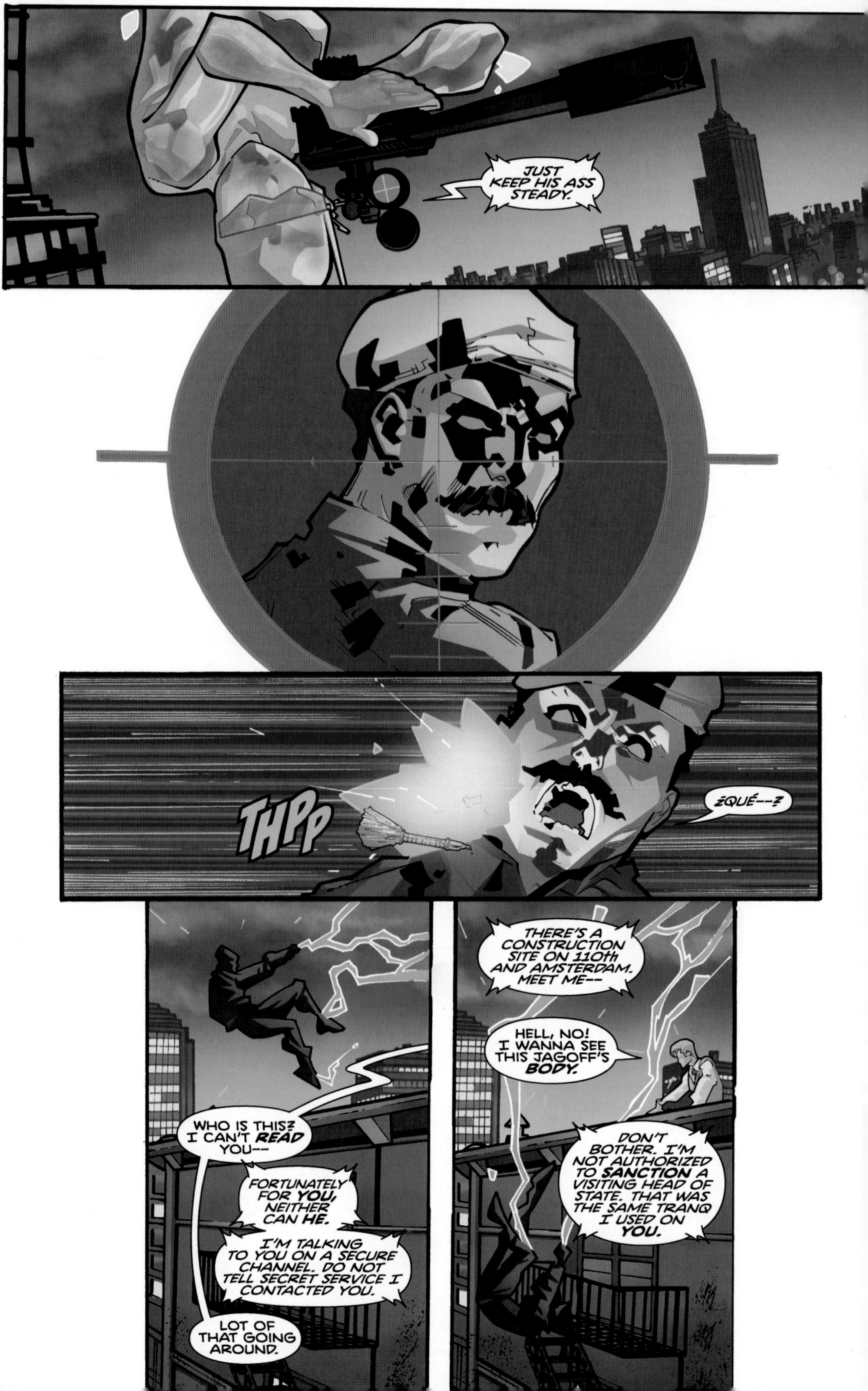
JUST KEEP HIS ASS STEADY.
THPP
¿QUÉ--?
WHO IS THIS? I CAN'T READ YOU--
FORTUNATELY FOR YOU, NEITHER CAN HE.
I'M TALKING TO YOU ON A SECURE CHANNEL. DO NOT TELL SECRET SERVICE I CONTACTED YOU.
LOT OF THAT GOING AROUND.
THERE'S A CONSTRUCTION SITE ON 110th AND AMSTERDAM. MEET ME--
HELL, NO! I WANNA SEE THIS JAGOFF'S BODY.
DON'T BOTHER. I'M NOT AUTHORIZED TO SANCTION A VISITING HEAD OF STATE. THAT WAS THE SAME TRANQ I USED ON YOU.

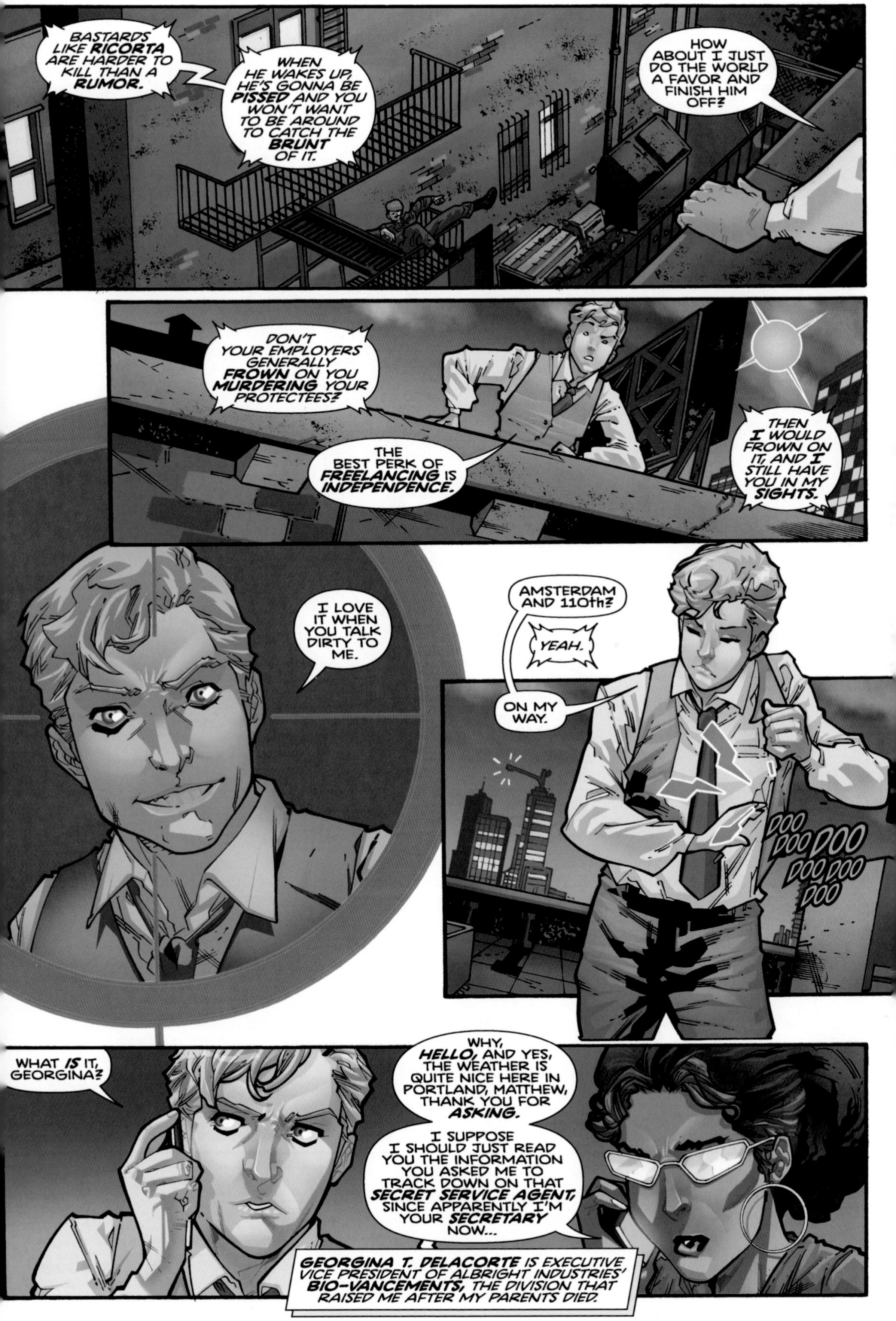
BASTARDS LIKE RICORTA ARE HARDER TO KILL THAN A RUMOR.
WHEN HE WAKES UP, HE'S GONNA BE PISSED AND YOU WON'T WANT TO BE AROUND TO CATCH THE BRUNT OF IT.
HOW ABOUT I JUST DO THE WORLD A FAVOR AND FINISH HIM OFF?
DON'T YOUR EMPLOYERS GENERALLY FROWN ON YOU MURDERING YOUR PROTECTEES?
THE BEST PERK OF FREELANCING IS INDEPENDENCE.
THEN I WOULD FROWN ON IT, AND I STILL HAVE YOU IN MY SIGHTS.
I LOVE IT WHEN YOU TALK DIRTY TO ME.
AMSTERDAM AND 110th?
YEAH.
ON MY WAY.
DOO DOO DOO DOO DOO DOO
WHAT IS IT, GEORGINA?
WHY, HELLO, AND YES, THE WEATHER IS QUITE NICE HERE IN PORTLAND, MATTHEW, THANK YOU FOR ASKING.
I SUPPOSE I SHOULD JUST READ YOU THE INFORMATION YOU ASKED ME TO TRACK DOWN ON THAT SECRET SERVICE AGENT, SINCE APPARENTLY I'M YOUR SECRETARY NOW...
GEORGINA T. DELACORTE IS EXECUTIVE VICE PRESIDENT OF ALBRIGHT INDUSTRIES' BIO-VANCEMENTS, THE DIVISION THAT RAISED ME AFTER MY PARENTS DIED.

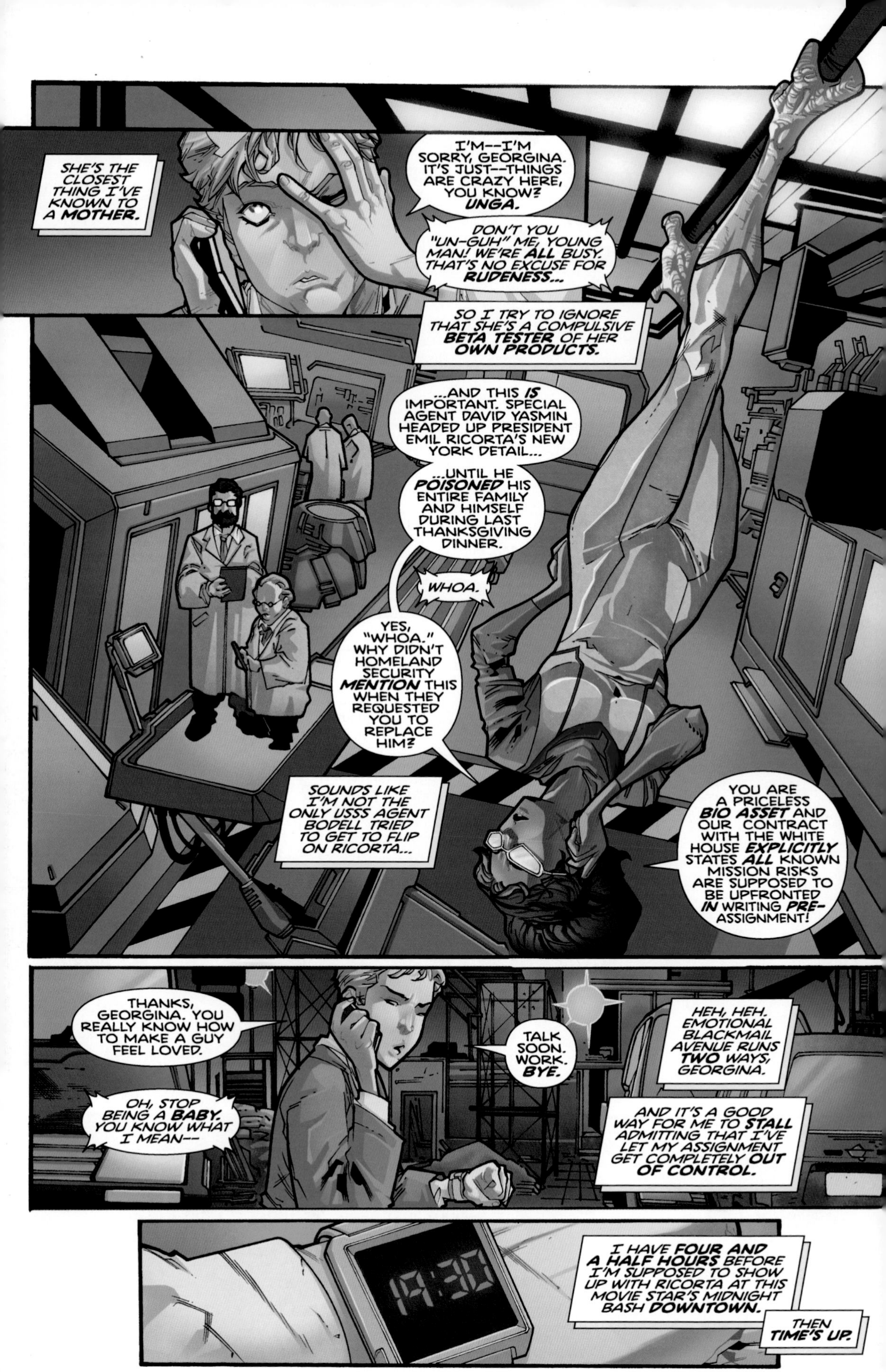

SHE'S THE CLOSEST THING I'VE KNOWN TO A MOTHER.
I'M--I'M SORRY, GEORGINA. IT'S JUST--THINGS ARE CRAZY HERE, YOU KNOW? UNGA.
DON'T YOU "UN-GUH" ME, YOUNG MAN! WE'RE ALL BUSY. THAT'S NO EXCUSE FOR RUDENESS...
SO I TRY TO IGNORE THAT SHE'S A COMPULSIVE BETA TESTER OF HER OWN PRODUCTS.
...AND THIS IS IMPORTANT. SPECIAL AGENT DAVID YASMIN HEADED UP PRESIDENT EMIL RICORTA'S NEW YORK DETAIL...
...UNTIL HE POISONED HIS ENTIRE FAMILY AND HIMSELF DURING LAST THANKSGIVING DINNER.
WHOA.
YES, "WHOA." WHY DIDN'T HOMELAND SECURITY MENTION THIS WHEN THEY REQUESTED YOU TO REPLACE HIM?
SOUNDS LIKE I'M NOT THE ONLY USSS AGENT BODELL TRIED TO GET TO FLIP ON RICORTA...
YOU ARE A PRICELESS BIO ASSET AND OUR CONTRACT WITH THE WHITE HOUSE EXPLICITLY STATES ALL KNOWN MISSION RISKS ARE SUPPOSED TO BE UPFRONTED IN WRITING PRE-ASSIGNMENT!
THANKS, GEORGINA. YOU REALLY KNOW HOW TO MAKE A GUY FEEL LOVED.
OH, STOP BEING A BABY. YOU KNOW WHAT I MEAN--
TALK SOON. WORK. BYE.
HEH, HEH. EMOTIONAL BLACKMAIL AVENUE RUNS TWO WAYS, GEORGINA.
AND IT'S A GOOD WAY FOR ME TO STALL ADMITTING THAT I'VE LET MY ASSIGNMENT GET COMPLETELY OUT OF CONTROL.
19:30
I HAVE FOUR AND A HALF HOURS BEFORE I'M SUPPOSED TO SHOW UP WITH RICORTA AT THIS MOVIE STAR'S MIDNIGHT BASH DOWNTOWN.
THEN TIME'S UP.

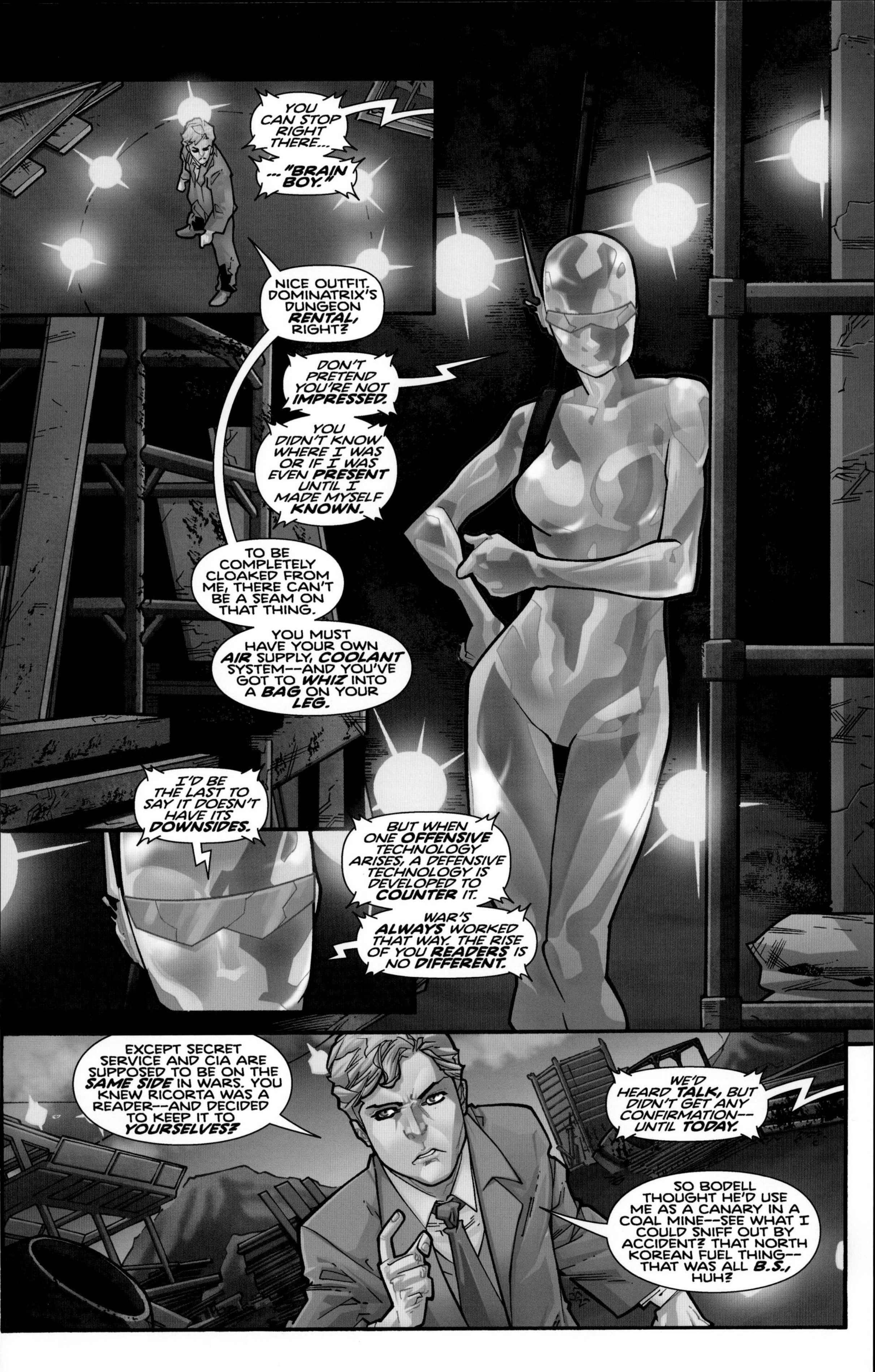

YOU CAN STOP RIGHT THERE...
..."BRAIN BOY."
NICE OUTFIT. DOMINATRIX'S DUNGEON RENTAL, RIGHT?
DON'T PRETEND YOU'RE NOT IMPRESSED.
YOU DIDN'T KNOW WHERE I WAS OR IF I WAS EVEN PRESENT UNTIL I MADE MYSELF KNOWN.
TO BE COMPLETELY CLOAKED FROM ME, THERE CAN'T BE A SEAM ON THAT THING.
YOU MUST HAVE YOUR OWN AIR SUPPLY, COOLANT SYSTEM--AND YOU'VE GOT TO WHIZ INTO A BAG ON YOUR LEG.
I'D BE THE LAST TO SAY IT DOESN'T HAVE ITS DOWNSIDES.
BUT WHEN ONE OFFENSIVE TECHNOLOGY ARISES, A DEFENSIVE TECHNOLOGY IS DEVELOPED TO COUNTER IT.
WAR'S ALWAYS WORKED THAT WAY. THE RISE OF YOU READERS IS NO DIFFERENT.
EXCEPT SECRET SERVICE AND CIA ARE SUPPOSED TO BE ON THE SAME SIDE IN WARS. YOU KNEW RICORTA WAS A READER--AND DECIDED TO KEEP IT TO YOURSELVES?
WE'D HEARD TALK, BUT DIDN'T GET ANY CONFIRMATION--UNTIL TODAY.
SO BODELL THOUGHT HE'D USE ME AS A CANARY IN A COAL MINE--SEE WHAT I COULD SNIFF OUT BY ACCIDENT? THAT NORTH KOREAN FUEL THING--THAT WAS ALL B.S., HUH?

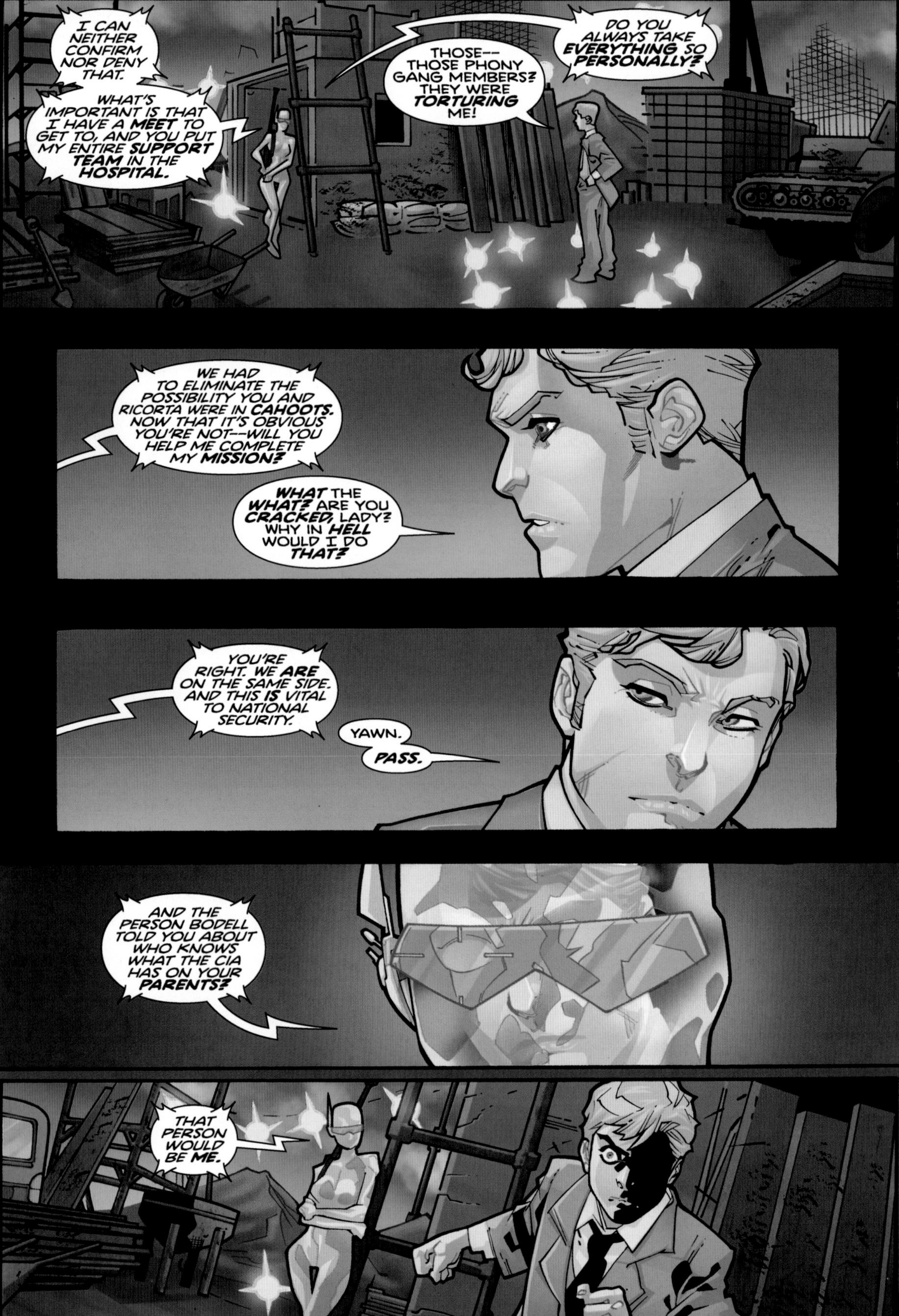
I CAN NEITHER CONFIRM NOR DENY THAT.
WHAT'S IMPORTANT IS THAT I HAVE A MEET TO GET TO, AND YOU PUT MY ENTIRE SUPPORT TEAM IN THE HOSPITAL.
THOSE-- THOSE PHONY GANG MEMBERS? THEY WERE TORTURING ME!
DO YOU ALWAYS TAKE EVERYTHING SO PERSONALLY?
WE HAD TO ELIMINATE THE POSSIBILITY YOU AND RICORTA WERE IN CAHOOTS. NOW THAT IT'S OBVIOUS YOU'RE NOT--WILL YOU HELP ME COMPLETE MY MISSION?
WHAT THE WHAT? ARE YOU CRACKED, LADY? WHY IN HELL WOULD I DO THAT?
YOU'RE RIGHT. WE ARE ON THE SAME SIDE. AND THIS IS VITAL TO NATIONAL SECURITY.
YAWN.
PASS.
AND THE PERSON BODELL TOLD YOU ABOUT WHO KNOWS WHAT THE CIA HAS ON YOUR PARENTS?
THAT PERSON WOULD BE ME.

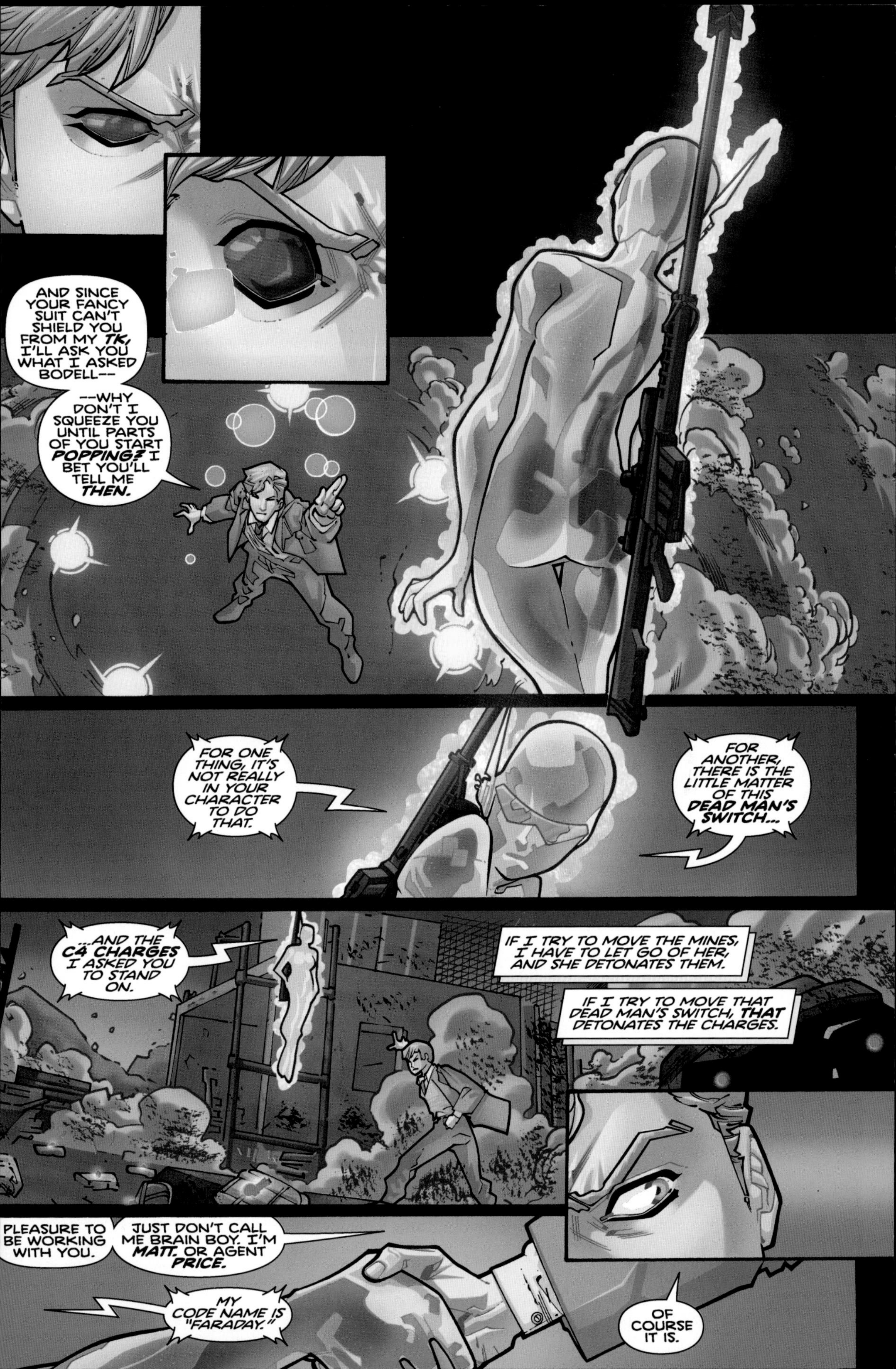
AND SINCE YOUR FANCY SUIT CAN'T SHIELD YOU FROM MY TK, I'LL ASK YOU WHAT I ASKED BODELL--
--WHY DON'T I SQUEEZE YOU UNTIL PARTS OF YOU START POPPING? I BET YOU'LL TELL ME THEN.
FOR ONE THING, IT'S NOT REALLY IN YOUR CHARACTER TO DO THAT.
FOR ANOTHER, THERE IS THE LITTLE MATTER OF THIS DEAD MAN'S SWITCH...
...AND THE C4 CHARGES I ASKED YOU TO STAND ON.
IF I TRY TO MOVE THE MINES, I HAVE TO LET GO OF HER, AND SHE DETONATES THEM.
IF I TRY TO MOVE THAT DEAD MAN'S SWITCH, THAT DETONATES THE CHARGES.
PLEASURE TO BE WORKING WITH YOU.
JUST DON'T CALL ME BRAIN BOY. I'M MATT. OR AGENT PRICE.
MY CODE NAME IS "FARADAY."
OF COURSE IT IS.

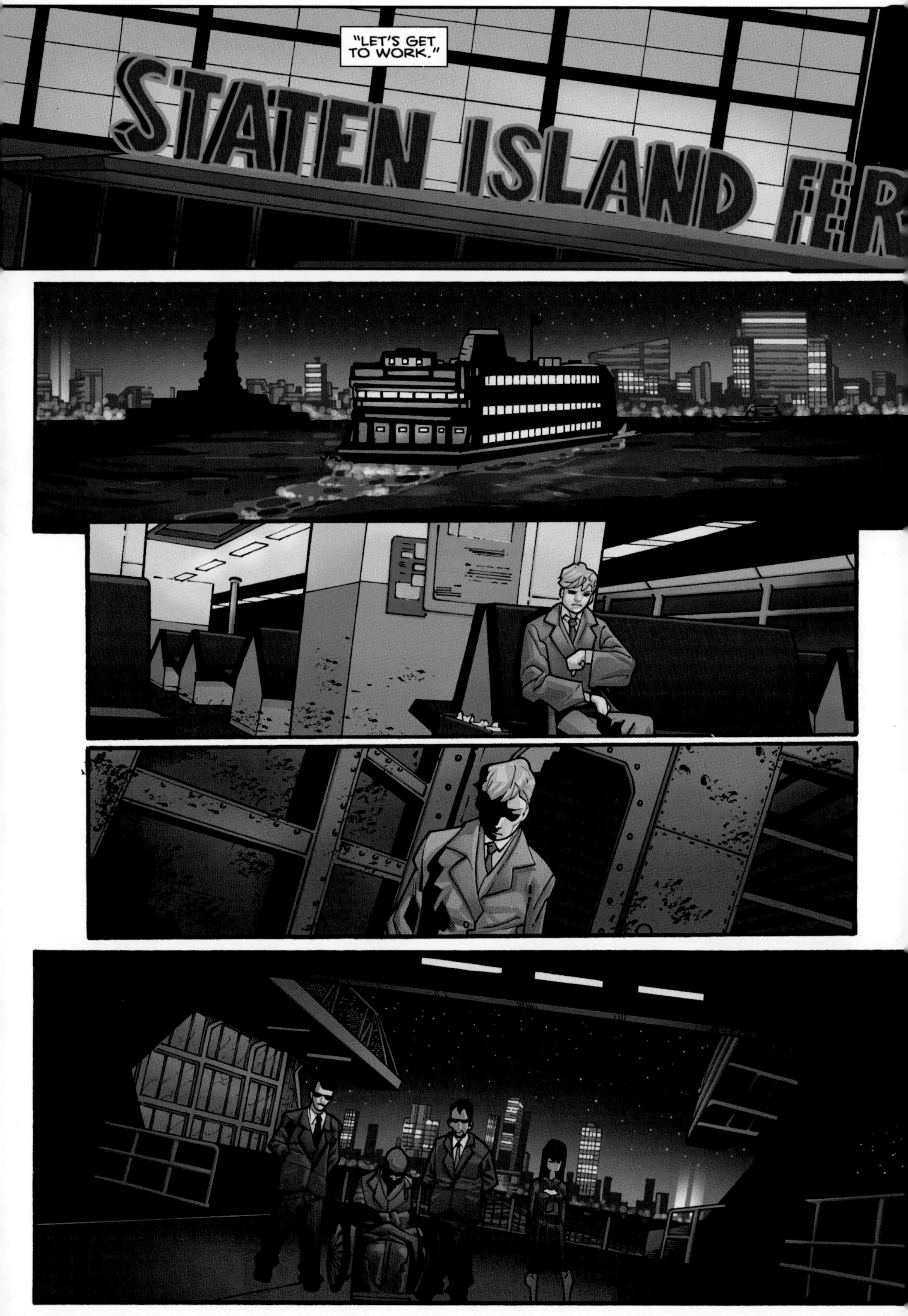
"LET'S GET TO WORK."
STATEN ISLAND FER

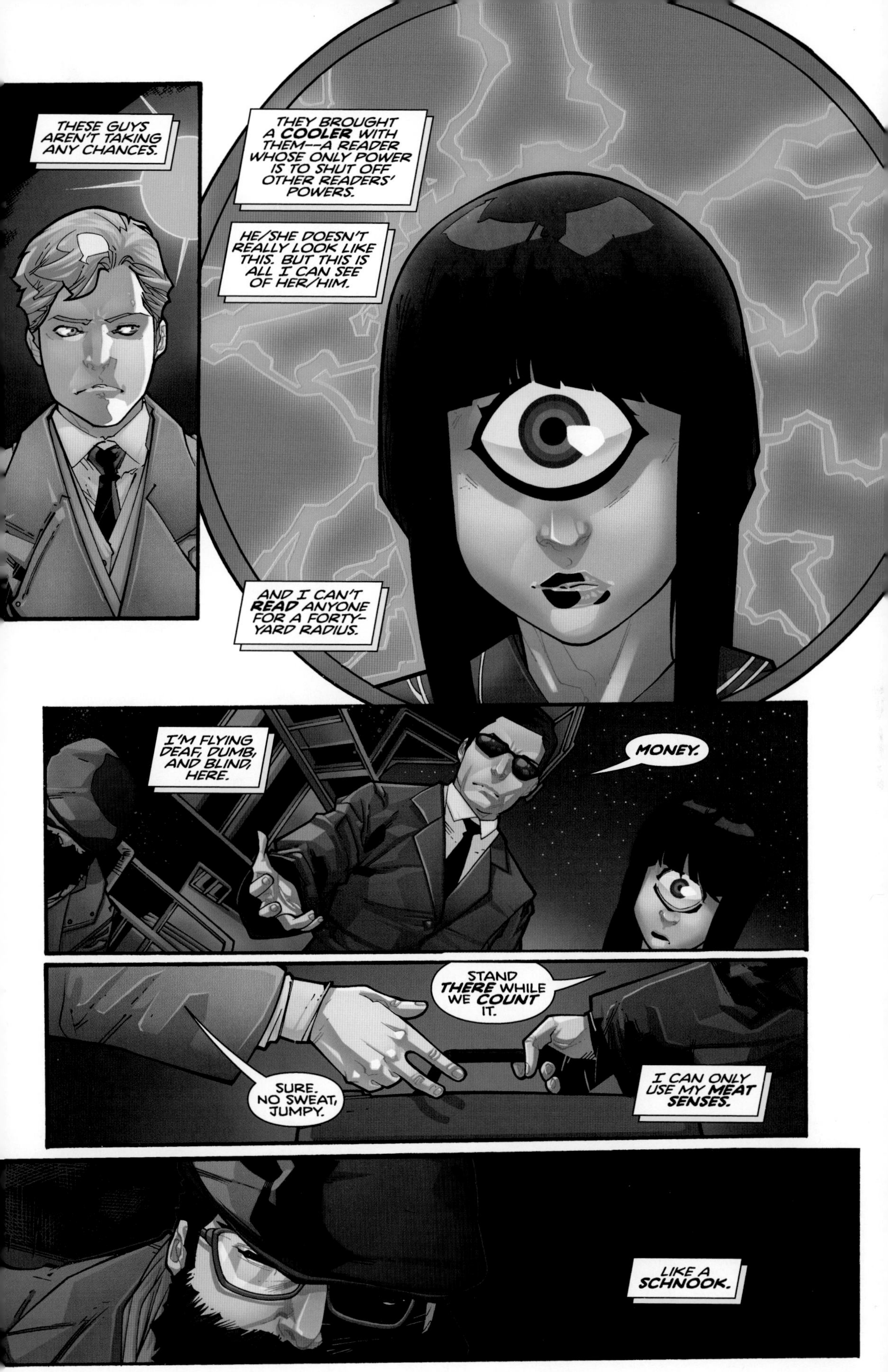
THESE GUYS AREN'T TAKING ANY CHANCES.
THEY BROUGHT A COOLER WITH THEM--A READER WHOSE ONLY POWER IS TO SHUT OFF OTHER READERS' POWERS.
HE/SHE DOESN'T REALLY LOOK LIKE THIS. BUT THIS IS ALL I CAN SEE OF HER/HIM.
AND I CAN'T READ ANYONE FOR A FORTY-YARD RADIUS.
I'M FLYING DEAF, DUMB, AND BLIND, HERE.
MONEY.
STAND THERE WHILE WE COUNT IT.
SURE. NO SWEAT, JUMPY.
I CAN ONLY USE MY MEAT SENSES.
LIKE A SCHNOOK.

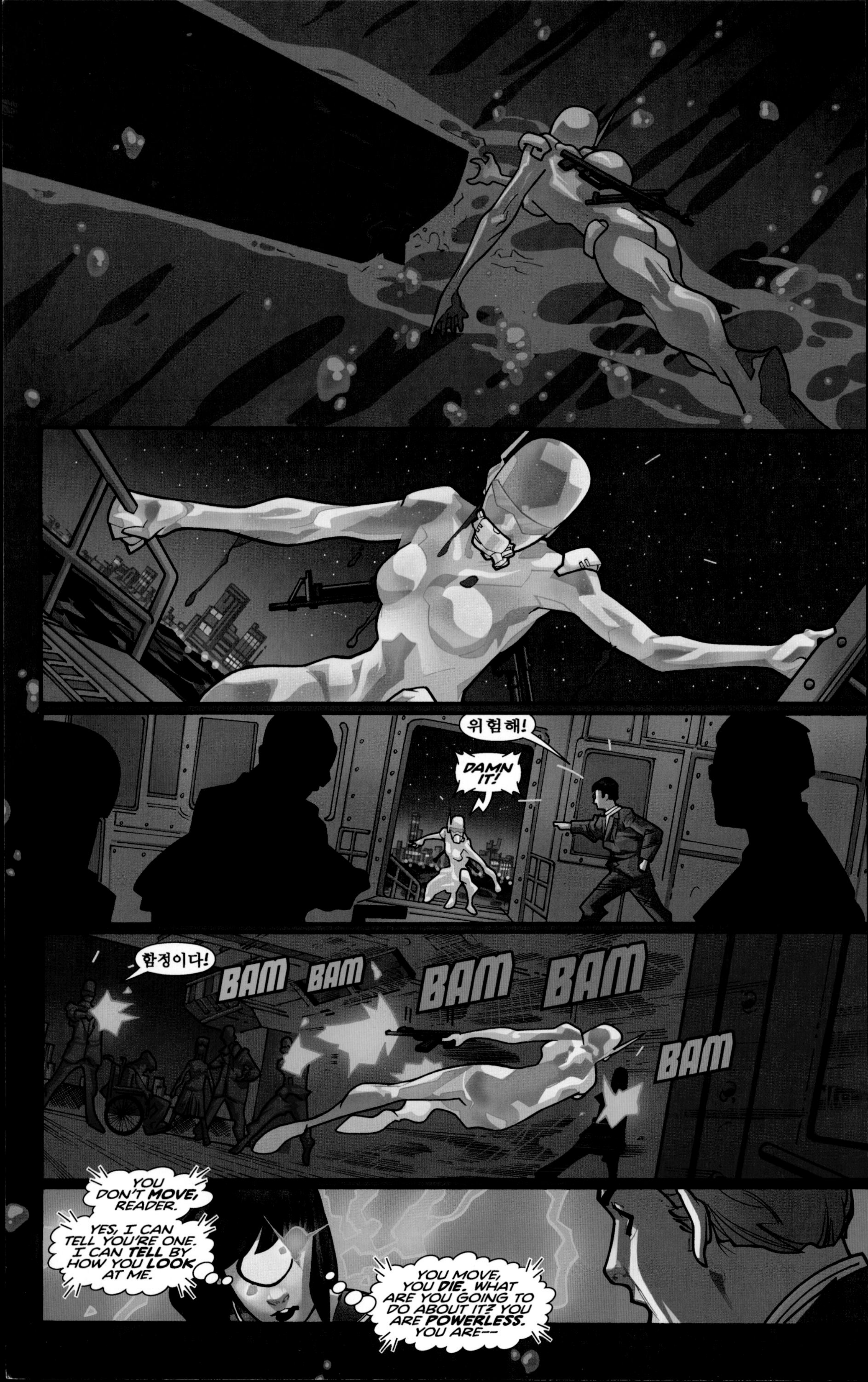
위험해!
DAMN IT!
함정이다!
BAM BAM BAM BAM
BAM
YOU DON'T MOVE, READER.
YES, I CAN TELL YOU'RE ONE. I CAN TELL BY HOW YOU LOOK AT ME.
YOU MOVE, YOU DIE. WHAT ARE YOU GOING TO DO ABOUT IT? YOU ARE POWERLESS. YOU ARE--

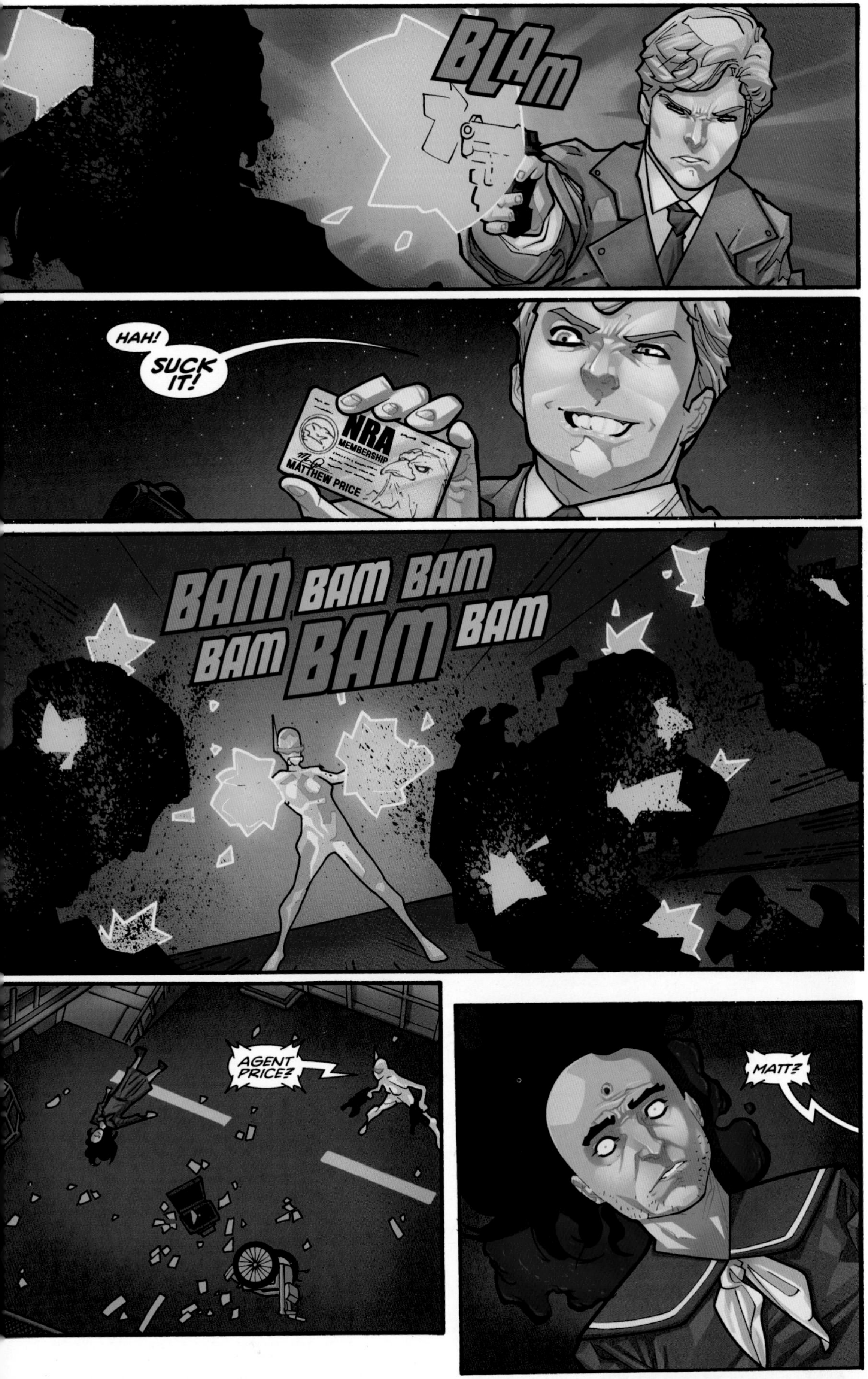
BLAM
HAH! SUCK IT!
NRA MEMBERSHIP
MATTHEW PRICE
BAM BAM BAM BAM BAM BAM
AGENT PRICE?
MATT?

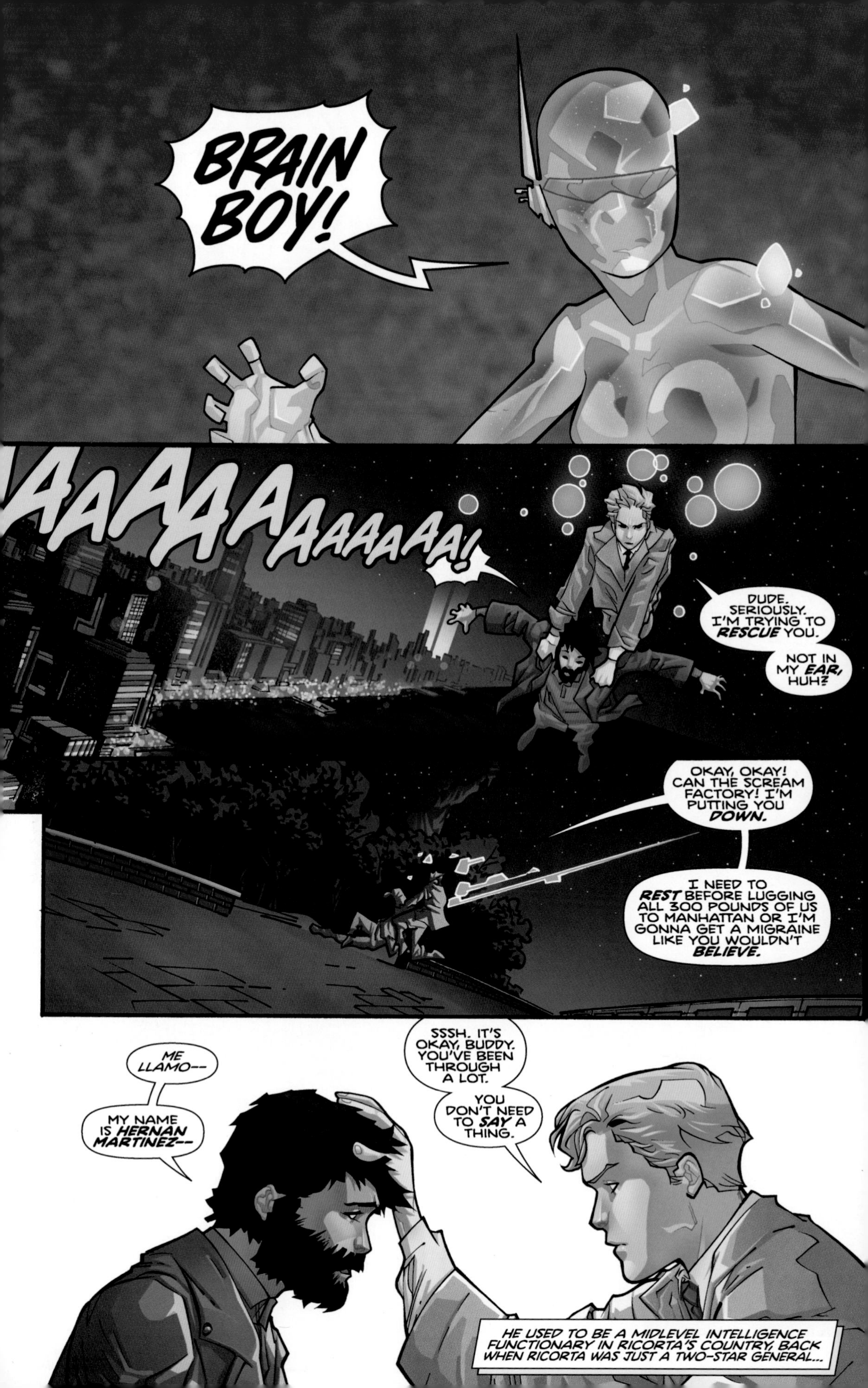
BRAIN BOY!
AAAAAAAAAAA!
DUDE. SERIOUSLY. I'M TRYING TO RESCUE YOU.
NOT IN MY EAR, HUH?
OKAY, OKAY! CAN THE SCREAM FACTORY! I'M PUTTING YOU DOWN.
I NEED TO REST BEFORE LUGGING ALL 300 POUNDS OF US TO MANHATTAN OR I'M GONNA GET A MIGRAINE LIKE YOU WOULDN'T BELIEVE.
ME LLAMO--
MY NAME IS HERNAN MARTINEZ--
SSSH. IT'S OKAY, BUDDY. YOU'VE BEEN THROUGH A LOT.
YOU DON'T NEED TO SAY A THING.
HE USED TO BE A MIDLEVEL INTELLIGENCE FUNCTIONARY IN RICORTA'S COUNTRY, BACK WHEN RICORTA WAS JUST A TWO-STAR GENERAL...

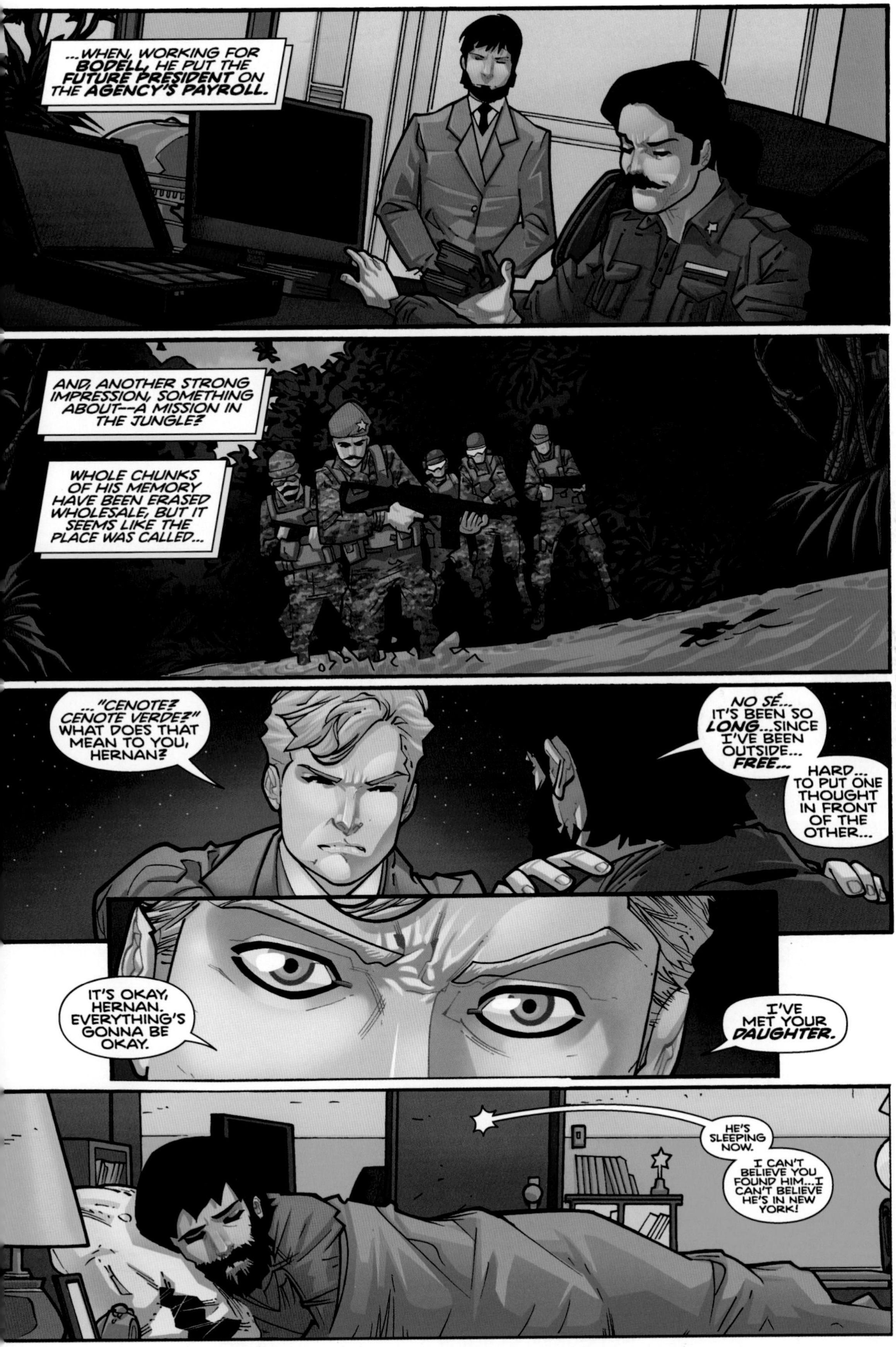
...WHEN, WORKING FOR BODELL, HE PUT THE FUTURE PRESIDENT ON THE AGENCY'S PAYROLL.
AND, ANOTHER STRONG IMPRESSION, SOMETHING ABOUT--A MISSION IN THE JUNGLE?
WHOLE CHUNKS OF HIS MEMORY HAVE BEEN ERASED WHOLESALE, BUT IT SEEMS LIKE THE PLACE WAS CALLED...
..."CENOTE? CENOTE VERDE?" WHAT DOES THAT MEAN TO YOU, HERNAN?
NO SÉ... IT'S BEEN SO LONG...SINCE I'VE BEEN OUTSIDE... FREE...
HARD... TO PUT ONE THOUGHT IN FRONT OF THE OTHER...
IT'S OKAY, HERNAN. EVERYTHING'S GONNA BE OKAY.
I'VE MET YOUR DAUGHTER.
HE'S SLEEPING NOW.
I CAN'T BELIEVE YOU FOUND HIM...I CAN'T BELIEVE HE'S IN NEW YORK!

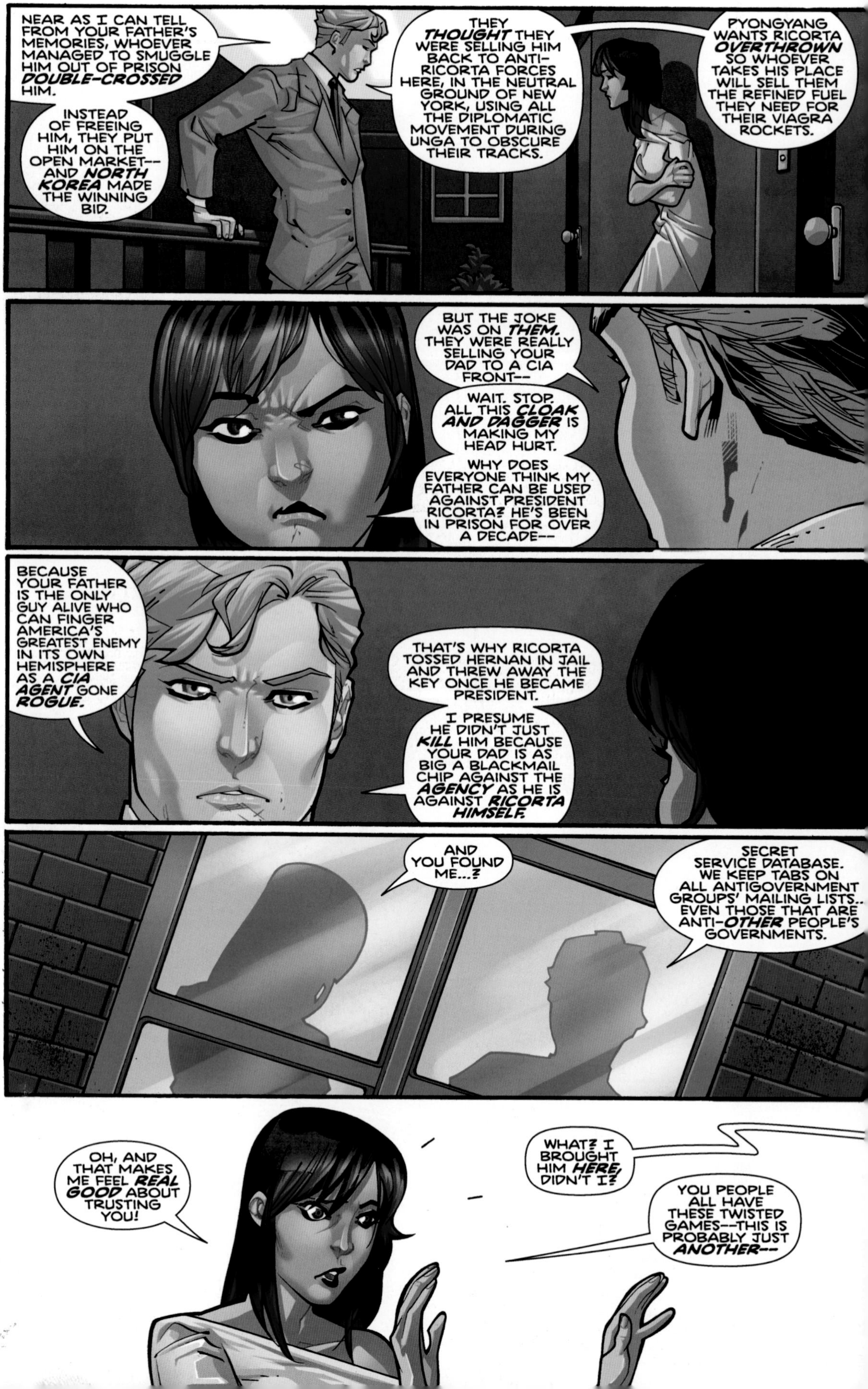
NEAR AS I CAN TELL FROM YOUR FATHER'S MEMORIES, WHOEVER MANAGED TO SMUGGLE HIM OUT OF PRISON DOUBLE-CROSSED HIM.
INSTEAD OF FREEING HIM, THEY PUT HIM ON THE OPEN MARKET-- AND NORTH KOREA MADE THE WINNING BID.
THEY THOUGHT THEY WERE SELLING HIM BACK TO ANTI-RICORTA FORCES HERE, IN THE NEUTRAL GROUND OF NEW YORK, USING ALL THE DIPLOMATIC MOVEMENT DURING UNGA TO OBSCURE THEIR TRACKS.
PYONGYANG WANTS RICORTA OVERTHROWN SO WHOEVER TAKES HIS PLACE WILL SELL THEM THE REFINED FUEL THEY NEED FOR THEIR VIAGRA ROCKETS.
BUT THE JOKE WAS ON THEM. THEY WERE REALLY SELLING YOUR DAD TO A CIA FRONT--
WAIT. STOP. ALL THIS CLOAK AND DAGGER IS MAKING MY HEAD HURT.
WHY DOES EVERYONE THINK MY FATHER CAN BE USED AGAINST PRESIDENT RICORTA? HE'S BEEN IN PRISON FOR OVER A DECADE--
BECAUSE YOUR FATHER IS THE ONLY GUY ALIVE WHO CAN FINGER AMERICA'S GREATEST ENEMY IN ITS OWN HEMISPHERE AS A CIA AGENT GONE ROGUE.
THAT'S WHY RICORTA TOSSED HERNAN IN JAIL AND THREW AWAY THE KEY ONCE HE BECAME PRESIDENT.
I PRESUME HE DIDN'T JUST KILL HIM BECAUSE YOUR DAD IS AS BIG A BLACKMAIL CHIP AGAINST THE AGENCY AS HE IS AGAINST RICORTA HIMSELF.
AND YOU FOUND ME...?
SECRET SERVICE DATABASE. WE KEEP TABS ON ALL ANTIGOVERNMENT GROUPS' MAILING LISTS.. EVEN THOSE THAT ARE ANTI-OTHER PEOPLE'S GOVERNMENTS.
OH, AND THAT MAKES ME FEEL REAL GOOD ABOUT TRUSTING YOU!
WHAT? I BROUGHT HIM HERE, DIDN'T I?
YOU PEOPLE ALL HAVE THESE TWISTED GAMES--THIS IS PROBABLY JUST ANOTHER--

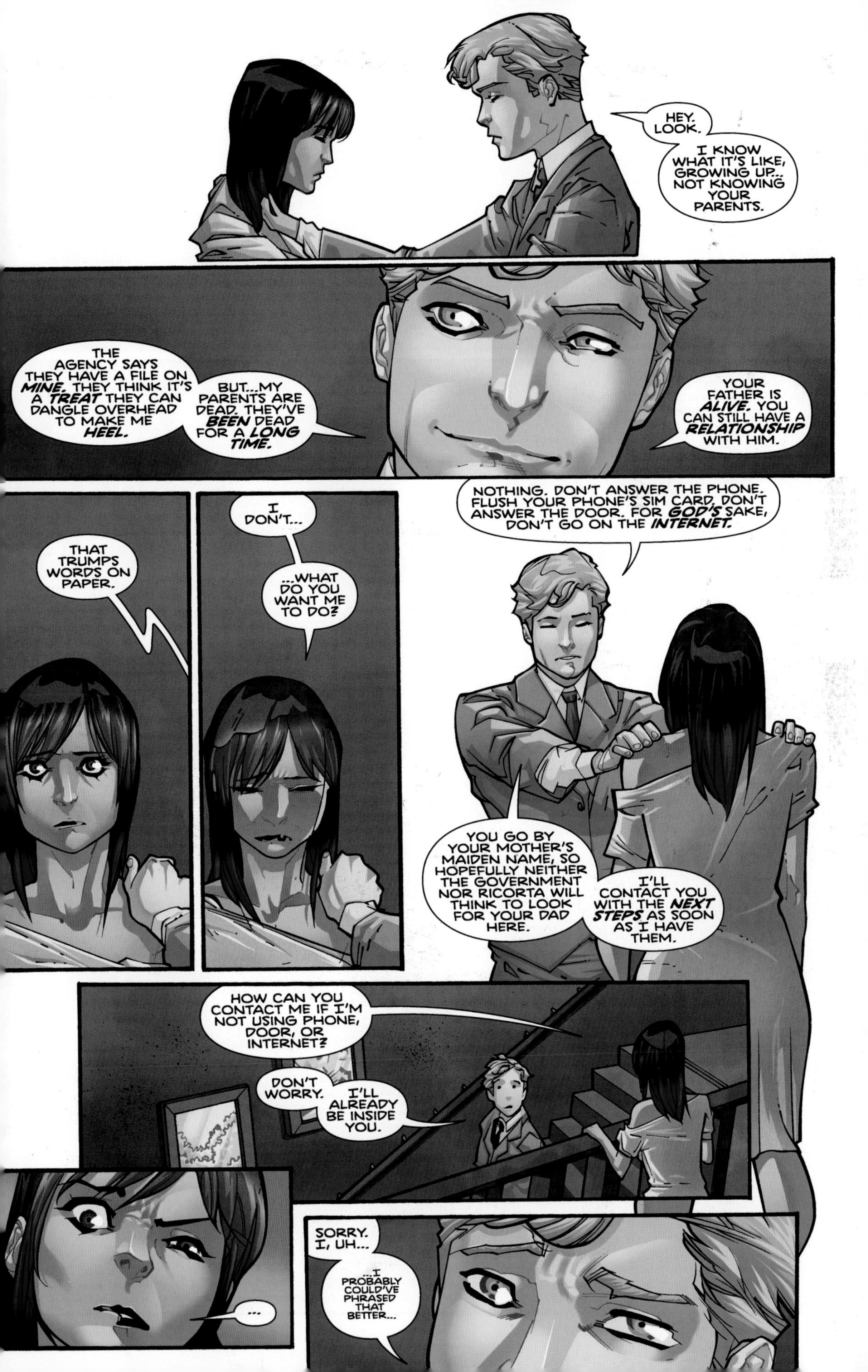
HEY. LOOK.
I KNOW WHAT IT'S LIKE, GROWING UP.. NOT KNOWING YOUR PARENTS.
THE AGENCY SAYS THEY HAVE A FILE ON MINE. THEY THINK IT'S A TREAT THEY CAN DANGLE OVERHEAD TO MAKE ME HEEL.
BUT...MY PARENTS ARE DEAD. THEY'VE BEEN DEAD FOR A LONG TIME.
YOUR FATHER IS ALIVE. YOU CAN STILL HAVE A RELATIONSHIP WITH HIM.
THAT TRUMPS WORDS ON PAPER.
I DON'T...
...WHAT DO YOU WANT ME TO DO?
NOTHING. DON'T ANSWER THE PHONE. FLUSH YOUR PHONE'S SIM CARD, DON'T ANSWER THE DOOR. FOR GOD'S SAKE, DON'T GO ON THE INTERNET.
YOU GO BY YOUR MOTHER'S MAIDEN NAME, SO HOPEFULLY NEITHER THE GOVERNMENT NOR RICORTA WILL THINK TO LOOK FOR YOUR DAD HERE.
I'LL CONTACT YOU WITH THE NEXT STEPS AS SOON AS I HAVE THEM.
HOW CAN YOU CONTACT ME IF I'M NOT USING PHONE, DOOR, OR INTERNET?
DON'T WORRY.
I'LL ALREADY BE INSIDE YOU.
...
SORRY. I, UH...
...I PROBABLY COULD'VE PHRASED THAT BETTER...

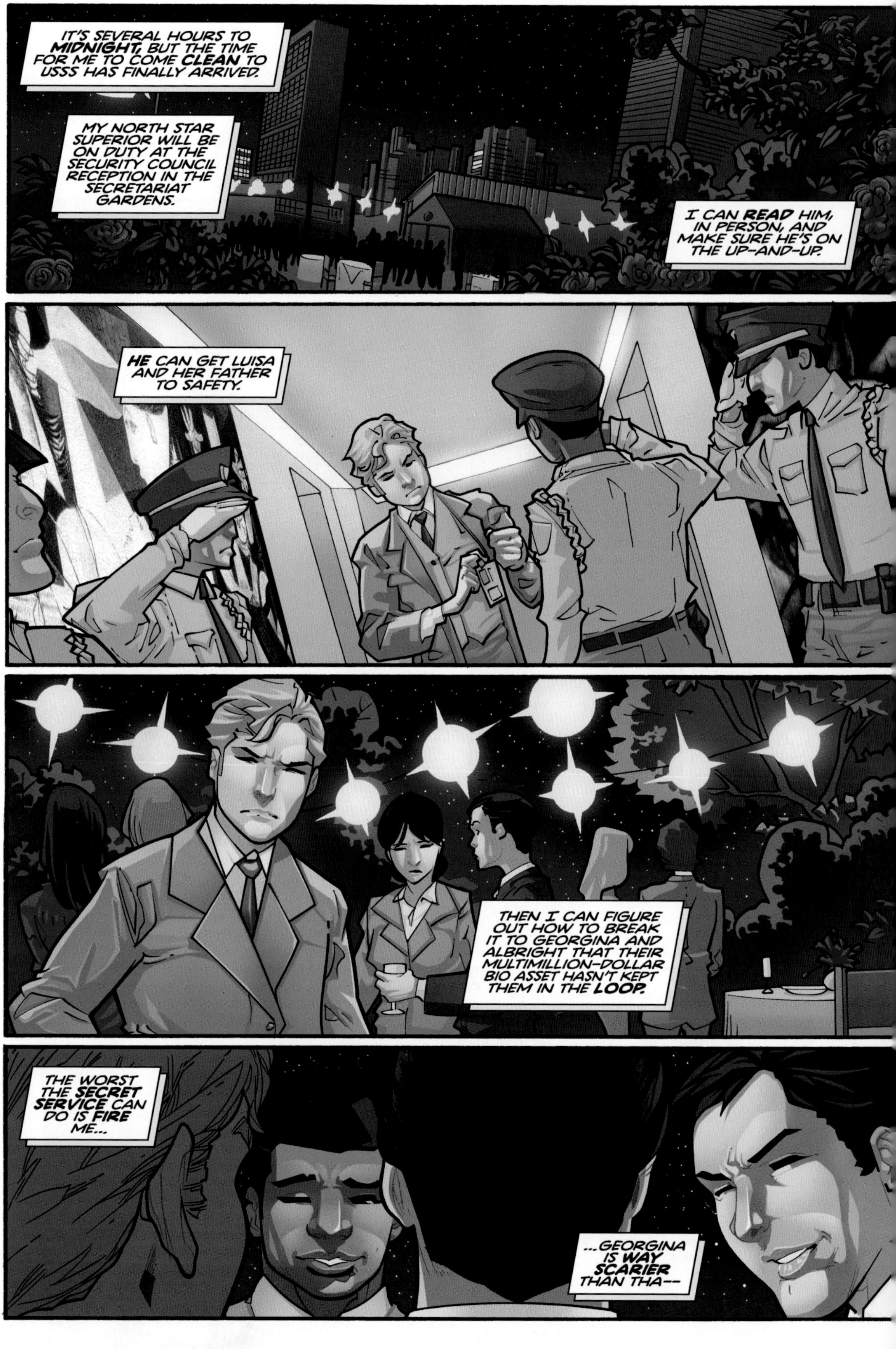
IT'S SEVERAL HOURS TO MIDNIGHT, BUT THE TIME FOR ME TO COME CLEAN TO USSS HAS FINALLY ARRIVED.
MY NORTH STAR SUPERIOR WILL BE ON DUTY AT THE SECURITY COUNCIL RECEPTION IN THE SECRETARIAT GARDENS.
I CAN READ HIM, IN PERSON, AND MAKE SURE HE'S ON THE UP-AND-UP.
HE CAN GET LUISA AND HER FATHER TO SAFETY.
THEN I CAN FIGURE OUT HOW TO BREAK IT TO GEORGINA AND ALBRIGHT THAT THEIR MULTIMILLION-DOLLAR BIO ASSET HASN'T KEPT THEM IN THE LOOP.
THE WORST THE SECRET SERVICE CAN DO IS FIRE ME...
...GEORGINA IS WAY SCARIER THAN THA--

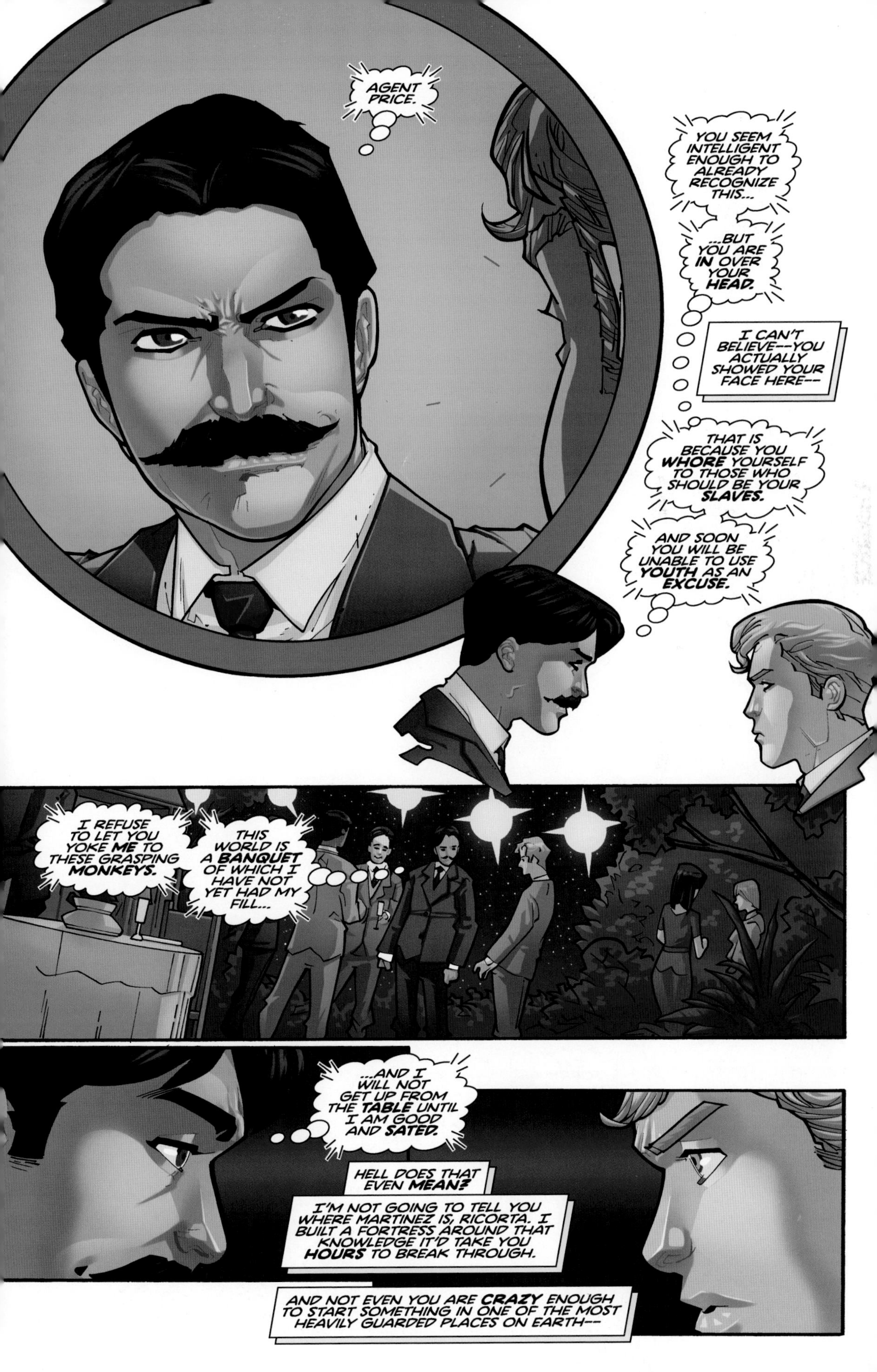
AGENT PRICE.
YOU SEEM INTELLIGENT ENOUGH TO ALREADY RECOGNIZE THIS...
...BUT YOU ARE IN OVER YOUR HEAD.
I CAN'T BELIEVE--YOU ACTUALLY SHOWED YOUR FACE HERE--
THAT IS BECAUSE YOU WHORE YOURSELF TO THOSE WHO SHOULD BE YOUR SLAVES.
AND SOON YOU WILL BE UNABLE TO USE YOUTH AS AN EXCUSE.
I REFUSE TO LET YOU YOKE ME TO THESE GRASPING MONKEYS.
THIS WORLD IS A BANQUET OF WHICH I HAVE NOT YET HAD MY FILL...
...AND I WILL NOT GET UP FROM THE TABLE UNTIL I AM GOOD AND SATED.
HELL DOES THAT EVEN MEAN?
I'M NOT GOING TO TELL YOU WHERE MARTINEZ IS, RICORTA. I BUILT A FORTRESS AROUND THAT KNOWLEDGE IT'D TAKE YOU HOURS TO BREAK THROUGH.
AND NOT EVEN YOU ARE CRAZY ENOUGH TO START SOMETHING IN ONE OF THE MOST HEAVILY GUARDED PLACES ON EARTH--

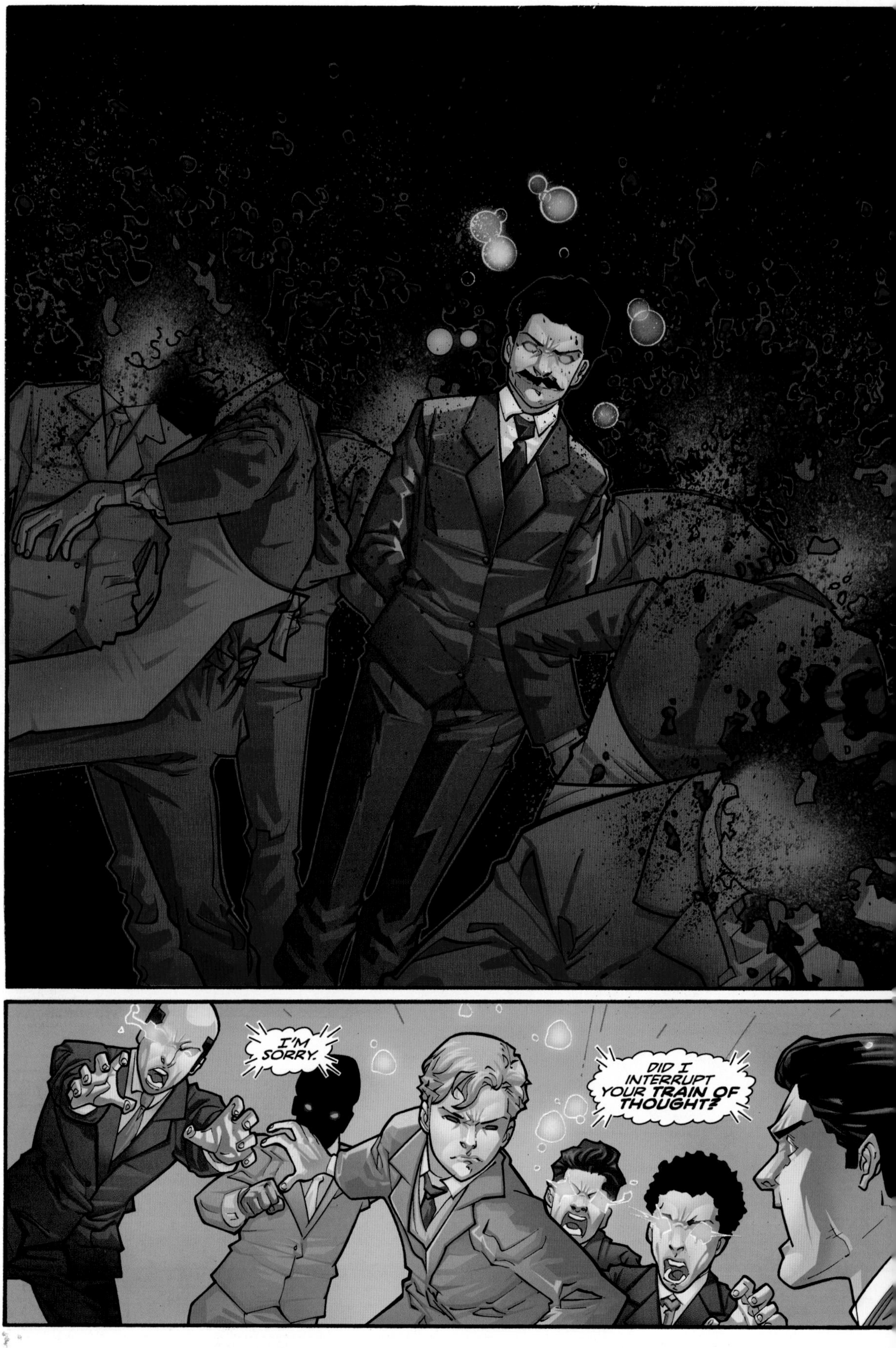
I'M SORRY.
DID I INTERRUPT YOUR TRAIN OF THOUGHT?

CHAPTER 3

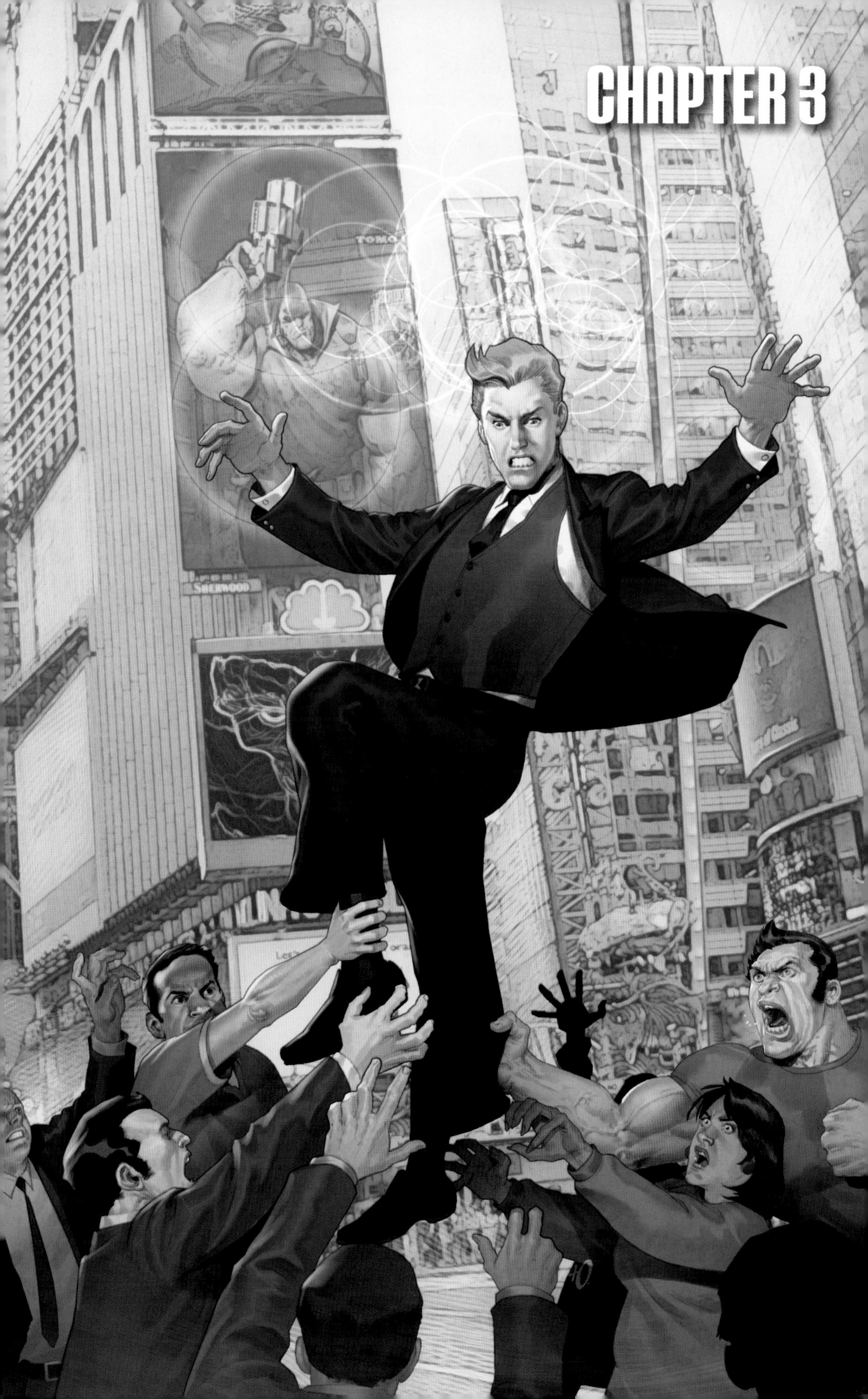
SHERWOOD

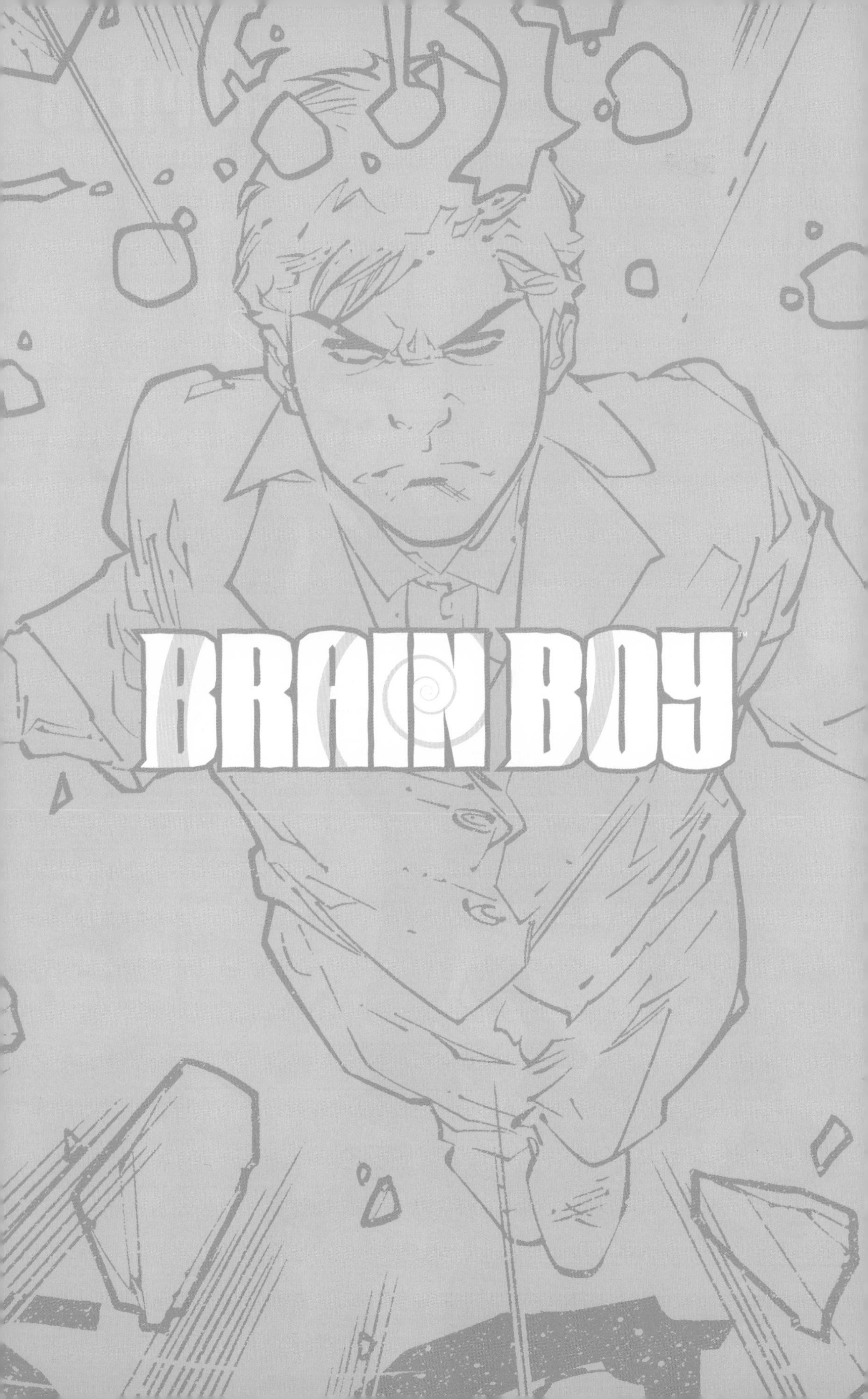
BRAIN BOY™

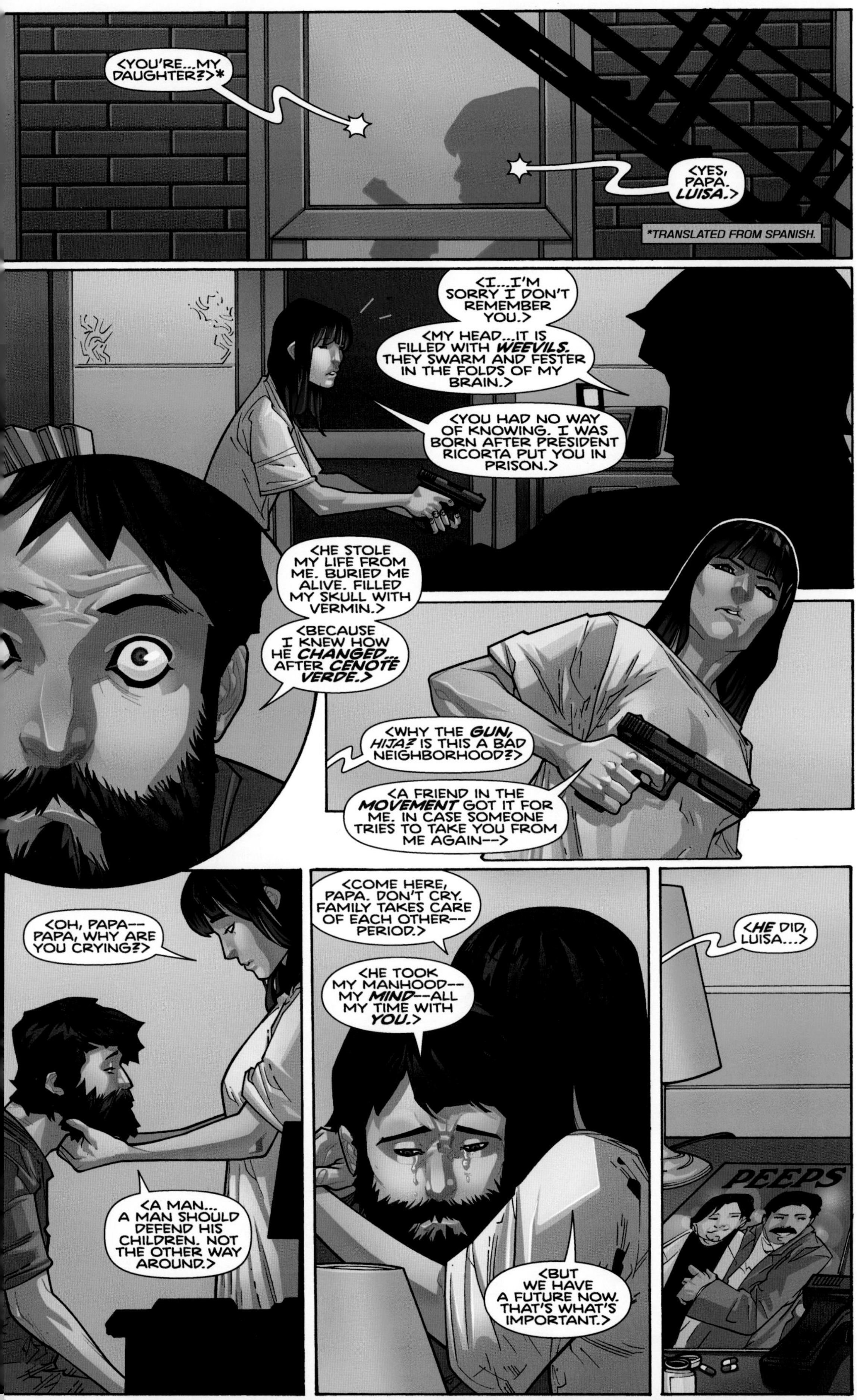
<YOU'RE...MY DAUGHTER?>*
<YES, PAPA. LUISA.>
*TRANSLATED FROM SPANISH.
<I...I'M SORRY I DON'T REMEMBER YOU.>
<MY HEAD...IT IS FILLED WITH WEEVILS. THEY SWARM AND FESTER IN THE FOLDS OF MY BRAIN.>
<YOU HAD NO WAY OF KNOWING. I WAS BORN AFTER PRESIDENT RICORTA PUT YOU IN PRISON.>
<HE STOLE MY LIFE FROM ME. BURIED ME ALIVE. FILLED MY SKULL WITH VERMIN.>
<BECAUSE I KNEW HOW HE CHANGED... AFTER CENOTE VERDE.>
<WHY THE GUN, HIJA? IS THIS A BAD NEIGHBORHOOD?>
<A FRIEND IN THE MOVEMENT GOT IT FOR ME. IN CASE SOMEONE TRIES TO TAKE YOU FROM ME AGAIN-->
<OH, PAPA-- PAPA, WHY ARE YOU CRYING?>
<A MAN... A MAN SHOULD DEFEND HIS CHILDREN. NOT THE OTHER WAY AROUND.>
<COME HERE, PAPA. DON'T CRY. FAMILY TAKES CARE OF EACH OTHER-- PERIOD.>
<HE TOOK MY MANHOOD-- MY MIND--ALL MY TIME WITH YOU.>
<BUT WE HAVE A FUTURE NOW. THAT'S WHAT'S IMPORTANT.>
<HE DID, LUISA...>
PEEPS

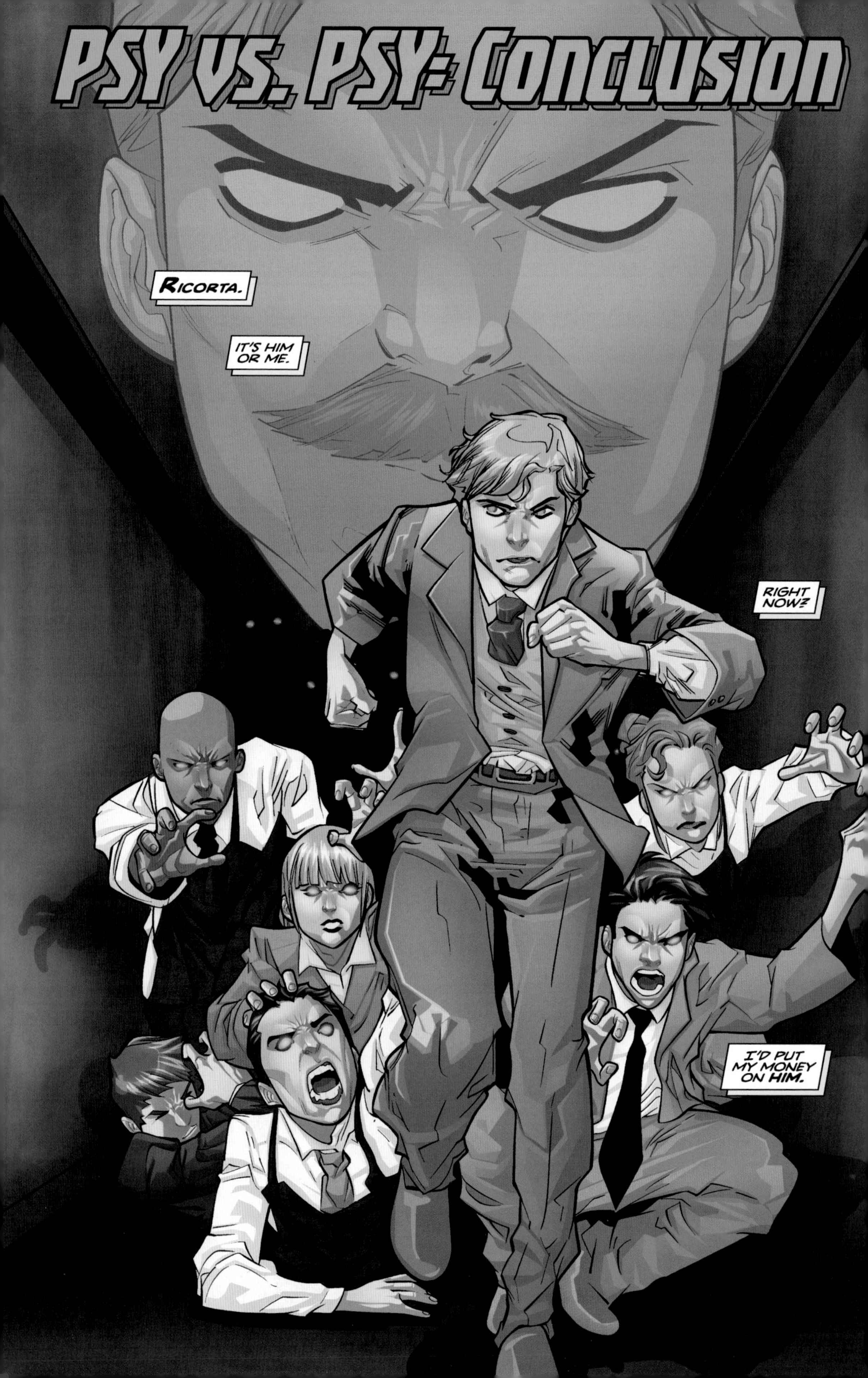
PSY VS. PSY: CONCLUSION
RICORTA.
IT'S HIM OR ME.
RIGHT NOW?
I'D PUT MY MONEY ON HIM.

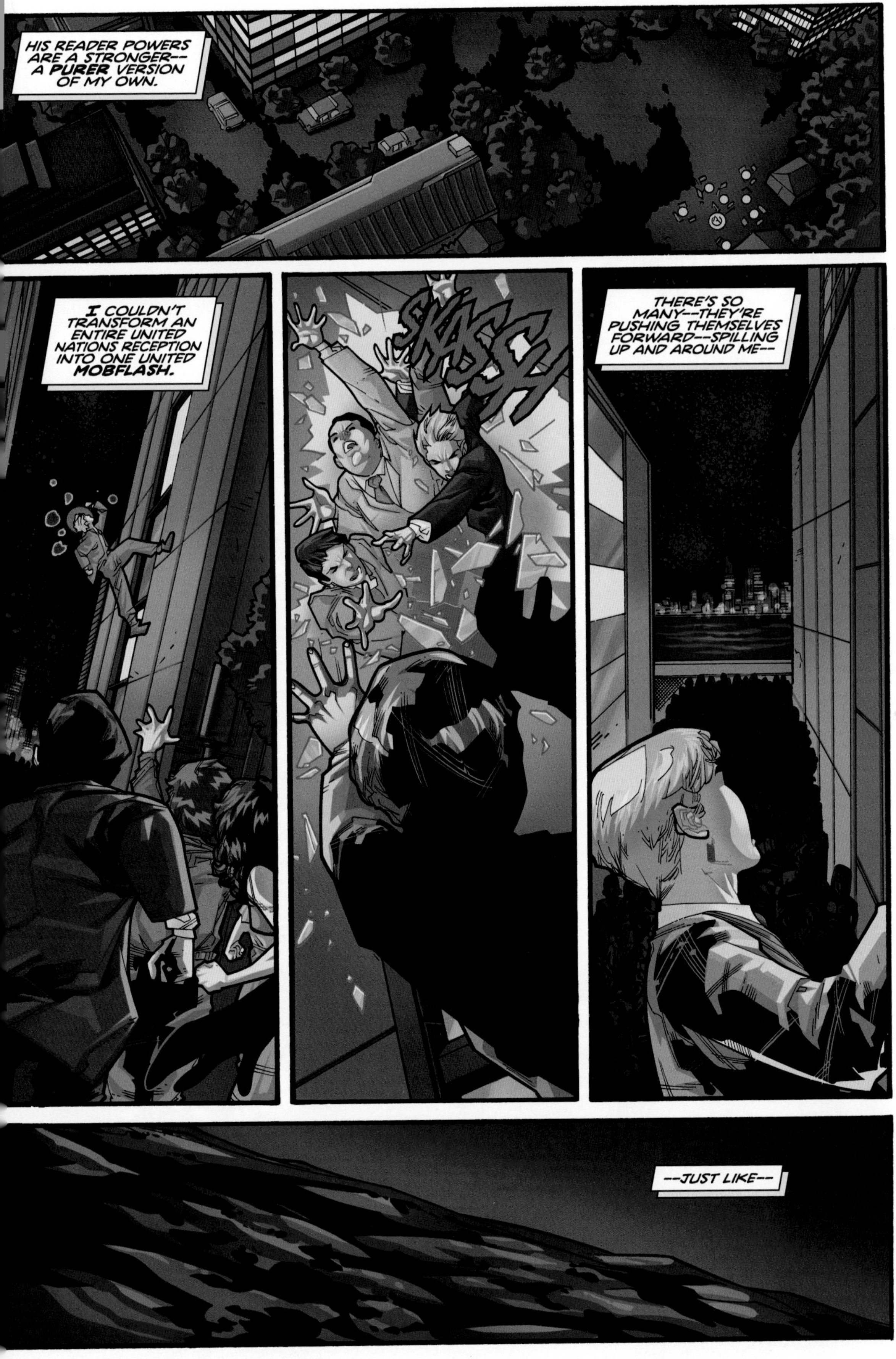
HIS READER POWERS ARE A STRONGER-- A PURER VERSION OF MY OWN.
I COULDN'T TRANSFORM AN ENTIRE UNITED NATIONS RECEPTION INTO ONE UNITED MOBFLASH.
SKASCH
THERE'S SO MANY--THEY'RE PUSHING THEMSELVES FORWARD--SPILLING UP AND AROUND ME--
--JUST LIKE--

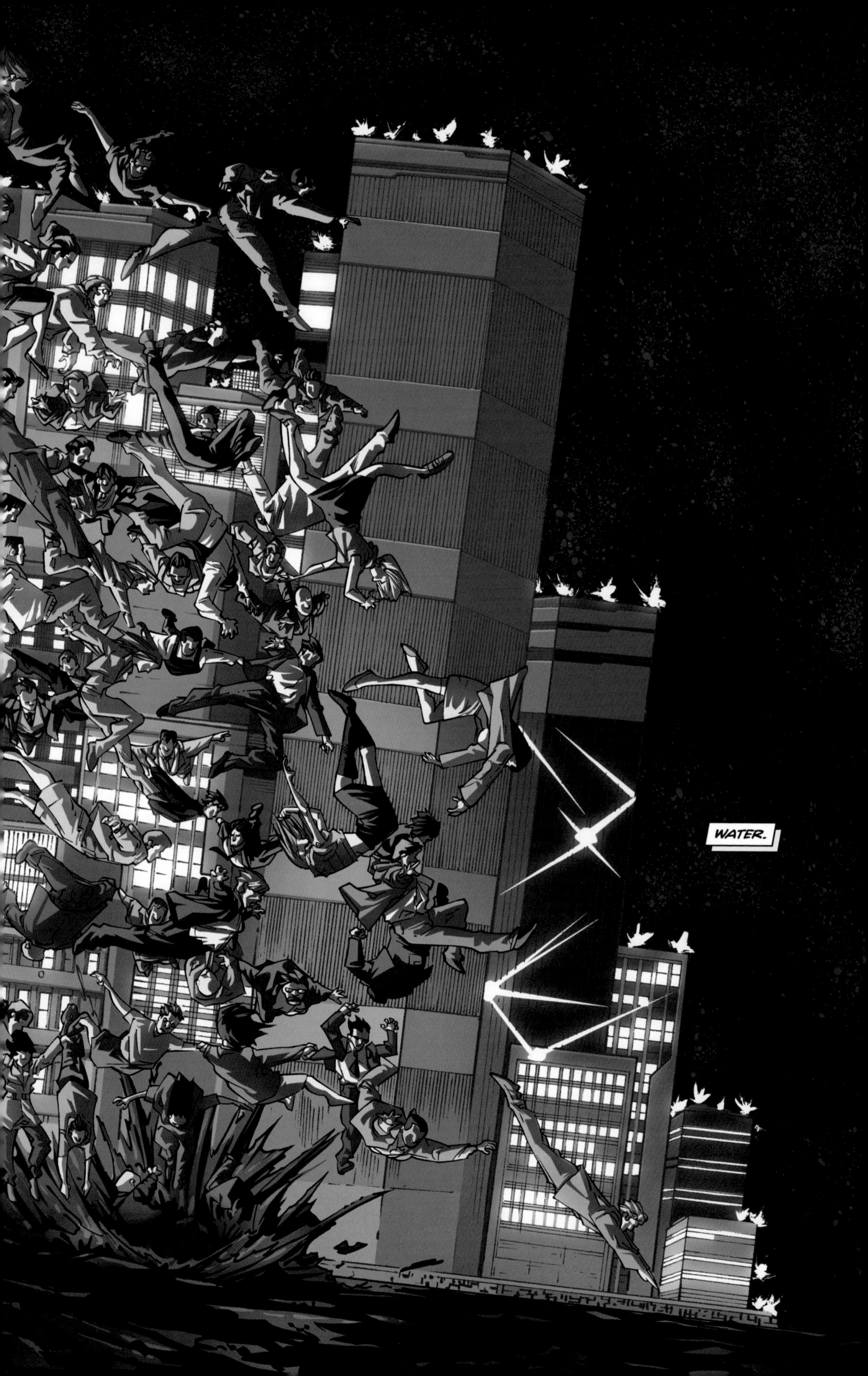
WATER.

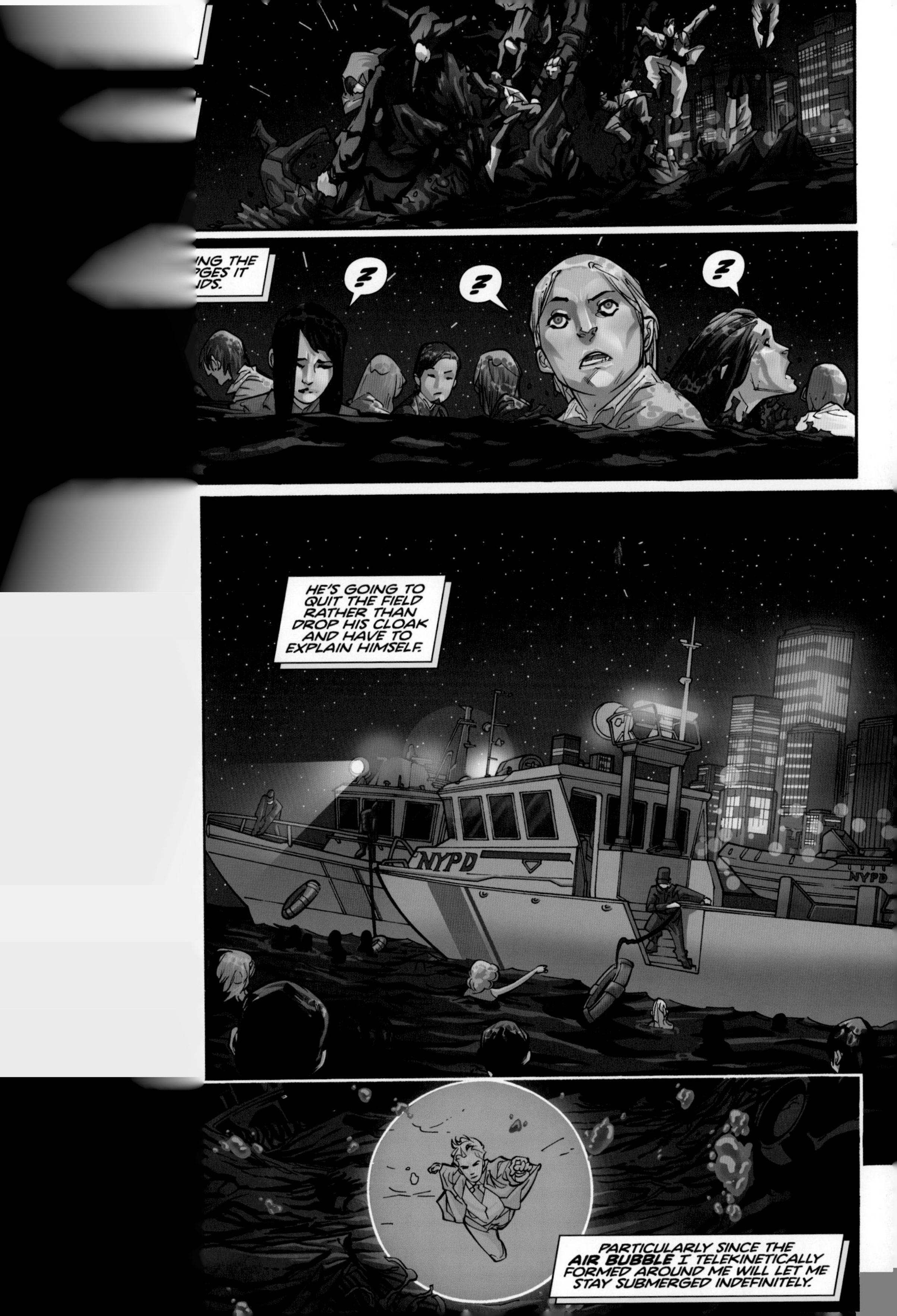
HE'S GOING TO QUIT THE FIELD RATHER THAN DROP HIS CLOAK AND HAVE TO EXPLAIN HIMSELF.
PARTICULARLY SINCE THE AIR BUBBLE I TELEKINETICALLY FORMED AROUND ME WILL LET ME STAY SUBMERGED INDEFINITELY.

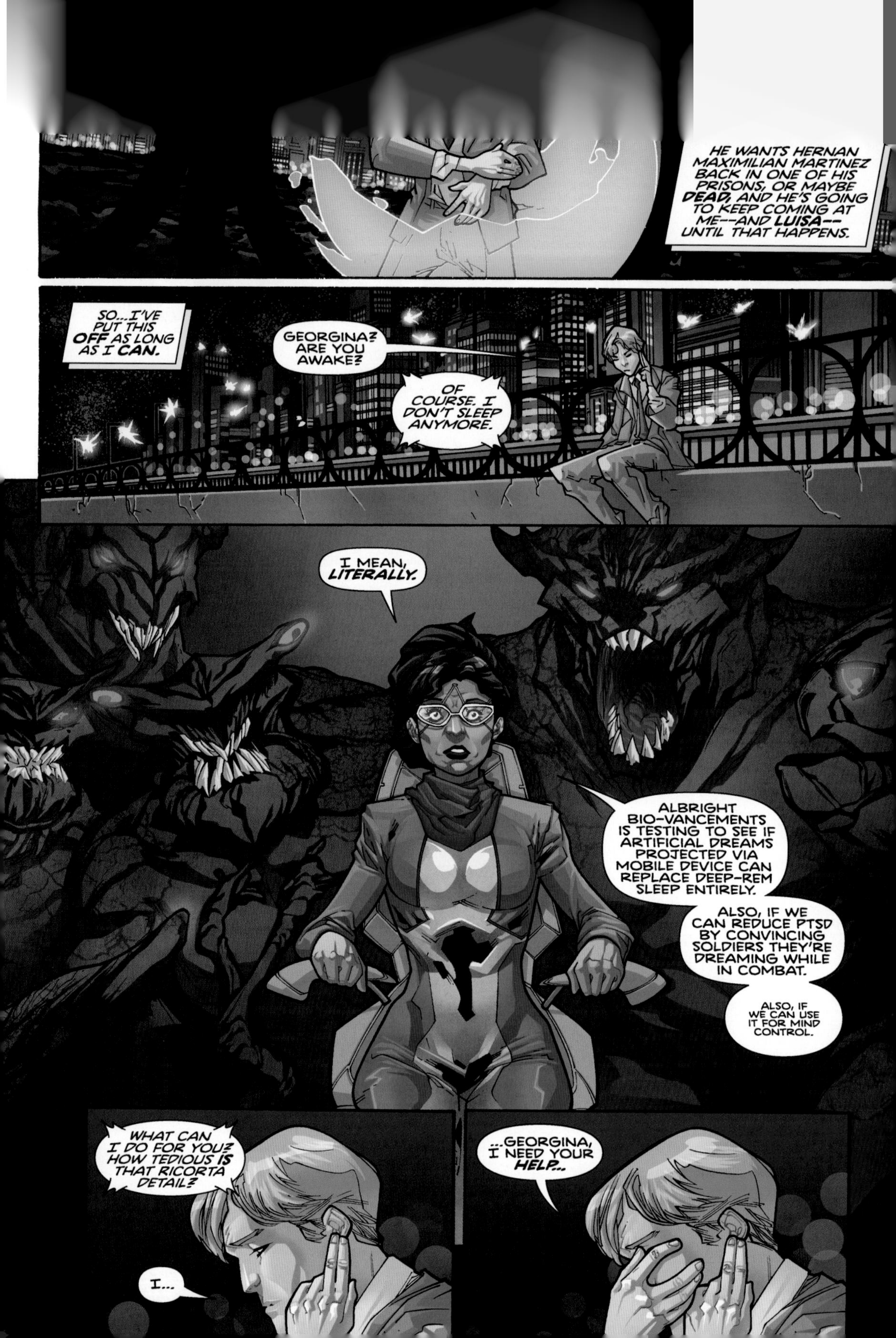
HE WANTS HERNAN MAXIMILIAN MARTINEZ BACK IN ONE OF HIS PRISONS, OR MAYBE DEAD, AND HE'S GOING TO KEEP COMING AT ME--AND LUISA-- UNTIL THAT HAPPENS.
SO...I'VE PUT THIS OFF AS LONG AS I CAN.
GEORGINA? ARE YOU AWAKE?
OF COURSE. I DON'T SLEEP ANYMORE.
I MEAN, LITERALLY.
ALBRIGHT BIO-VANCEMENTS IS TESTING TO SEE IF ARTIFICIAL DREAMS PROJECTED VIA MOBILE DEVICE CAN REPLACE DEEP-REM SLEEP ENTIRELY.
ALSO, IF WE CAN REDUCE PTSD BY CONVINCING SOLDIERS THEY'RE DREAMING WHILE IN COMBAT.
ALSO, IF WE CAN USE IT FOR MIND CONTROL.
WHAT CAN I DO FOR YOU? HOW TEDIOUS IS THAT RICORTA DETAIL?
I...
...GEORGINA, I NEED YOUR HELP...

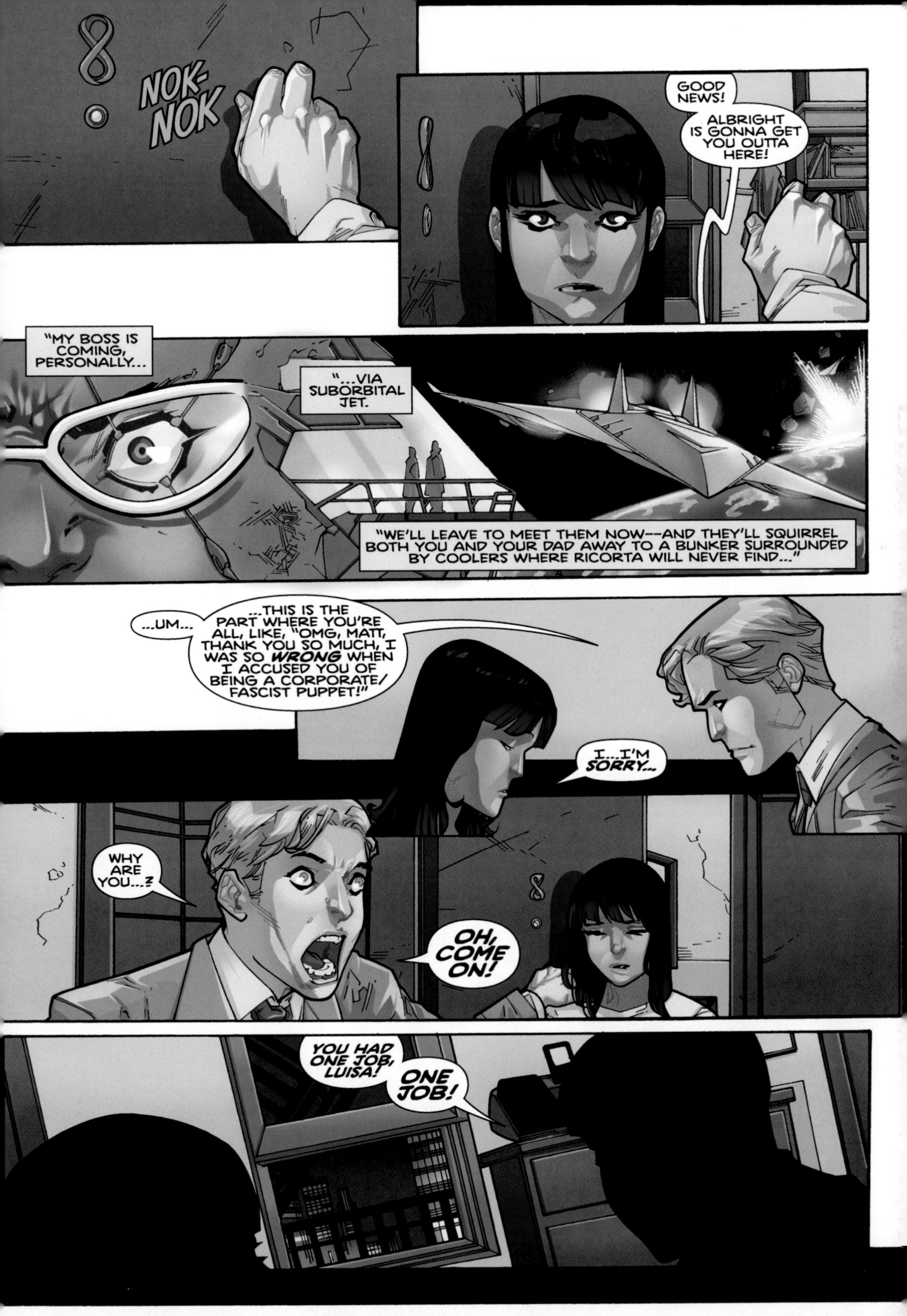
NOK-NOK
GOOD NEWS!
ALBRIGHT IS GONNA GET YOU OUTTA HERE!
"MY BOSS IS COMING, PERSONALLY...
"...VIA SUBORBITAL JET.
"WE'LL LEAVE TO MEET THEM NOW--AND THEY'LL SQUIRREL BOTH YOU AND YOUR DAD AWAY TO A BUNKER SURROUNDED BY COOLERS WHERE RICORTA WILL NEVER FIND..."
...THIS IS THE PART WHERE YOU'RE ALL, LIKE, "OMG, MATT, THANK YOU SO MUCH, I WAS SO WRONG WHEN I ACCUSED YOU OF BEING A CORPORATE/ FASCIST PUPPET!"
...UM...
I...I'M SORRY...
WHY ARE YOU...?
OH, COME ON!
YOU HAD ONE JOB, LUISA!
ONE JOB!

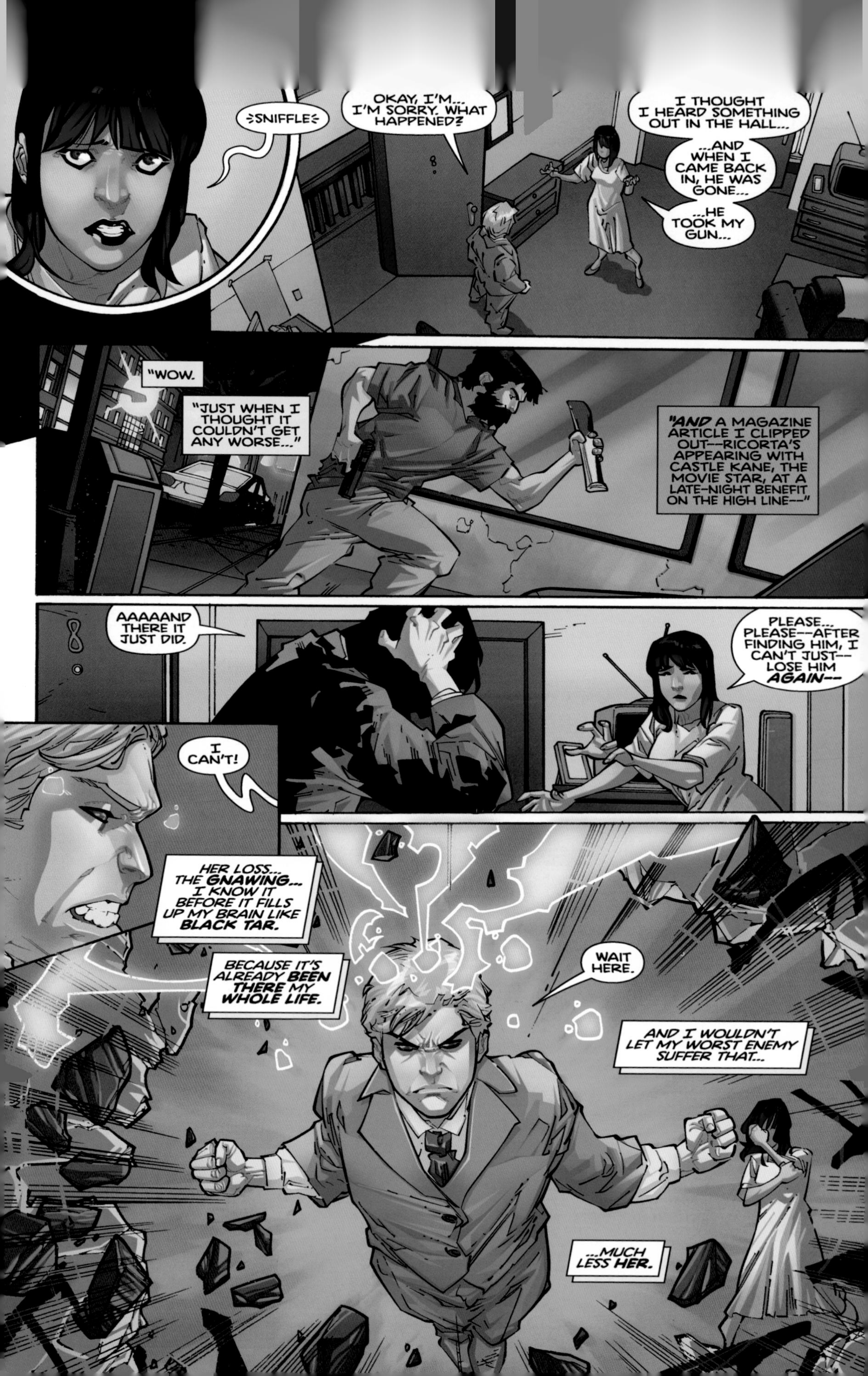

SNIFFLE
OKAY, I'M... I'M SORRY. WHAT HAPPENED?
I THOUGHT I HEARD SOMETHING OUT IN THE HALL...
...AND WHEN I CAME BACK IN, HE WAS GONE...
...HE TOOK MY GUN...
"WOW.
"JUST WHEN I THOUGHT IT COULDN'T GET ANY WORSE..."
"AND A MAGAZINE ARTICLE I CLIPPED OUT--RICORTA'S APPEARING WITH CASTLE KANE, THE MOVIE STAR, AT A LATE-NIGHT BENEFIT ON THE HIGH LINE--"
AAAAAND THERE IT JUST DID.
PLEASE... PLEASE--AFTER FINDING HIM, I CAN'T JUST--LOSE HIM AGAIN--
I CAN'T!
HER LOSS... THE GNAWING... I KNOW IT BEFORE IT FILLS UP MY BRAIN LIKE BLACK TAR.
BECAUSE IT'S ALREADY BEEN THERE MY WHOLE LIFE.
WAIT HERE.
AND I WOULDN'T LET MY WORST ENEMY SUFFER THAT...
...MUCH LESS HER.

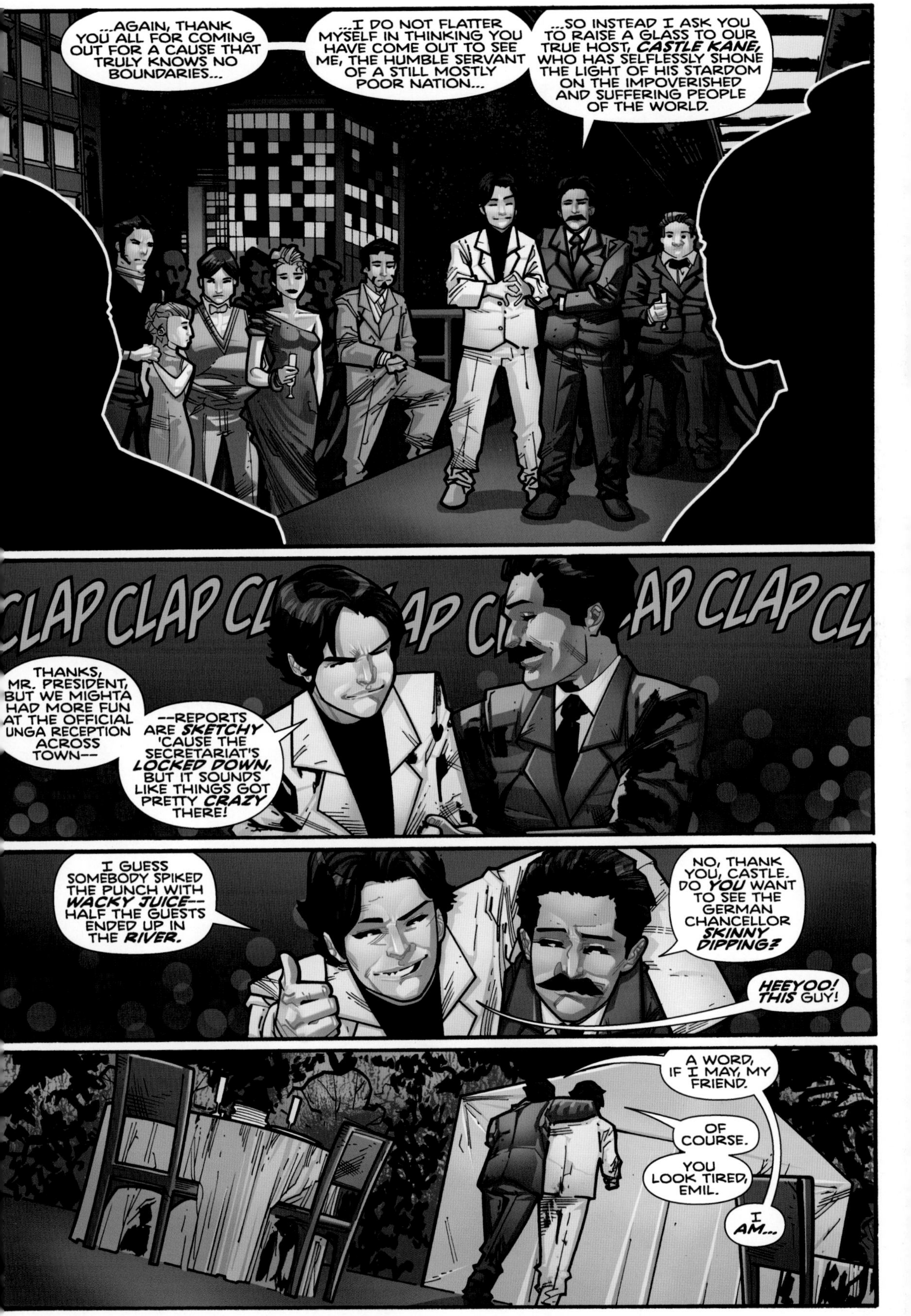
...AGAIN, THANK YOU ALL FOR COMING OUT FOR A CAUSE THAT TRULY KNOWS NO BOUNDARIES...
...I DO NOT FLATTER MYSELF IN THINKING YOU HAVE COME OUT TO SEE ME, THE HUMBLE SERVANT OF A STILL MOSTLY POOR NATION...
...SO INSTEAD I ASK YOU TO RAISE A GLASS TO OUR TRUE HOST, CASTLE KANE, WHO HAS SELFLESSLY SHONE THE LIGHT OF HIS STARDOM ON THE IMPOVERISHED AND SUFFERING PEOPLE OF THE WORLD.
CLAP CLAP CL AP CL AP CLAP CL
THANKS, MR. PRESIDENT, BUT WE MIGHTA HAD MORE FUN AT THE OFFICIAL UNGA RECEPTION ACROSS TOWN--
--REPORTS ARE SKETCHY 'CAUSE THE SECRETARIAT'S LOCKED DOWN, BUT IT SOUNDS LIKE THINGS GOT PRETTY CRAZY THERE!
I GUESS SOMEBODY SPIKED THE PUNCH WITH WACKY JUICE--HALF THE GUESTS ENDED UP IN THE RIVER.
NO, THANK YOU, CASTLE. DO YOU WANT TO SEE THE GERMAN CHANCELLOR SKINNY DIPPING?
HEEYOO! THIS GUY!
A WORD, IF I MAY, MY FRIEND.
OF COURSE.
YOU LOOK TIRED, EMIL.
I AM...

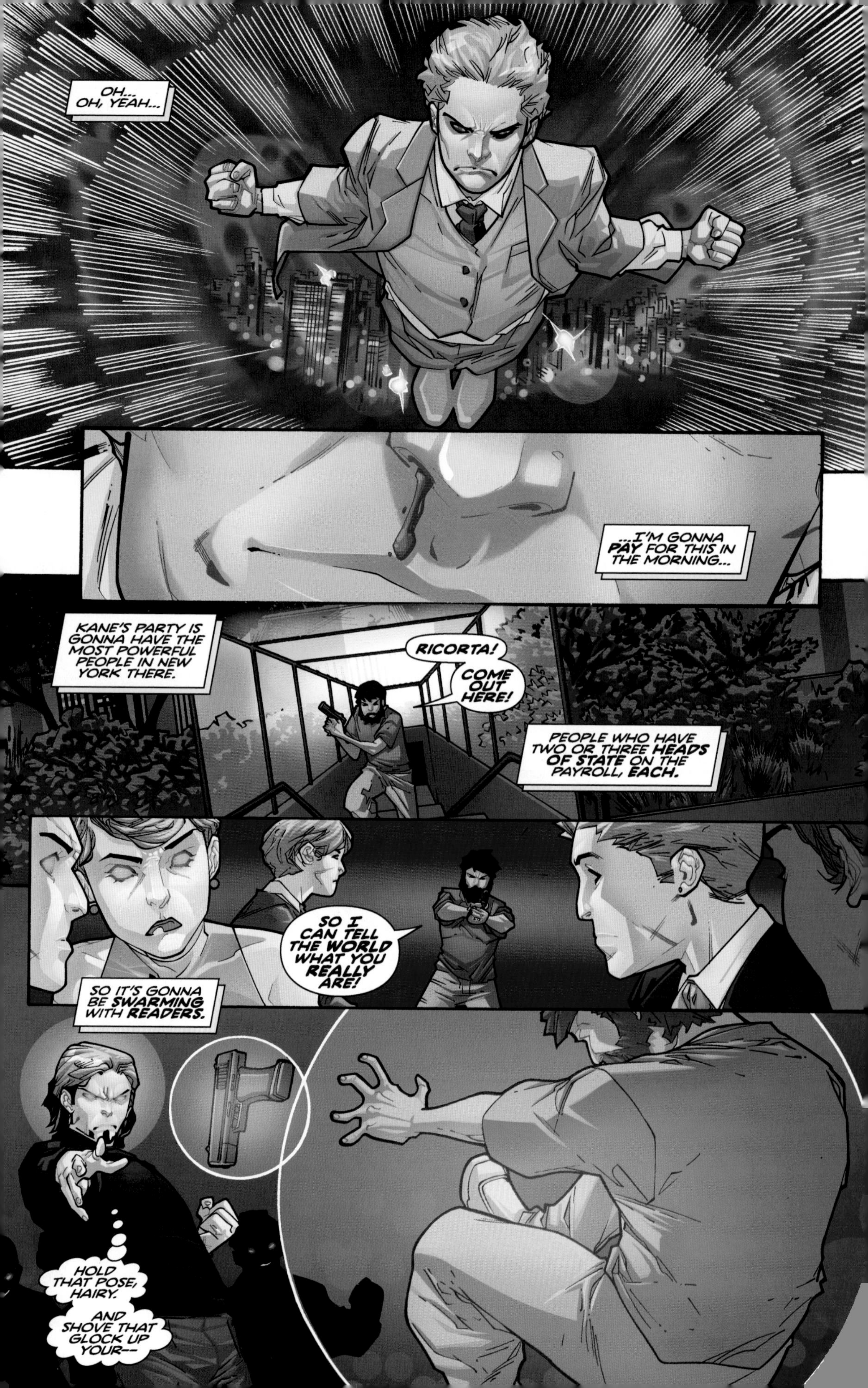
OH... OH, YEAH...
...I'M GONNA PAY FOR THIS IN THE MORNING...
KANE'S PARTY IS GONNA HAVE THE MOST POWERFUL PEOPLE IN NEW YORK THERE.
RICORTA!
COME OUT HERE!
PEOPLE WHO HAVE TWO OR THREE HEADS OF STATE ON THE PAYROLL, EACH.
SO I CAN TELL THE WORLD WHAT YOU REALLY ARE!
SO IT'S GONNA BE SWARMING WITH READERS.
HOLD THAT POSE, HAIRY.
AND SHOVE THAT GLOCK UP YOUR--

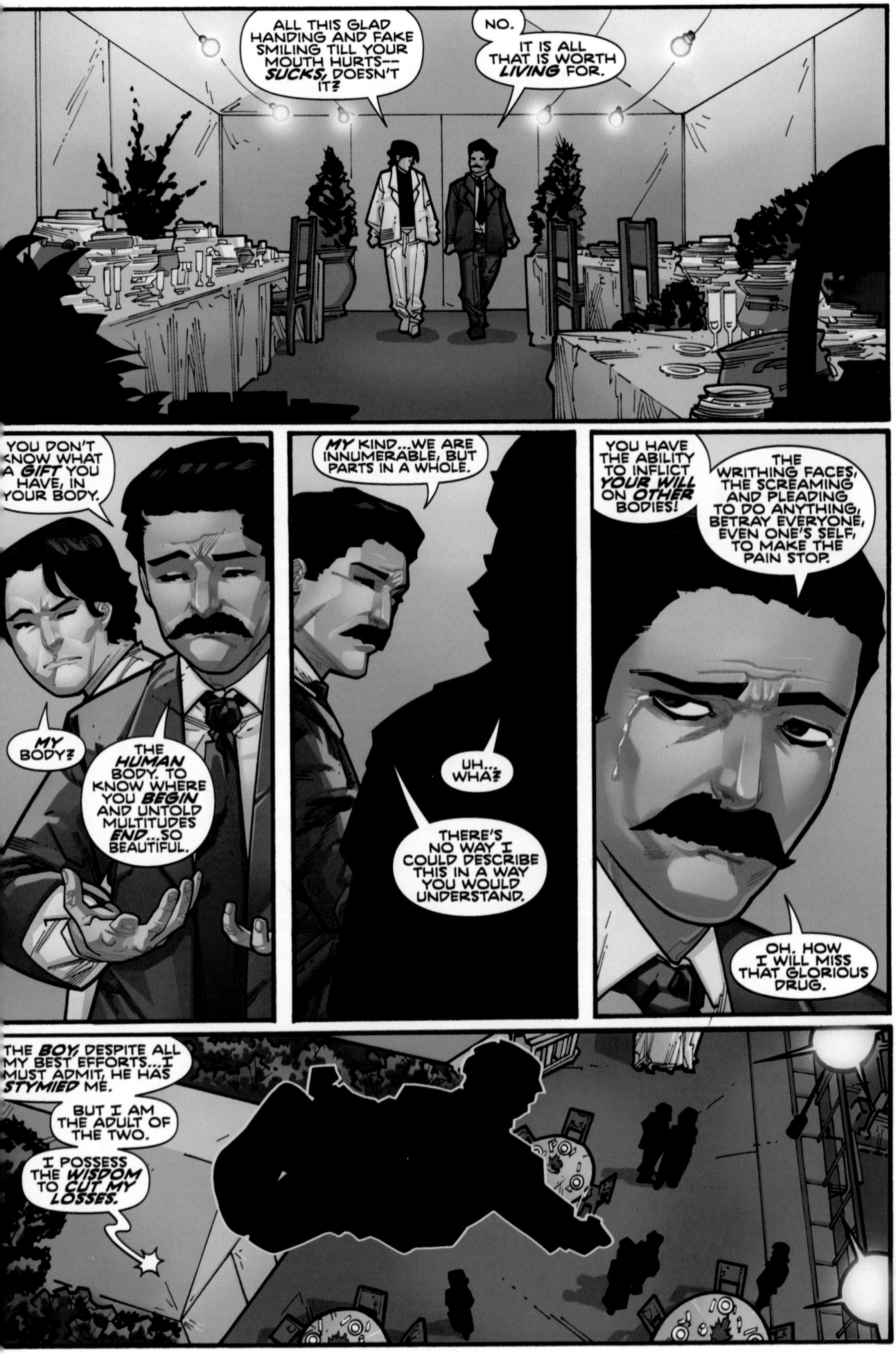
ALL THIS GLAD HANDING AND FAKE SMILING TILL YOUR MOUTH HURTS-- SUCKS, DOESN'T IT?
NO.
IT IS ALL THAT IS WORTH LIVING FOR.
YOU DON'T KNOW WHAT A GIFT YOU HAVE, IN YOUR BODY.
MY BODY?
THE HUMAN BODY. TO KNOW WHERE YOU BEGIN AND UNTOLD MULTITUDES END...SO BEAUTIFUL.
MY KIND...WE ARE INNUMERABLE, BUT PARTS IN A WHOLE.
UH... WHA?
THERE'S NO WAY I COULD DESCRIBE THIS IN A WAY YOU WOULD UNDERSTAND.
YOU HAVE THE ABILITY TO INFLICT YOUR WILL ON OTHER BODIES!
THE WRITHING FACES, THE SCREAMING AND PLEADING TO DO ANYTHING, BETRAY EVERYONE, EVEN ONE'S SELF, TO MAKE THE PAIN STOP.
OH, HOW I WILL MISS THAT GLORIOUS DRUG.
THE BOY, DESPITE ALL MY BEST EFFORTS...I MUST ADMIT, HE HAS STYMIED ME.
BUT I AM THE ADULT OF THE TWO.
I POSSESS THE WISDOM TO CUT MY LOSSES.

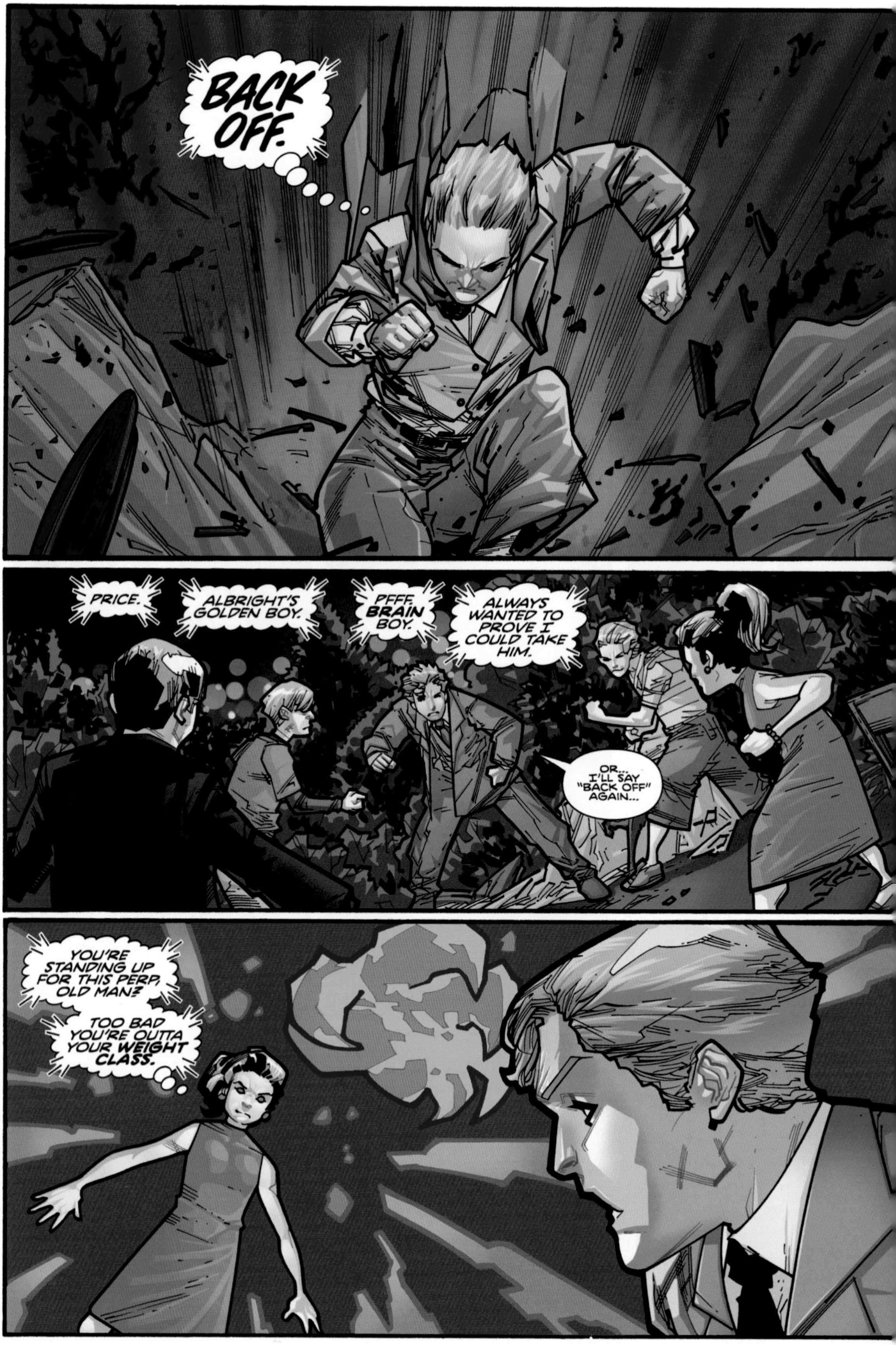
BACK OFF.
PRICE.
ALBRIGHT'S GOLDEN BOY.
PFFF. BRAIN BOY.
ALWAYS WANTED TO PROVE I COULD TAKE HIM.
OR... I'LL SAY "BACK OFF" AGAIN...
YOU'RE STANDING UP FOR THIS PERP, OLD MAN?
TOO BAD YOU'RE OUTTA YOUR WEIGHT CLASS.

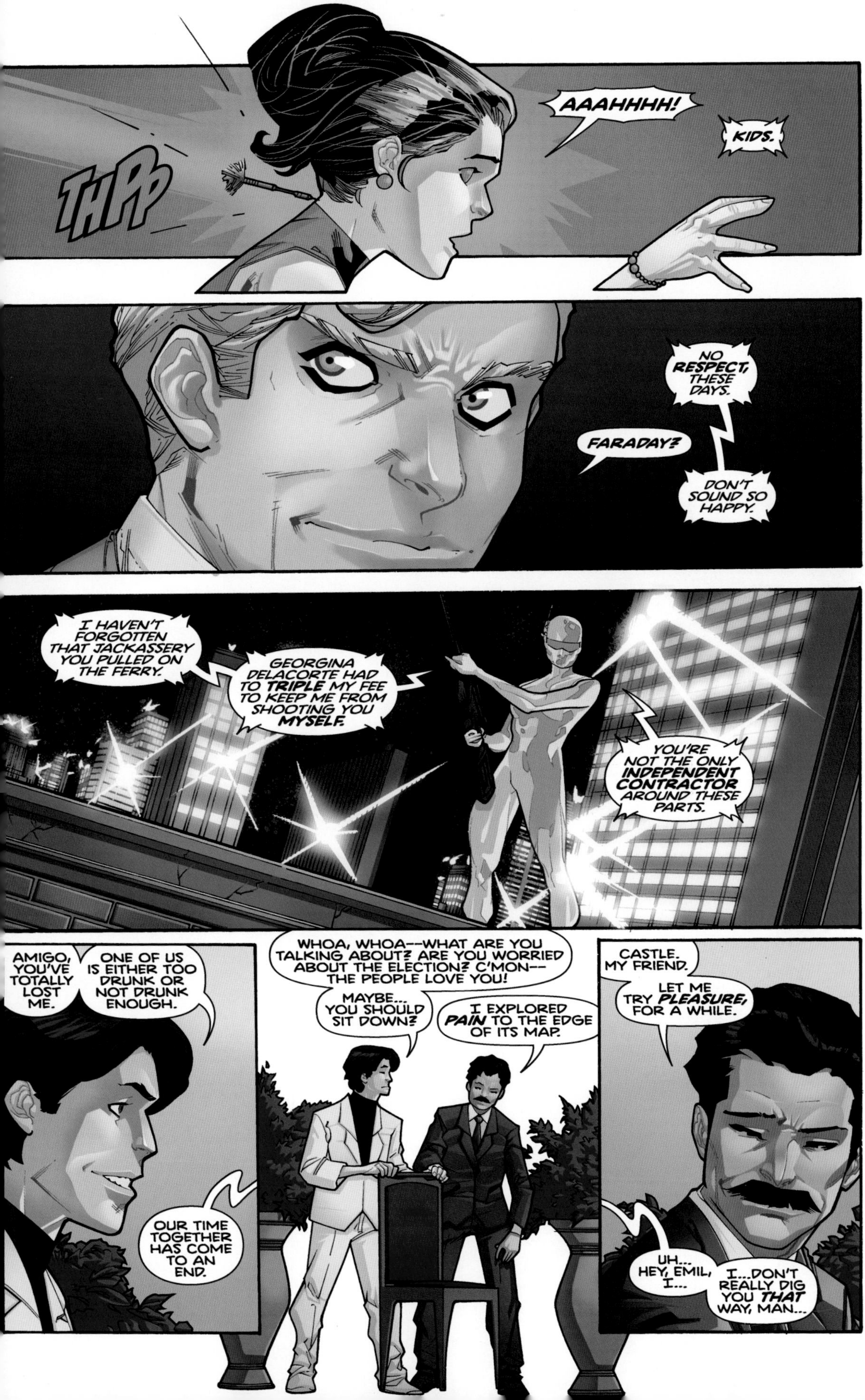
THPP
AAAHHHH!
KIDS.
NO RESPECT, THESE DAYS.
FARADAY?
DON'T SOUND SO HAPPY.
I HAVEN'T FORGOTTEN THAT JACKASSERY YOU PULLED ON THE FERRY.
GEORGINA DELACORTE HAD TO TRIPLE MY FEE TO KEEP ME FROM SHOOTING YOU MYSELF.
YOU'RE NOT THE ONLY INDEPENDENT CONTRACTOR AROUND THESE PARTS.
AMIGO, YOU'VE TOTALLY LOST ME.
ONE OF US IS EITHER TOO DRUNK OR NOT DRUNK ENOUGH.
OUR TIME TOGETHER HAS COME TO AN END.
WHOA, WHOA--WHAT ARE YOU TALKING ABOUT? ARE YOU WORRIED ABOUT THE ELECTION? C'MON-- THE PEOPLE LOVE YOU!
MAYBE... YOU SHOULD SIT DOWN?
I EXPLORED PAIN TO THE EDGE OF ITS MAP.
CASTLE. MY FRIEND.
LET ME TRY PLEASURE, FOR A WHILE.
UH... HEY, EMIL, I...
I...DON'T REALLY DIG YOU THAT WAY, MAN...

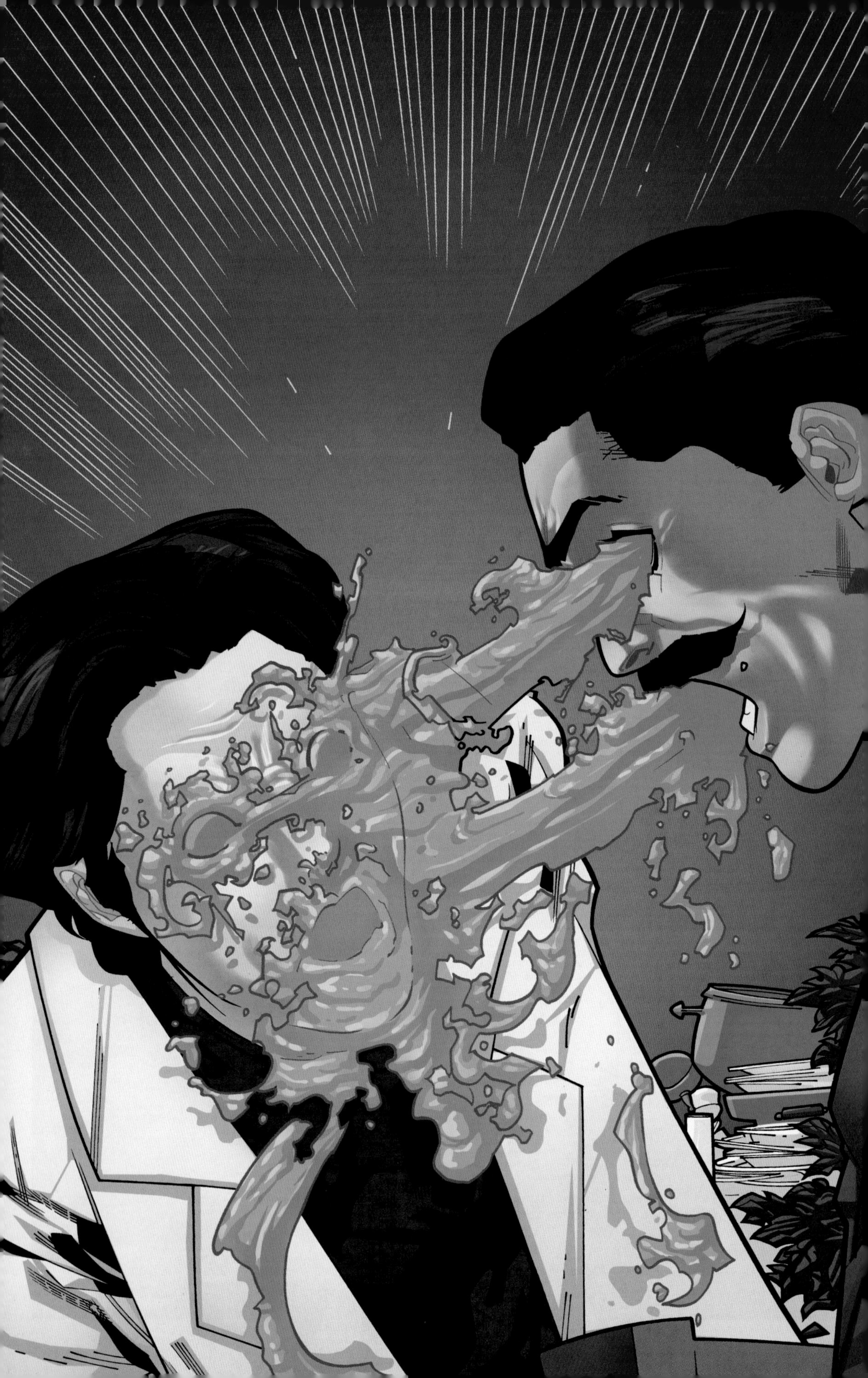

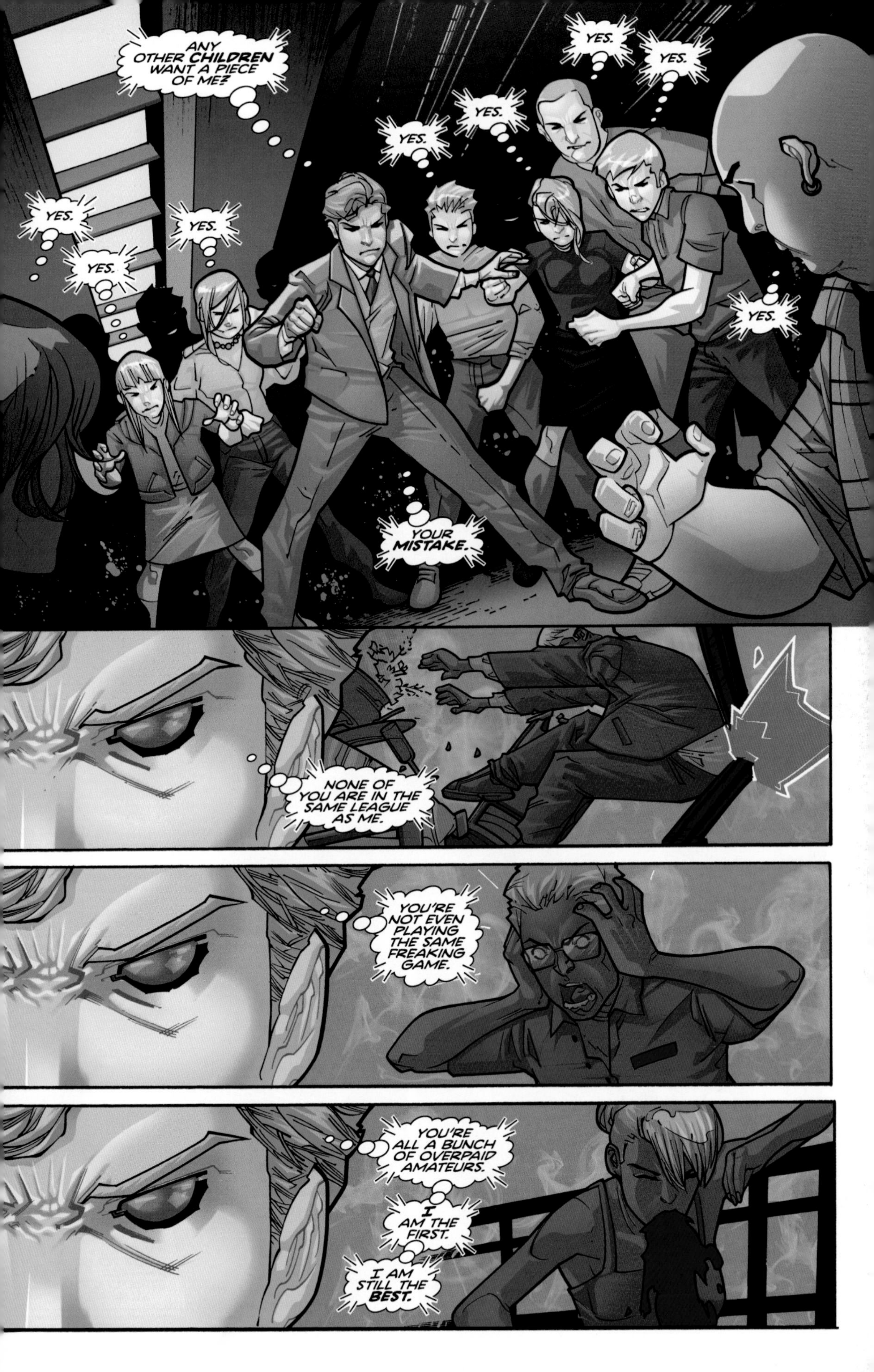
ANY OTHER CHILDREN WANT A PIECE OF ME?
YES.
YES.
YES.
YES.
YES.
YES.
YES.
YES.
YOUR MISTAKE.
NONE OF YOU ARE IN THE SAME LEAGUE AS ME.
YOU'RE NOT EVEN PLAYING THE SAME FREAKING GAME.
YOU'RE ALL A BUNCH OF OVERPAID AMATEURS.
I AM THE FIRST.
I AM STILL THE BEST.

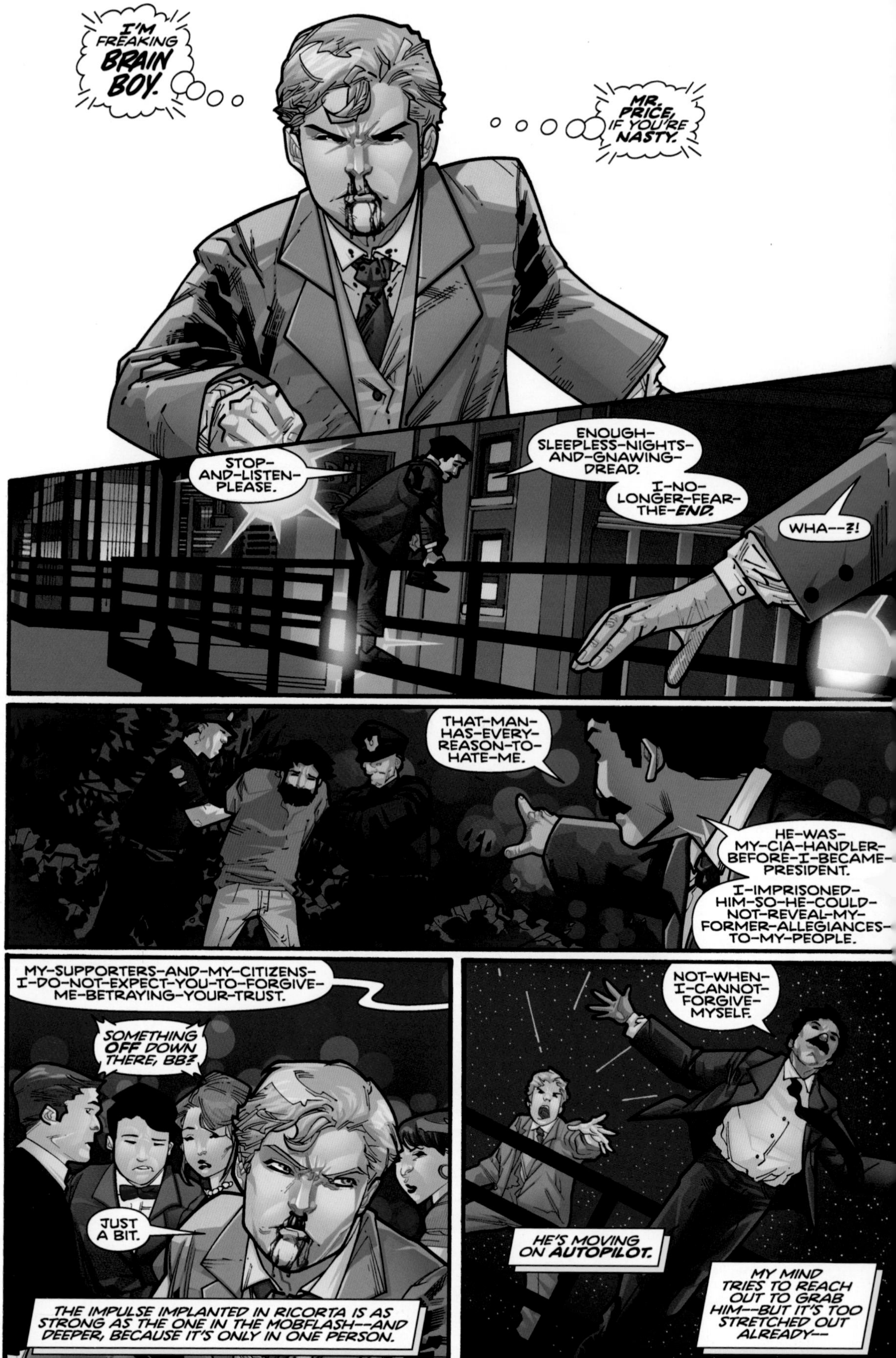
I'M FREAKING BRAIN BOY.
MR. PRICE, IF YOU'RE NASTY.
STOP-AND-LISTEN-PLEASE.
ENOUGH-SLEEPLESS-NIGHTS-AND-GNAWING-DREAD.
I-NO-LONGER-FEAR-THE-END.
WHA--?!
THAT-MAN-HAS-EVERY-REASON-TO-HATE-ME.
HE-WAS-MY-CIA-HANDLER-BEFORE-I-BECAME-PRESIDENT.
I-IMPRISONED-HIM-SO-HE-COULD-NOT-REVEAL-MY-FORMER-ALLEGIANCES-TO-MY-PEOPLE.
MY-SUPPORTERS-AND-MY-CITIZENS-I-DO-NOT-EXPECT-YOU-TO-FORGIVE-ME-BETRAYING-YOUR-TRUST.
SOMETHING OFF DOWN THERE, BB?
JUST A BIT.
THE IMPULSE IMPLANTED IN RICORTA IS AS STRONG AS THE ONE IN THE MOBFLASH--AND DEEPER, BECAUSE IT'S ONLY IN ONE PERSON.
NOT-WHEN-I-CANNOT-FORGIVE-MYSELF.
HE'S MOVING ON AUTOPILOT.
MY MIND TRIES TO REACH OUT TO GRAB HIM--BUT IT'S TOO STRETCHED OUT ALREADY--

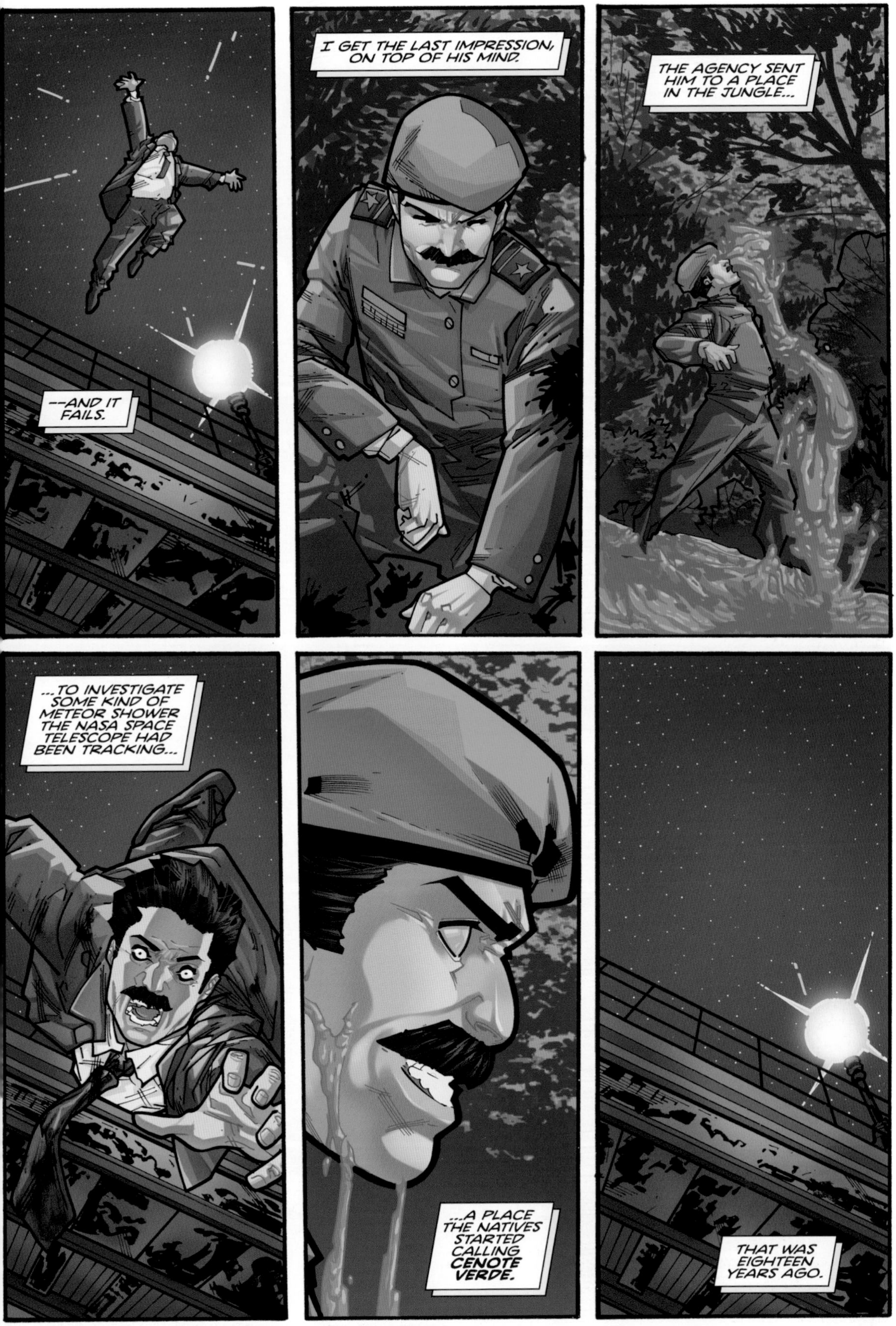
--AND IT FAILS.
I GET THE LAST IMPRESSION, ON TOP OF HIS MIND.
THE AGENCY SENT HIM TO A PLACE IN THE JUNGLE...
...TO INVESTIGATE SOME KIND OF METEOR SHOWER THE NASA SPACE TELESCOPE HAD BEEN TRACKING...
...A PLACE THE NATIVES STARTED CALLING **CENOTE VERDE.**
THAT WAS EIGHTEEN YEARS AGO.

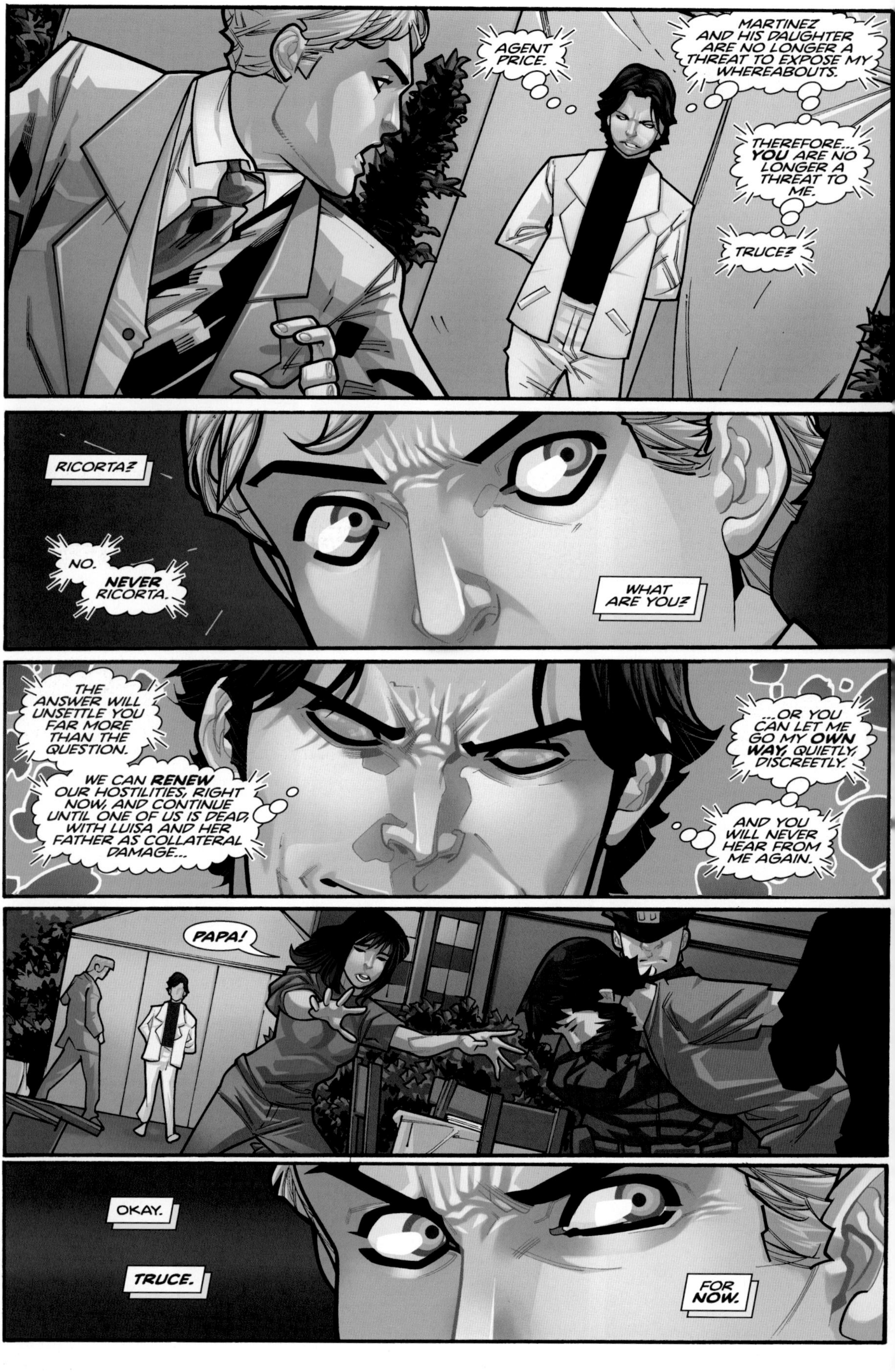
AGENT PRICE.
MARTINEZ AND HIS DAUGHTER ARE NO LONGER A THREAT TO EXPOSE MY WHEREABOUTS.
THEREFORE... YOU ARE NO LONGER A THREAT TO ME.
TRUCE?
RICORTA?
NO. NEVER RICORTA.
WHAT ARE YOU?
THE ANSWER WILL UNSETTLE YOU FAR MORE THAN THE QUESTION.
WE CAN RENEW OUR HOSTILITIES, RIGHT NOW, AND CONTINUE UNTIL ONE OF US IS DEAD, WITH LUISA AND HER FATHER AS COLLATERAL DAMAGE...
...OR YOU CAN LET ME GO MY OWN WAY, QUIETLY, DISCREETLY.
AND YOU WILL NEVER HEAR FROM ME AGAIN.
PAPA!
OKAY.
TRUCE.
FOR NOW.

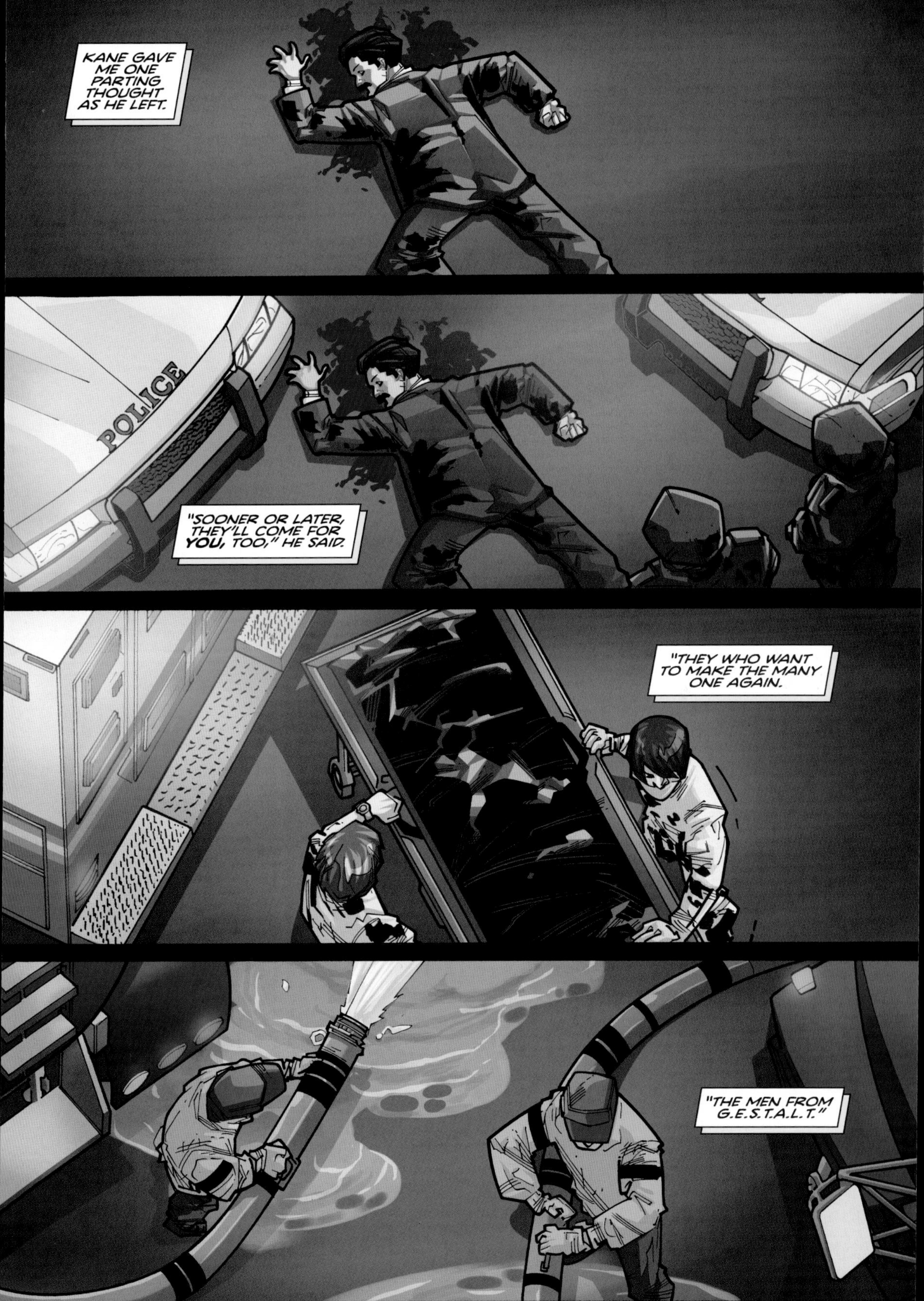
KANE GAVE ME ONE PARTING THOUGHT AS HE LEFT.
POLICE
"SOONER OR LATER, THEY'LL COME FOR **YOU,** TOO," HE SAID.
"THEY WHO WANT TO MAKE THE MANY ONE AGAIN.
"THE MEN FROM G.E.S.T.A.L.T."

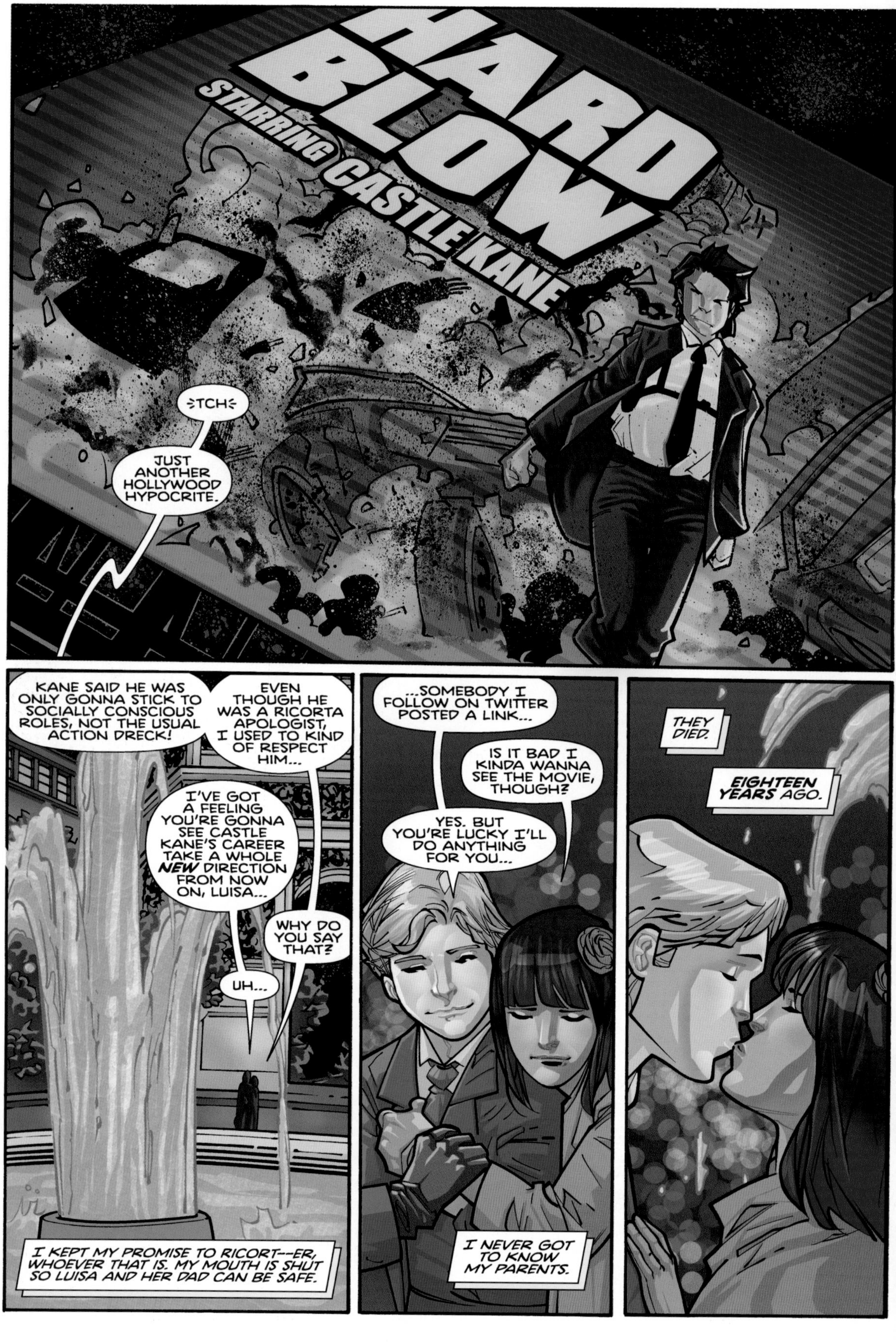
HARD BLOW
STARRING CASTLE KANE
TCH
JUST ANOTHER HOLLYWOOD HYPOCRITE.
KANE SAID HE WAS ONLY GONNA STICK TO SOCIALLY CONSCIOUS ROLES, NOT THE USUAL ACTION DRECK!
EVEN THOUGH HE WAS A RICORTA APOLOGIST, I USED TO KIND OF RESPECT HIM...
I'VE GOT A FEELING YOU'RE GONNA SEE CASTLE KANE'S CAREER TAKE A WHOLE NEW DIRECTION FROM NOW ON, LUISA...
WHY DO YOU SAY THAT?
UH...
I KEPT MY PROMISE TO RICORT--ER, WHOEVER THAT IS. MY MOUTH IS SHUT SO LUISA AND HER DAD CAN BE SAFE.
...SOMEBODY I FOLLOW ON TWITTER POSTED A LINK...
IS IT BAD I KINDA WANNA SEE THE MOVIE, THOUGH?
YES. BUT YOU'RE LUCKY I'LL DO ANYTHING FOR YOU...
I NEVER GOT TO KNOW MY PARENTS.
THEY DIED.
EIGHTEEN YEARS AGO.

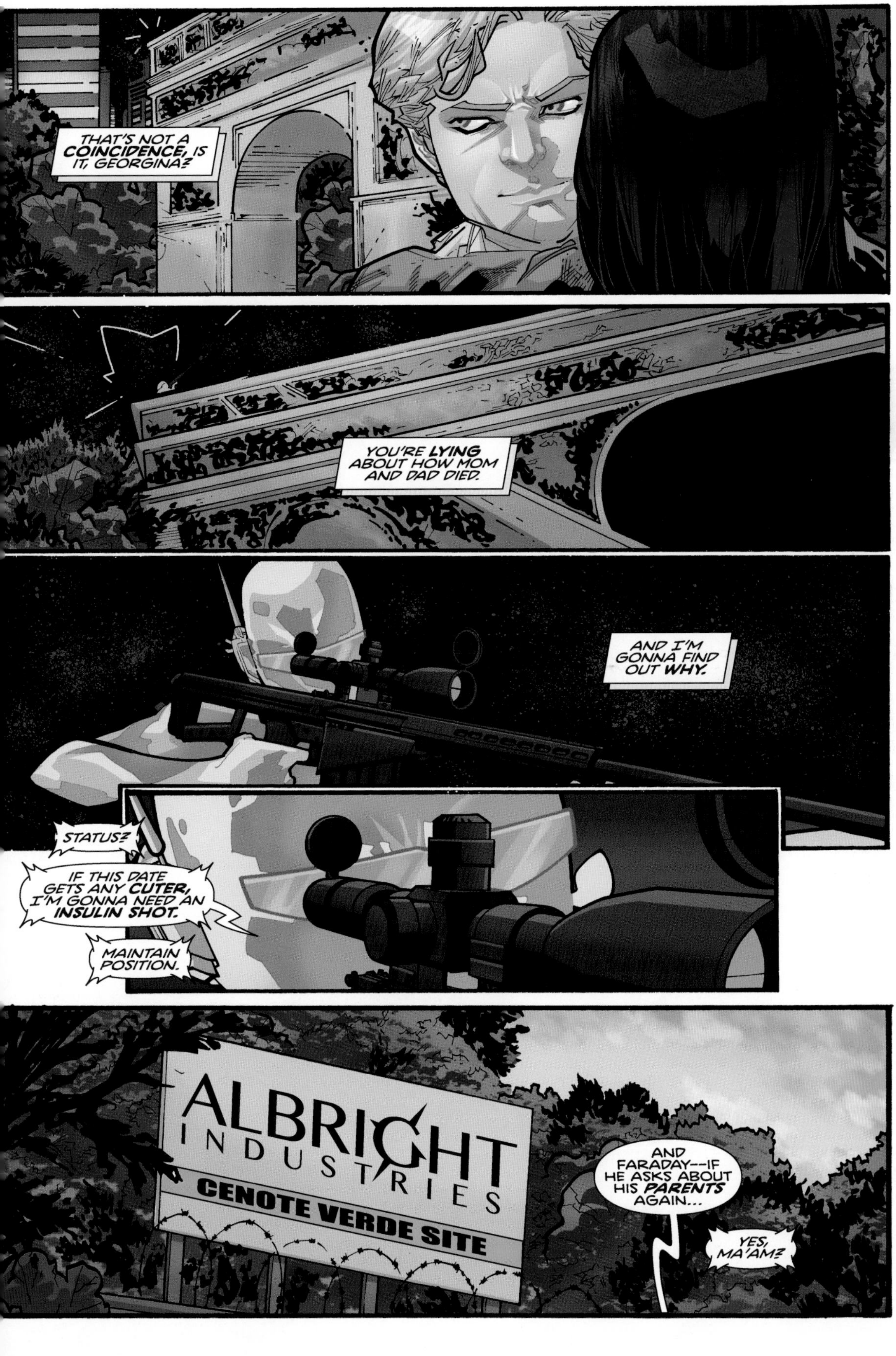
THAT'S NOT A COINCIDENCE, IS IT, GEORGINA?
YOU'RE LYING ABOUT HOW MOM AND DAD DIED.
AND I'M GONNA FIND OUT WHY.
STATUS?
IF THIS DATE GETS ANY CUTER, I'M GONNA NEED AN INSULIN SHOT.
MAINTAIN POSITION.
ALBRIGHT INDUSTRIES
CENOTE VERDE SITE
AND FARADAY--IF HE ASKS ABOUT HIS PARENTS AGAIN...
YES, MA'AM?

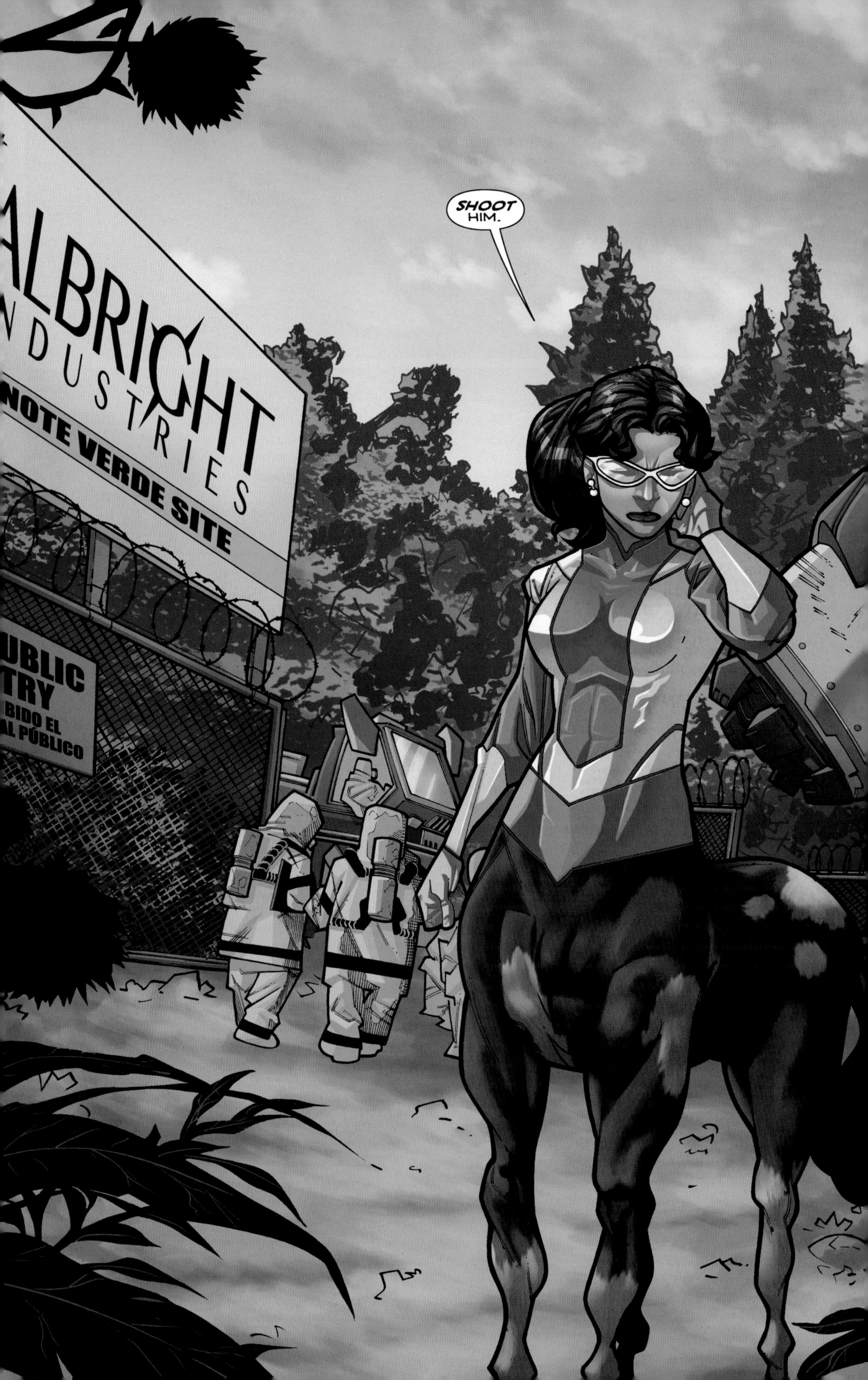
ALBRIGHT
NDUSTRIES
NOTE VERDE SITE
UBLIC
TRY
BIDO EL
AL PÚBLICO
SHOOT HIM.

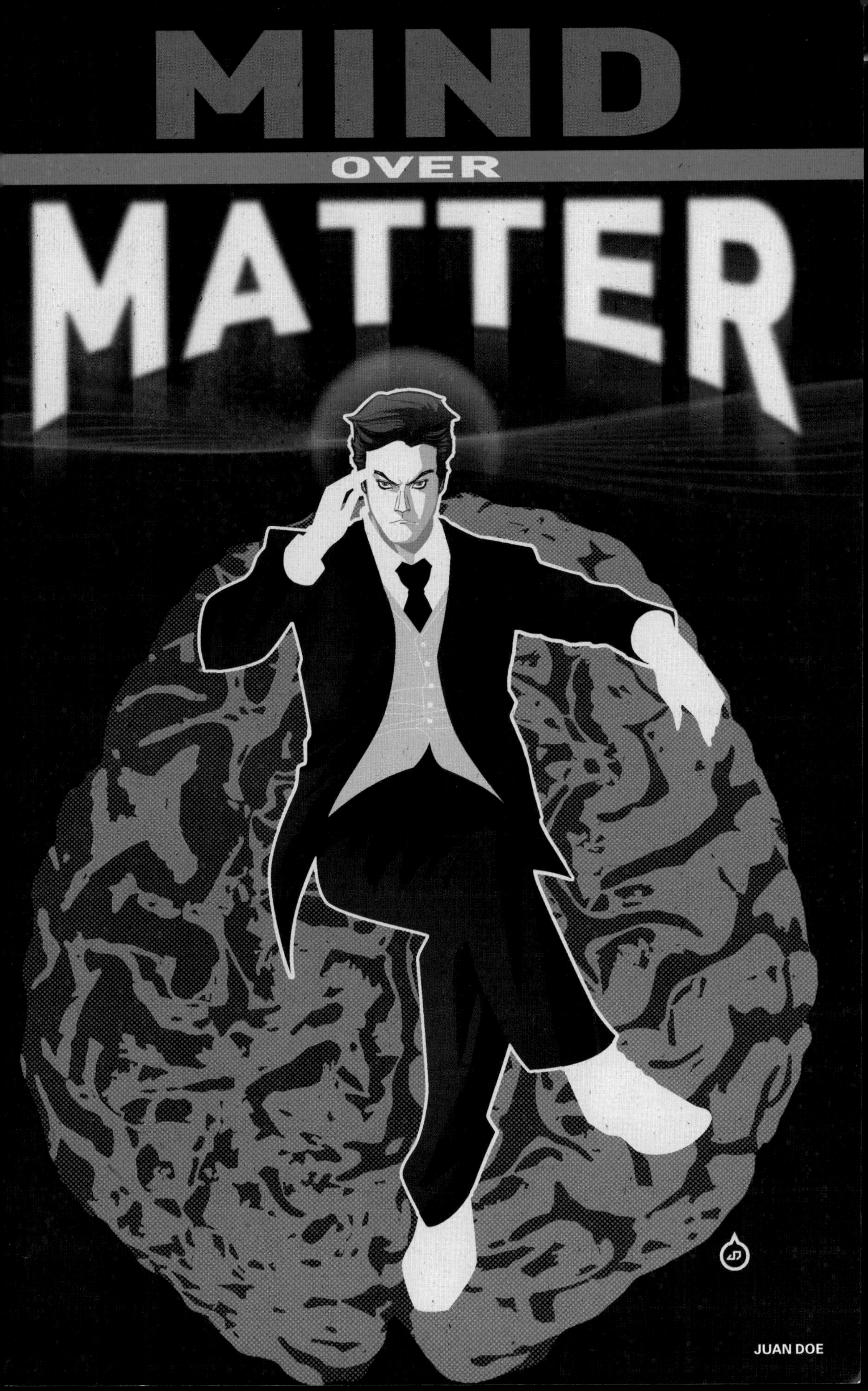
MIND
OVER
MATTER
JUAN DOE

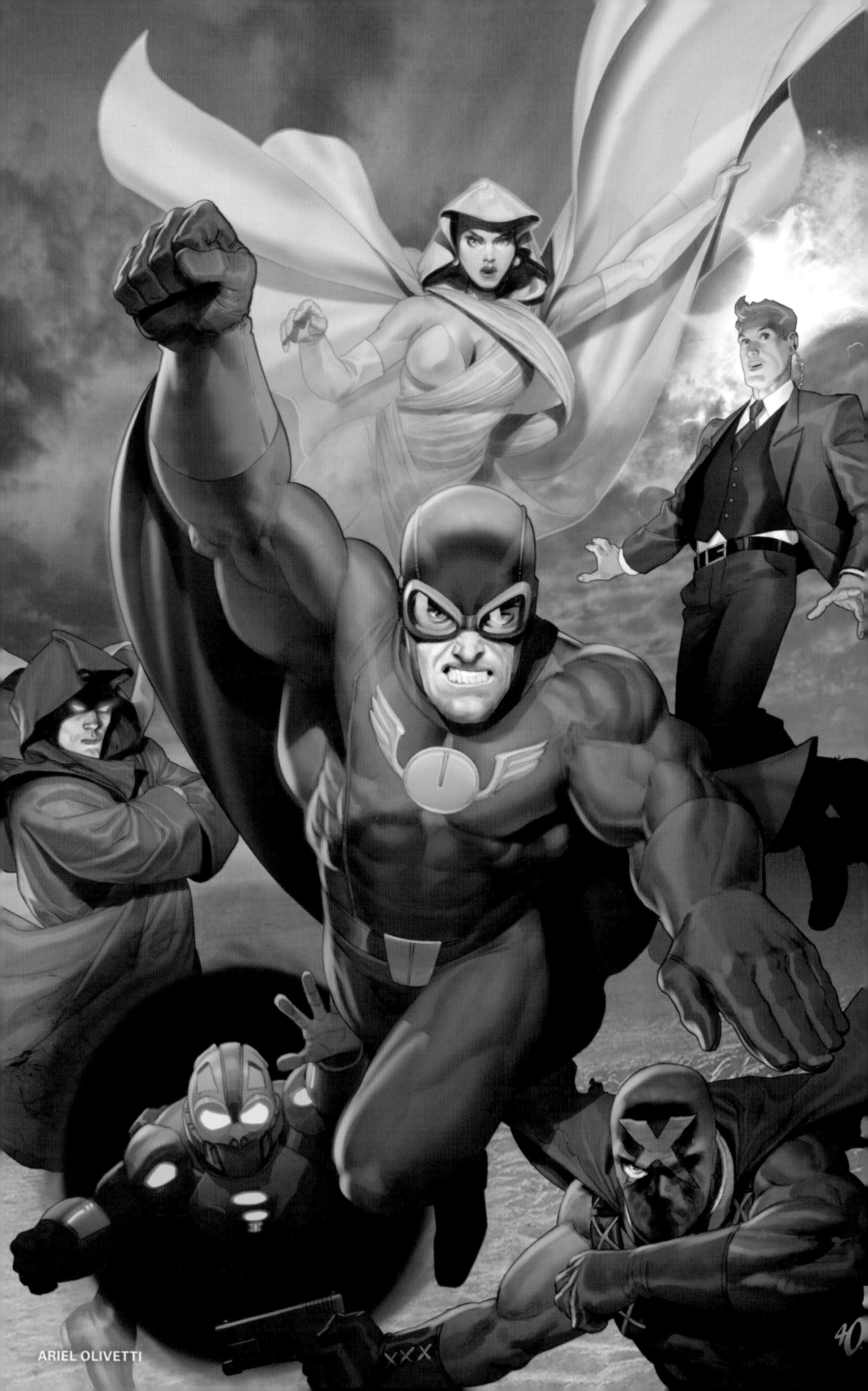

ARIEL OLIVETTI

BRAIN BOY™ SKETCHBOOK

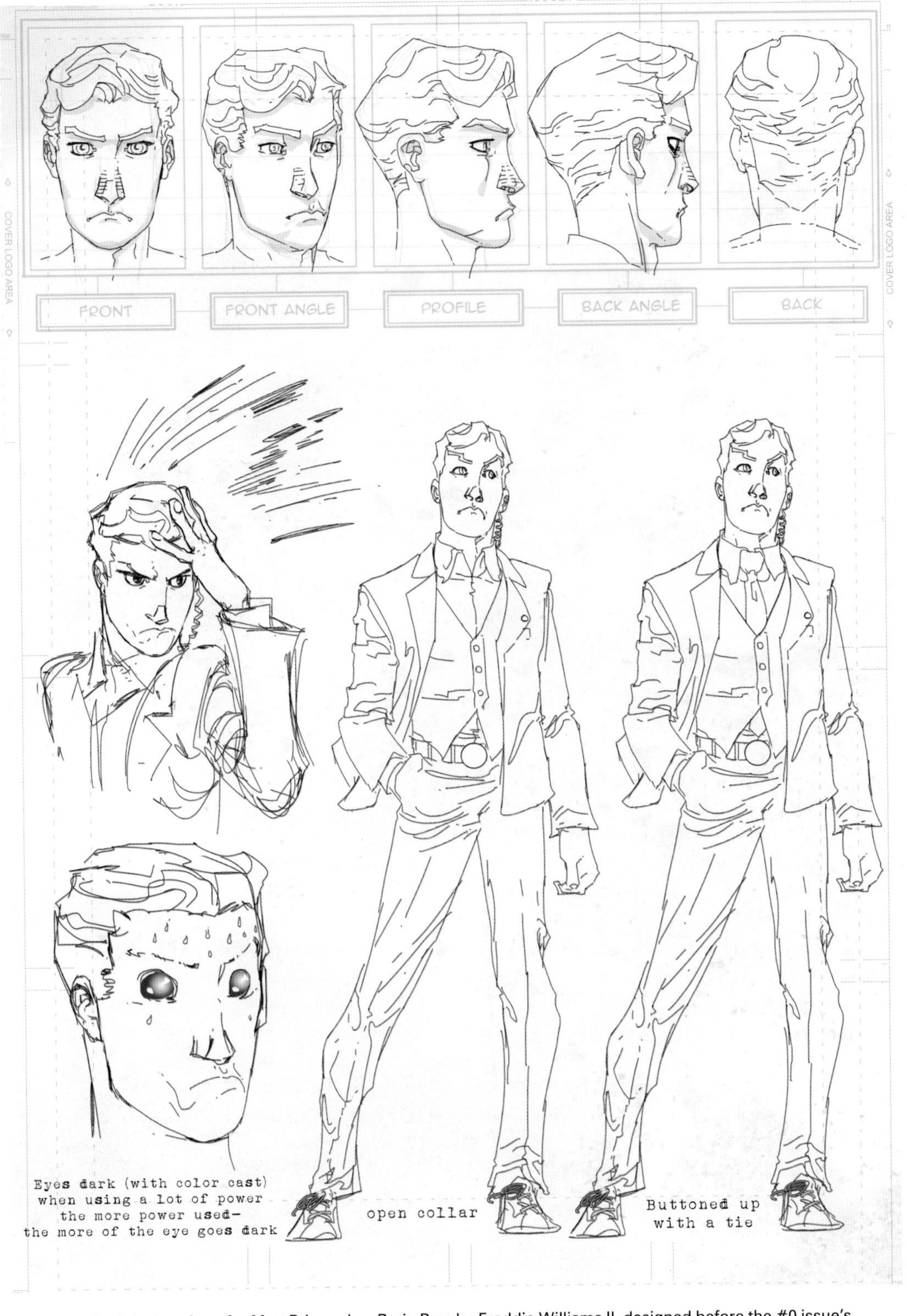

FRONT
FRONT ANGLE
PROFILE
BACK ANGLE
BACK
COVER LOGO AREA
Eyes dark (with color cast) when using a lot of power the more power used- the more of the eye goes dark
open collar
Buttoned up with a tie

This is the final design sheet for Matt Price, a.k.a. Brain Boy, by Freddie Williams II, designed before the #0 issue's content ran in *Dark Horse Presents* #23–#25. It was decided that Matt, being a wealthy Albright Industries asset, would have a much nicer suit than the average Secret Service agent.

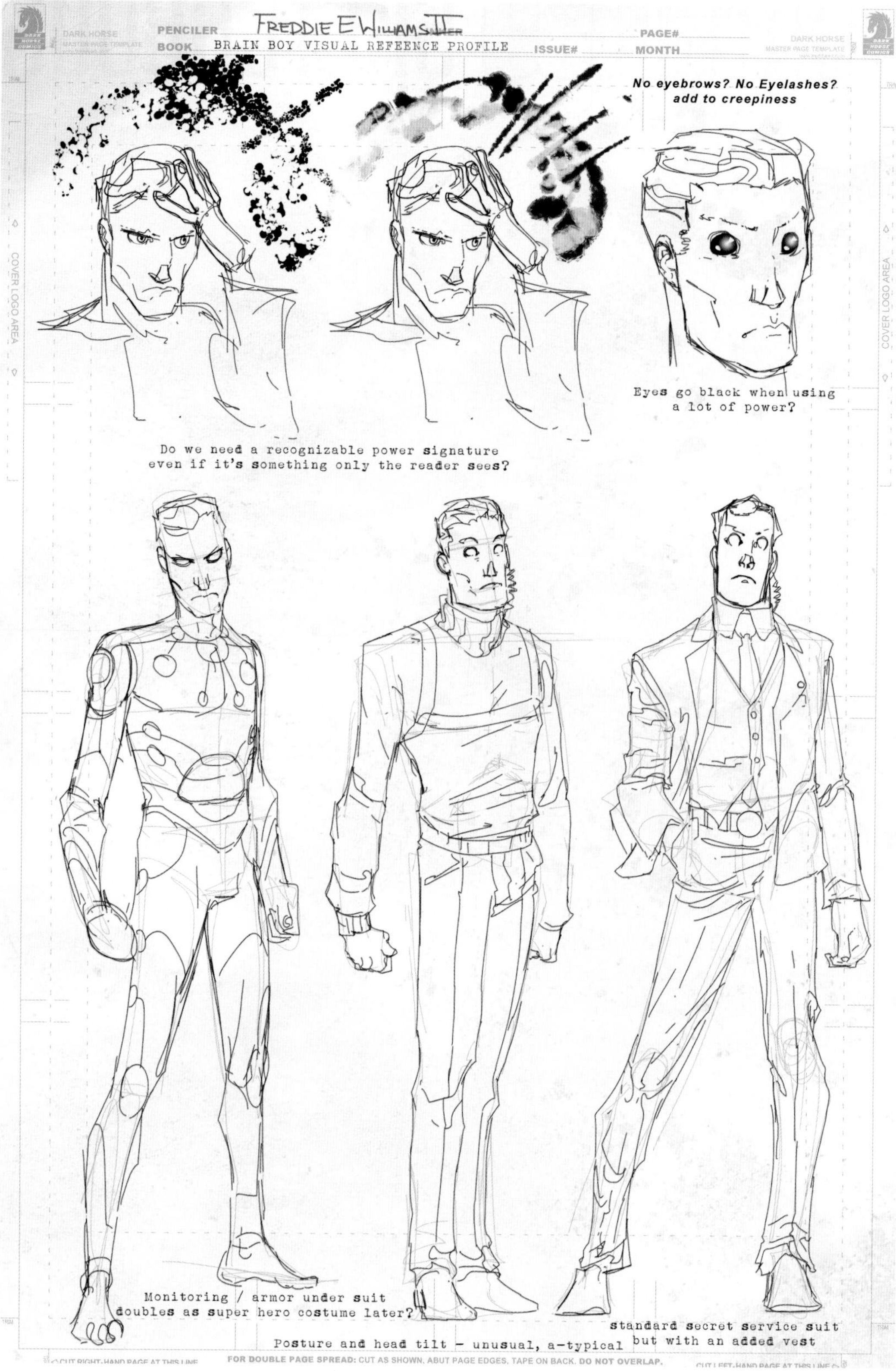
DARK HORSE
MASTER PAGE TEMPLATE
PENCILER FREDDIE E WILLIAMS II
BOOK BRAIN BOY VISUAL REFEENCE PROFILE
ISSUE#
PAGE#
MONTH
No eyebrows? No Eyelashes? add to creepiness
Eyes go black when using a lot of power?
Do we need a recognizable power signature even if it's something only the reader sees?
COVER LOGO AREA
Monitoring / armor under suit doubles as super hero costume later?
Posture and head tilt - unusual, a-typical
standard secret service suit but with an added vest
FOR DOUBLE PAGE SPREAD: CUT AS SHOWN, ABUT PAGE EDGES, TAPE ON BACK. DO NOT OVERLAP.

You can see some variations Freddie was playing around with to showcase Brain Boy's powers, which eventually led to the signature circles used throughout this volume. Though short lived, Dell Comics' original *Brain Boy* series (which ran from 1962 to 1963) was unique in that it featured a superhero who wore no costume. Matt Price's new look was heavily informed by that idea.

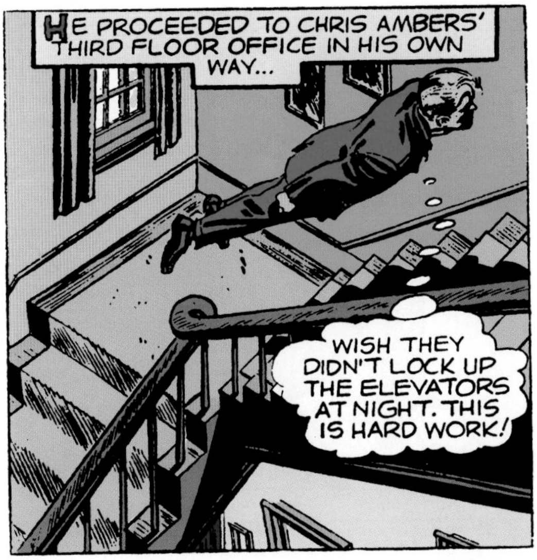
HE PROCEEDED TO CHRIS AMBERS' THIRD FLOOR OFFICE IN HIS OWN WAY...
WISH THEY DIDN'T LOCK UP THE ELEVATORS AT NIGHT. THIS IS HARD WORK!

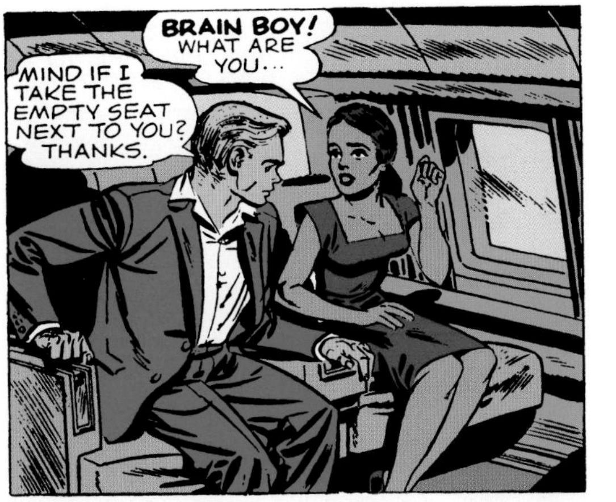
MIND IF I TAKE THE EMPTY SEAT NEXT TO YOU? THANKS.
BRAIN BOY! WHAT ARE YOU...

Though Freddie Williams II tried a number of different looks, as seen below, all were informed by the novel idea of a costumeless superhero.

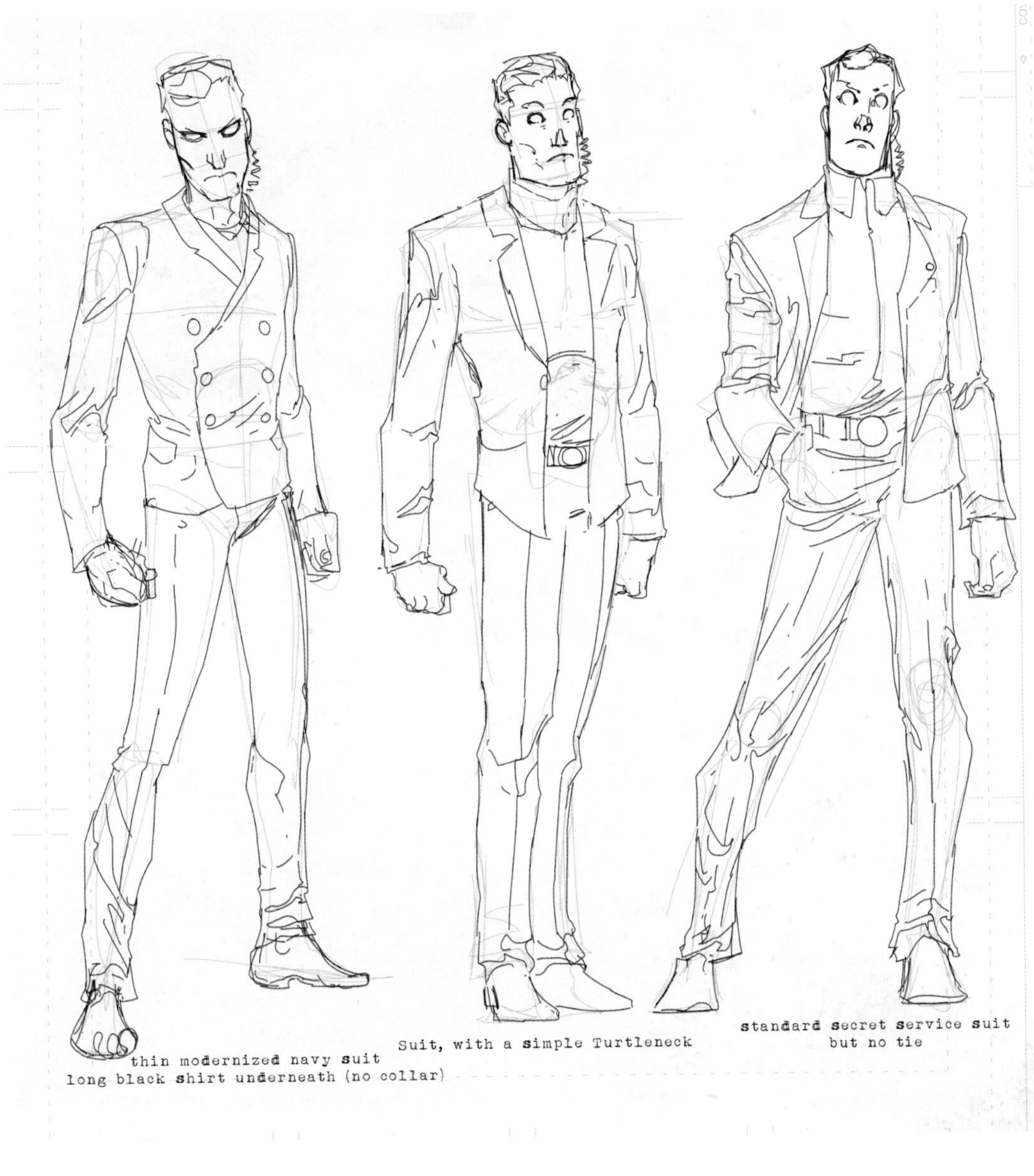
thin modernized navy suit
long black shirt underneath (no collar)
Suit, with a simple Turtleneck
standard secret service suit
but no tie

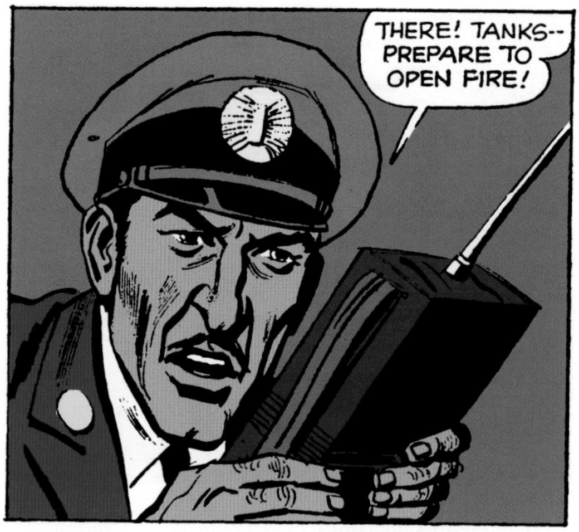
THERE! TANKS-- PREPARE TO OPEN FIRE!

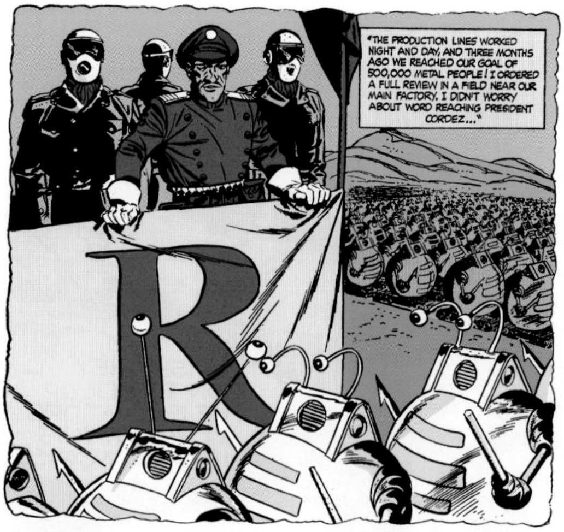
"THE PRODUCTION LINES WORKED NIGHT AND DAY, AND THREE MONTHS AGO WE REACHED OUR GOAL OF 500,000 METAL PEOPLE! I ORDERED A FULL REVIEW IN A FIELD NEAR OUR MAIN FACTORY. I DIDN'T WORRY ABOUT WORD REACHING PRESIDENT CORDEZ..."

A Fidel Castro analog in the original Cold War–era run of *Brain Boy*, Ricorta was Matt Price's archenemy.

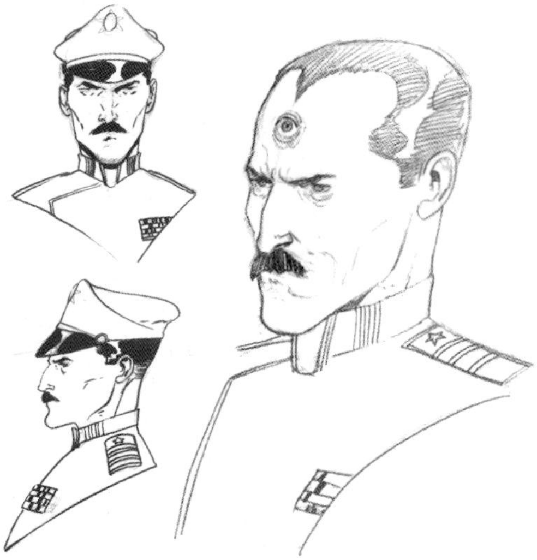

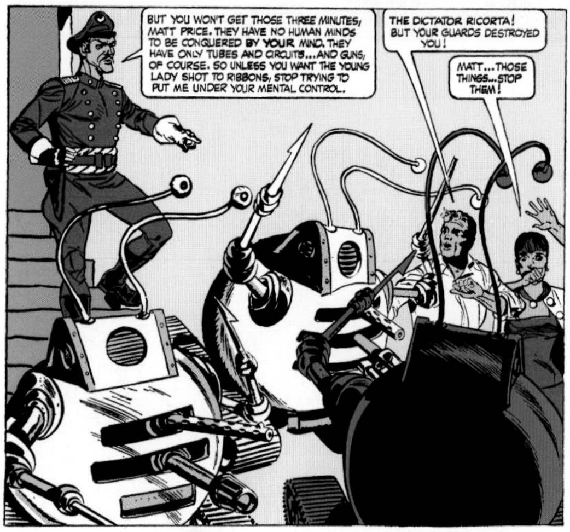
BUT YOU WON'T GET THOSE THREE MINUTES, MATT PRICE. THEY HAVE NO HUMAN MINDS TO BE CONQUERED BY YOUR MIND. THEY HAVE ONLY TUBES AND CIRCUITS...AND GUNS, OF COURSE. SO UNLESS YOU WANT THE YOUNG LADY SHOT TO RIBBONS, STOP TRYING TO PUT ME UNDER YOUR MENTAL CONTROL.
THE DICTATOR RICORTA! BUT YOUR GUARDS DESTROYED YOU!
MATT...THOSE THINGS...STOP THEM!

As a fan of both comics history and actual history, writer Fred Van Lente modernized the character to be a counterpart to similar modern political figures.

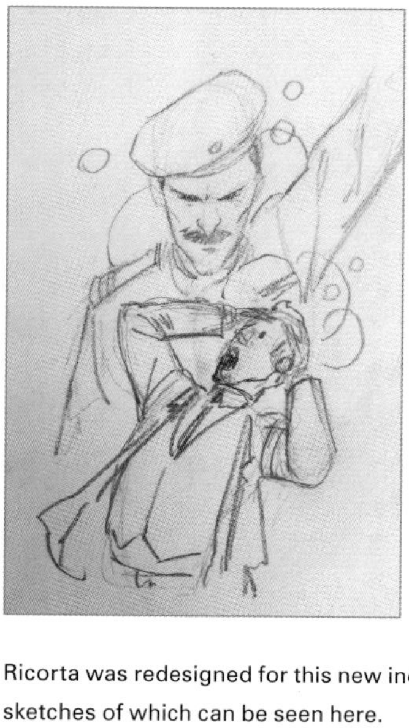

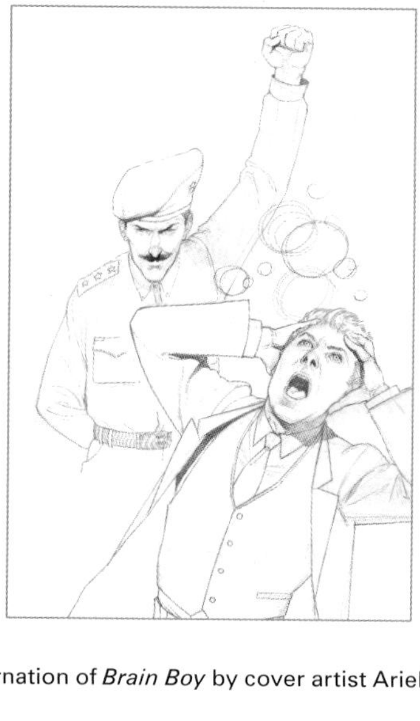

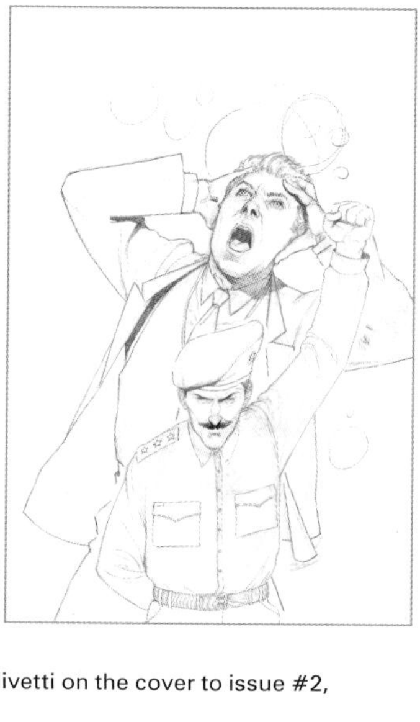

Ricorta was redesigned for this new incarnation of *Brain Boy* by cover artist Ariel Olivetti on the cover to issue #2, sketches of which can be seen here.

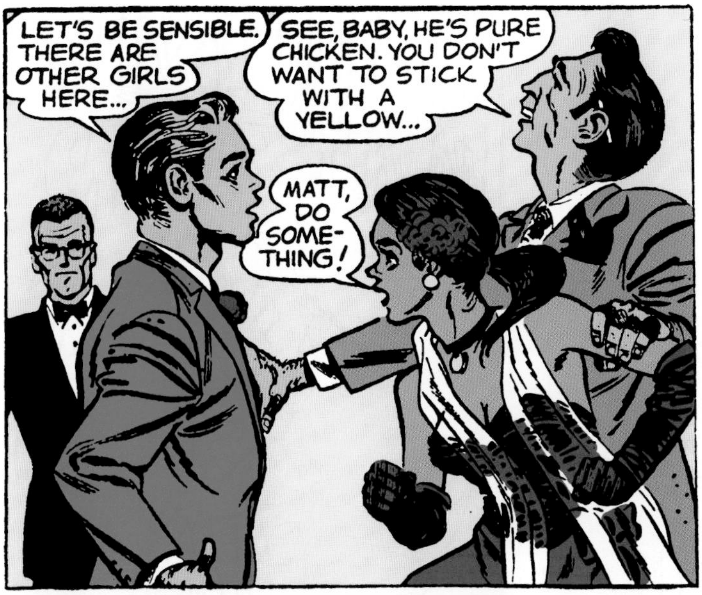
LET'S BE SENSIBLE. THERE ARE OTHER GIRLS HERE...
SEE, BABY, HE'S PURE CHICKEN. YOU DON'T WANT TO STICK WITH A YELLOW...
MATT, DO SOME-THING!

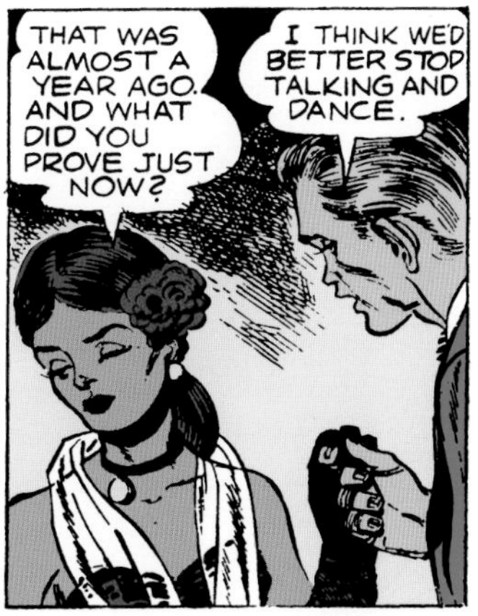
THAT WAS ALMOST A YEAR AGO. AND WHAT DID YOU PROVE JUST NOW?
I THINK WE'D BETTER STOP TALKING AND DANCE.

Another interesting element from the original Dell run that Van Lente latched onto was the idea that Matt Price's girlfriend was Hispanic—which was very progressive for a comic from the sixties.

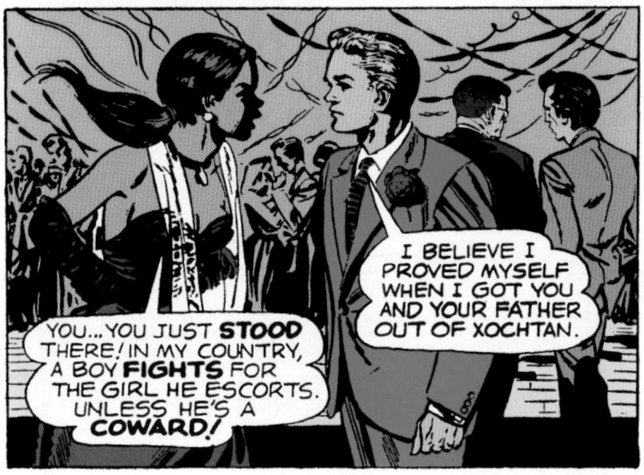
YOU...YOU JUST STOOD THERE! IN MY COUNTRY, A BOY FIGHTS FOR THE GIRL HE ESCORTS. UNLESS HE'S A COWARD!
I BELIEVE I PROVED MYSELF WHEN I GOT YOU AND YOUR FATHER OUT OF XOCHTAN.

In both runs, Ricorta is the force that brings the lovebirds together. Even though Matt's a mind reader, we can see that doesn't exactly make him a perfect boyfriend.

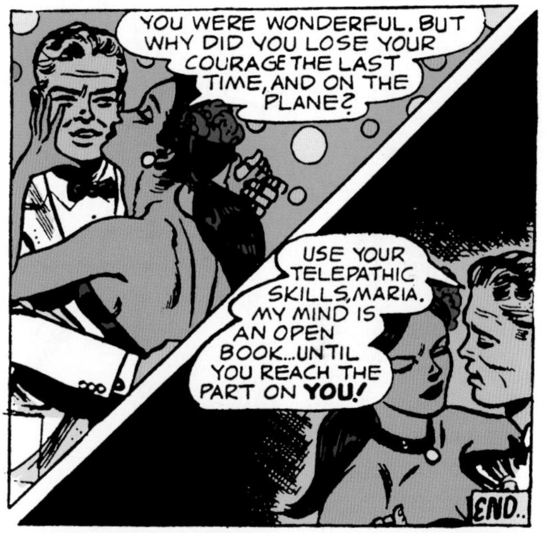
YOU WERE WONDERFUL. BUT WHY DID YOU LOSE YOUR COURAGE THE LAST TIME, AND ON THE PLANE?
USE YOUR TELEPATHIC SKILLS, MARIA. MY MIND IS AN OPEN BOOK...UNTIL YOU REACH THE PART ON YOU!
END..

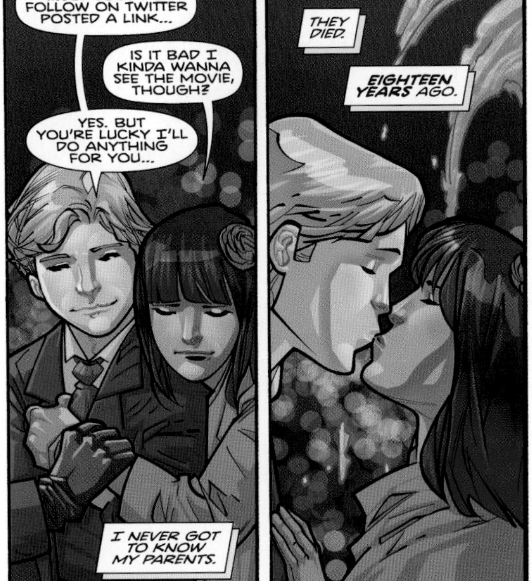
...SOMEBODY I FOLLOW ON TWITTER POSTED A LINK...
IS IT BAD I KINDA WANNA SEE THE MOVIE, THOUGH?
YES. BUT YOU'RE LUCKY I'LL DO ANYTHING FOR YOU...
I NEVER GOT TO KNOW MY PARENTS.
THEY DIED.
EIGHTEEN YEARS AGO.

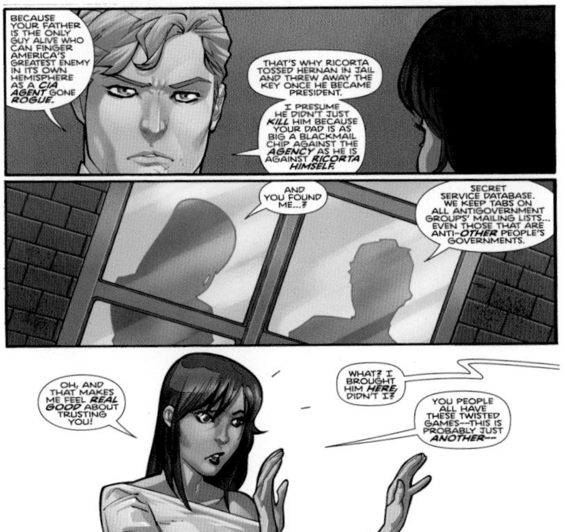
BECAUSE YOUR FATHER IS THE ONLY GUY ALIVE WHO CAN FINGER AMERICA'S GREATEST ENEMY IN ITS OWN HEMISPHERE AS A CIA AGENT GONE ROGUE.
THAT'S WHY RICORTA TOSSED HERNAN IN JAIL AND THREW AWAY THE KEY ONCE HE BECAME PRESIDENT.
I PRESUME HE DIDN'T JUST KILL HIM BECAUSE YOUR DAD IS AS BIG A BLACKMAIL CHIP AGAINST THE AGENCY AS HE IS AGAINST RICORTA HIMSELF.
AND YOU FOUND ME...?
SECRET SERVICE DATABASE. WE KEEP TABS ON ALL ANTIGOVERNMENT GROUPS' MAILING LISTS... EVEN THOSE THAT ARE ANTI-OTHER PEOPLE'S GOVERNMENTS.
OH, AND THAT MAKES ME FEEL REAL GOOD ABOUT TRUSTING YOU!
WHAT? I BROUGHT HIM HERE, DIDN'T I?
YOU PEOPLE ALL HAVE THESE TWISTED GAMES--THIS IS PROBABLY JUST ANOTHER--

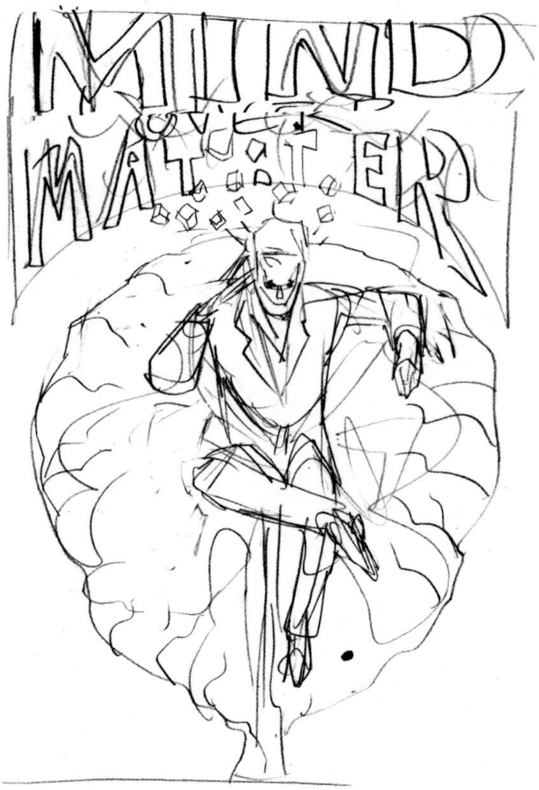
MIND
OVER
MATTER

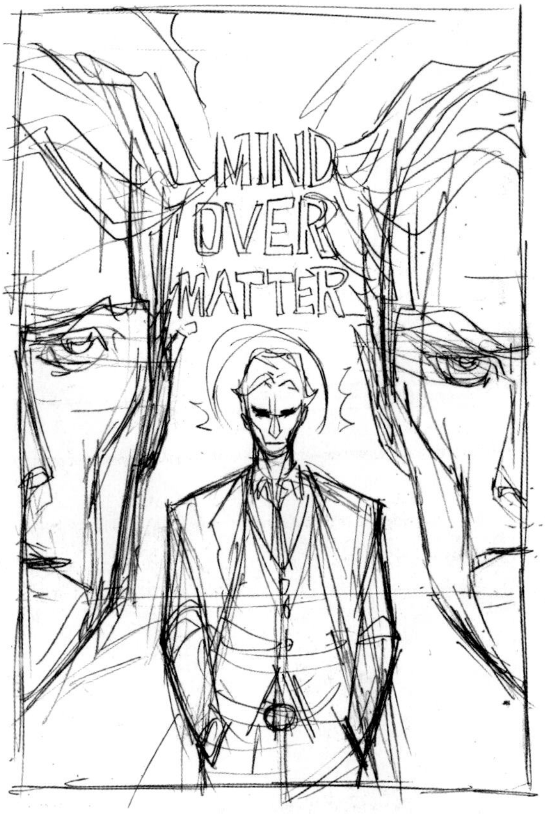
MIND
OVER
MATTER

Artist Juan Doe was hired to create the variant cover for *Brain Boy* #1, seen on page 103, as part of a series of propaganda-style variants. Here are Juan's original sketches.

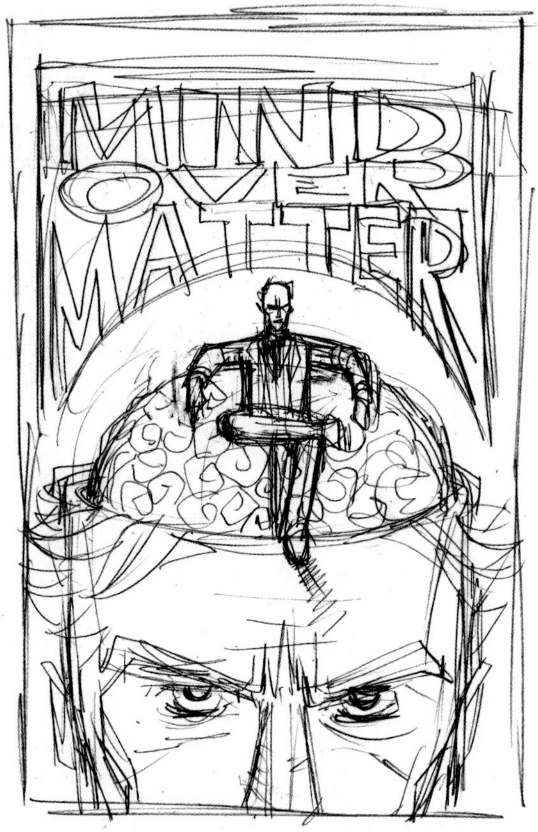
MIND
OVER
MATTER

PROJECT BLACK SKY

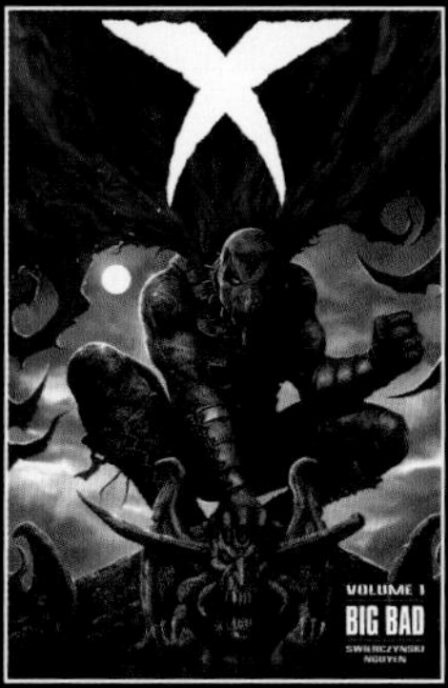
X
VOLUME 1
BIG BAD

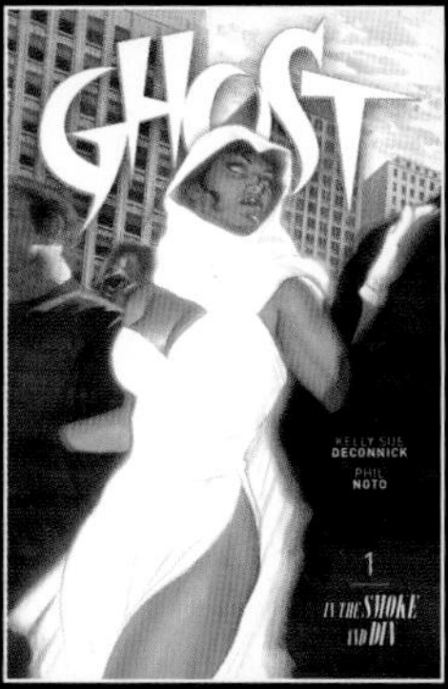
GHOST
DECONNICK
NOTO
1

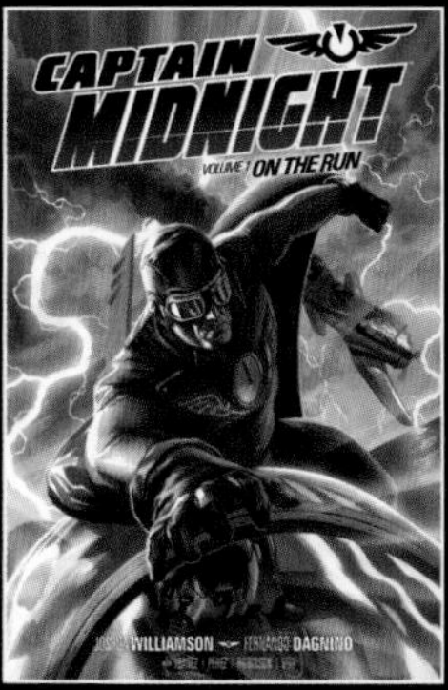
CAPTAIN MIDNIGHT
VOLUME 1 ON THE RUN
WILLIAMSON
DAGNINO

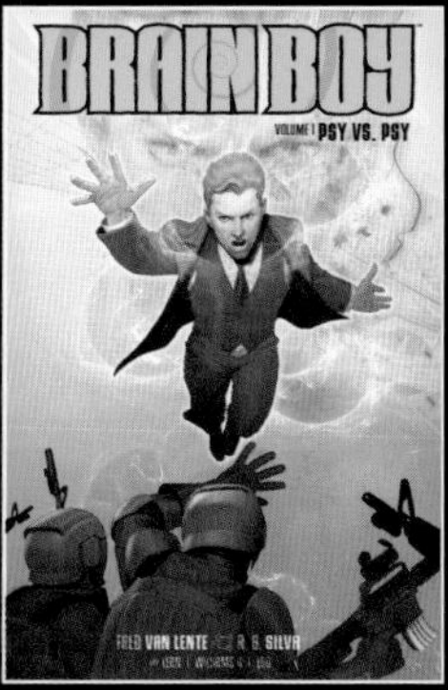
BRAIN BOY
VOLUME 1 PSY VS. PSY
FRED VAN LENTE
R. B. SILVA

X VOLUME 1: BIG BAD
Duane Swierczynski and Eric Nguyen
A masked vigilante dispenses justice without mercy to the criminals of the decaying city of Arcadia. Nonstop, visceral action, with Dark Horse's most brutal and exciting character—X!
978-1-61655-241-1 | $14.99

GHOST VOLUME 1: IN THE SMOKE AND DIN
Kelly Sue DeConnick, Phil Noto, Alex Ross, and Jenny Frison
Paranormal investigators accidentally summon a ghostly woman. The search for her identity uncovers a deadly alliance between political corruption and demonic science! In the middle stands a woman trapped between two worlds!
978-1-61655-121-6 | $14.99

THE OCCULTIST VOLUME 1
Mike Richardson, Tim Seeley, Victor Drujiniu, Jason Gorder, Andrew Dalhouse, and Steve Morris
With a team of hit mages hired by a powerful sorcerer after him, it's trial by fire for the new Occultist, as he learns to handle his powerful magical tome, or suffer at the hands of deadly enemies. From the mind of Dark Horse founder Mike Richardson (*The Secret*, *Cut*, *The Mask*)!
978-1-59582-745-6 | $16.99

CAPTAIN MIDNIGHT VOLUME 1: ON THE RUN
Joshua Williamson, Fernando Dagnino, Victor Ibáñez, Pere Pérez, and Roger Robinson
In the forties, he was an American hero, a daredevil fighter pilot, a technological genius . . . a superhero. Since he rifled out of the Bermuda Triangle and into the present day, Captain Midnight has been labeled a threat to homeland security. Can Captain Midnight survive in the modern world, with the US government on his heels and an old enemy out for revenge?
978-1-61655-229-9 | $14.99

BRAIN BOY VOLUME 1: PSY VS. PSY
Fred Van Lente, Freddie Williams II, and R.B. Silva
Ambushed while protecting an important statesman, Matt Price Jr., a.k.a. Brain Boy, finds himself wrapped up in political intrigue that could derail a key United Nations conference and sets the psychic spy on a collision course with a man whose mental powers rival his own!
978-1-61655-317-3 | $14.99

SUPER:POWERED BY CREATORS!

"These superheroes ain't no boy scouts in spandex. They're a high-octane blend of the damaged, quixotic heroes of pulp and detective fiction and the do-gooders in capes from the Golden and Silver Ages." —Duane Swierczynski

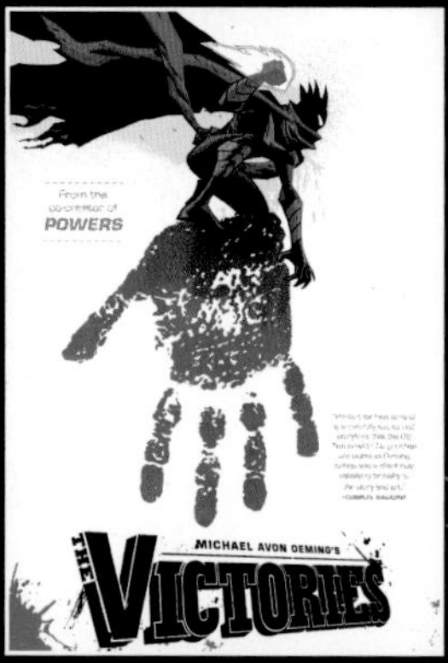
From the co-creator of POWERS
MICHAEL AVON OEMING'S
THE VICTORIES

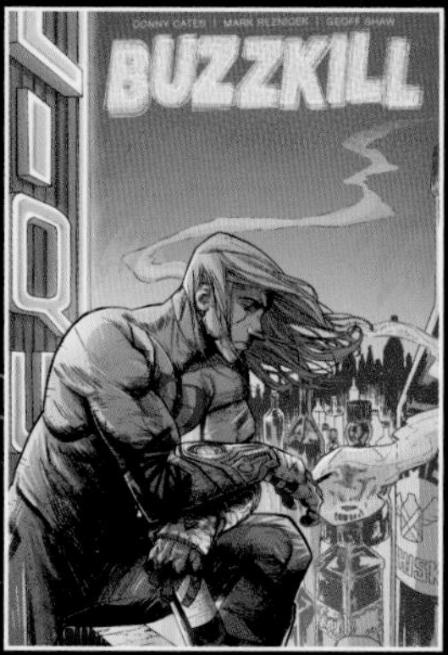
DONNY CATES | MARK REZNICEK | GEOFF SHAW
BUZZKILL

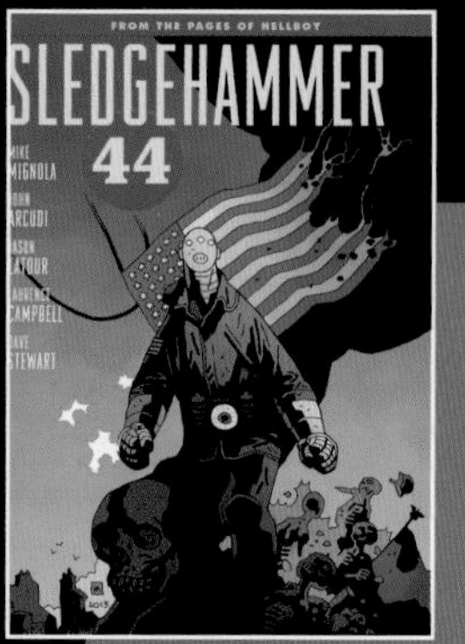
FROM THE PAGES OF HELLBOY
SLEDGEHAMMER
44

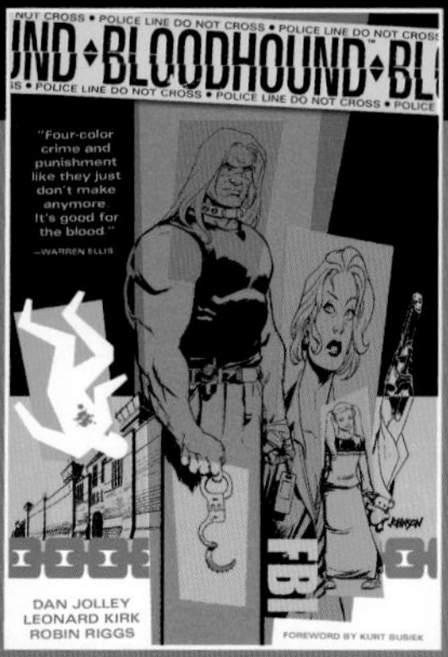
POLICE LINE DO NOT CROSS • POLICE LINE DO NOT CROSS
BLOODHOUND
"Four-color crime and punishment like they just don't make anymore It's good for the blood."
—WARREN ELLIS
FBI
DAN JOLLEY
LEONARD KIRK
ROBIN RIGGS
FOREWORD BY KURT BUSIEK

SLEDGEHAMMER 44
Mike Mignola, John Arcudi, and Jason Latour
ISBN 978-1-61655-395-1 | $19.99

DREAM THIEF
Jai Nitz and Greg Smallwood
ISBN 978-1-61655-283-1 | $17.99

BUZZKILL
Mark Reznicek, Donny Cates, and Geoff Shaw
ISBN 978-1-61655-305-0 | $14.99

THE BLACK BEETLE
Francesco Francavilla
VOLUME 1: NO WAY OUT
ISBN 978-1-61655-202-2 | $19.99

THE ANSWER!
Mike Norton and Dennis Hopeless
ISBN 978-1-61655-197-1 | $12.99

BLOODHOUND
Dan Jolley, Leonard Kirk, and Robin Riggs
VOLUME 1: BRASS KNUCKLE PSYCHOLOGY
ISBN 978-1-61655-125-4 | $19.99

MICHAEL AVON OEMING'S THE VICTORIES
Michael Avon Oeming
VOLUME 1: TOUCHED
ISBN 978-1-61655-100-1 | $9.99
VOLUME 2: TRANSHUMAN
ISBN 978-1-61655-214-5 | $17.99

ORIGINAL VISIONS— THRILLING TALES!

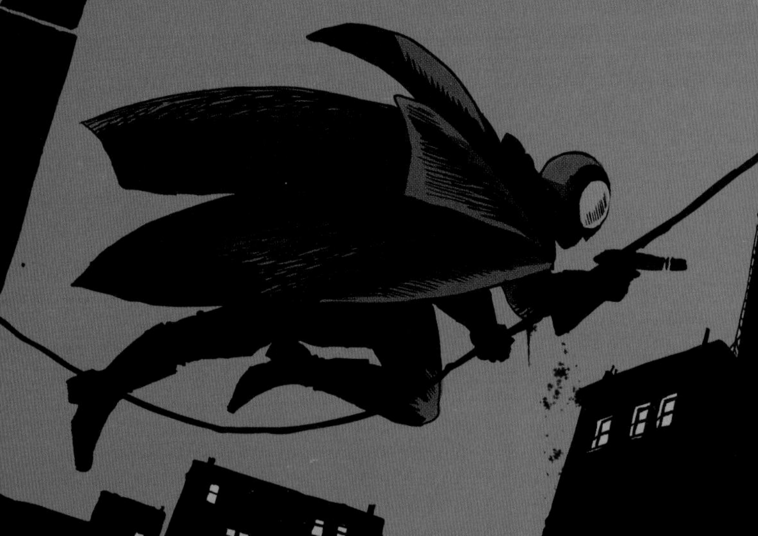

AVAILABLE AT YOUR LOCAL COMICS SHOP OR BOOKSTORE! • To find a comics shop in your area, call 1-888-266-4226.
For more information or to order direct visit DarkHorse.com or call 1-800-862-0052 Mon.–Fri. 9 a.m. to 5 p.m. Pacific Time. Prices and availability subject to change without notice.

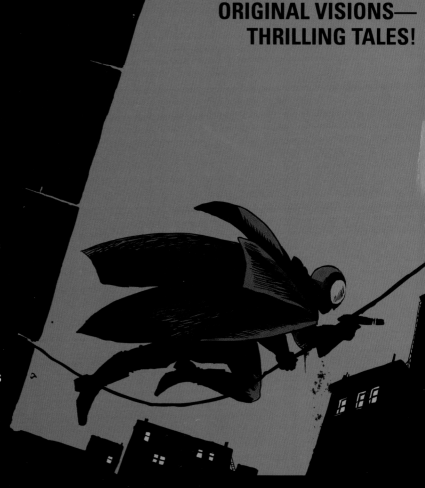